K$H

GOVERNMENT GANGSTERS

THE DEEP STATE, the TRUTH, and the BATTLE for OUR DEMOCRACY

KASH PRAMOD PATEL

Post Hill
PRESS

A POST HILL PRESS BOOK

ISBN: 978-1-63758-824-6
ISBN (eBook): 978-1-63758-825-3

Government Gangsters:
The Deep State, the Truth, and the Battle for Our Democracy
© 2023 by Kash Pramod Patel
All Rights Reserved

Cover design by Conroy Accord

This is a work of nonfiction. All people, locations, events, and situation are portrayed to the best of the author's memory.

Post Hill Press
New York • Nashville
posthillpress.com

Published in the United States of America

DEPARTMENT OF DEFENSE
DEFENSE OFFICE OF PREPUBLICATION AND SECURITY REVIEW
1155 DEFENSE PENTAGON
WASHINGTON, DC 20301-1155

Ref: **23-SB-0032**
June 7, 2023

Kash Patel
▮▮▮▮▮▮▮▮▮▮▮▮▮▮

Dear Mr. Patel:

This is in response to your December 2, 2022, correspondence requesting public release clearance for the manuscript titled, "Government Gangsters". The manuscript submitted for prepublication security review is **CLEARED AS AMENDED** for public release. Enclosed are copies of the "cleared as amended" manuscript pages. The amendments are clearly identified with blacked out text; where applicable, cleared alternative language is provided in the margins. Also enclosed is a stamped copy of the first page of the manuscript.

The amendments protect from release classified national security information and unclassified information that may lead to the compromise of classified information. The amendments may not be exclusive to the Department of Defense (DoD), as manuscript reviews often require consultation with other federal agencies that own information in the manuscript.

This office requires that you add the following disclaimers prior to publishing the manuscript: "The views expressed in this publication are those of the author and do not necessarily reflect the official policy or position of the Department of Defense or the U.S. government. The public release clearance of this publication by the Department of Defense does not imply Department of Defense endorsement or factual accuracy of the material".

This clearance does not include any photograph, picture, exhibit, caption, or other supplemental material not specifically approved by this office, nor does this clearance imply DoD endorsement or factual accuracy of the material. You are responsible for sourcing and acknowledgement of all photos in your manuscript, to include any stock footage you use of military equipment. The appearance of external hyperlinks does not constitute endorsement by the DoD of the linked websites, or the information, products or services contained therein. The DoD does not exercise any editorial, security, or other control over the information found at these locations.

This office notes that your manuscript may include the names and other personally identifiable information (PII) of former or active duty Service members, DoD employees, and third party individuals, the release of which could be a violation of the privacy rights of these individuals. As the author, you are solely responsible for the release of any PII and its legal implications. If you have not done so already, you may wish to consult these individuals and obtain permission to include their PII in the manuscript.

If you are not satisfied with this determination, please have your counsel contact the Department of Justice counsel assigned to the litigation captioned *Patel v. Department of Defense*, No. 23-cv-1255-CRC (D.D.C.). Additionally, you may rewrite portions of the redacted information and resubmit the manuscript for reconsideration.

The point of contact for this review is ▮▮▮▮▮▮▮▮▮▮▮▮▮▮▮▮▮▮ email
▮▮▮▮▮▮▮▮▮▮▮▮▮

Sincerely,
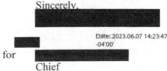

Date: 2023.06.07 14:23:47
-04'00'

for ▮▮▮▮▮▮▮▮▮▮
Chief

A NOTE FROM THE AUTHOR ON THE GOVERNMENT GANGSTERS

Unsurprisingly, the government gangsters that I expose in these pages didn't want this book to come out. Yet, by law, I needed their approval before we could publish.

Contractually, all former government employees with high-level security clearances who write a book must submit the manuscript to the government for prepublication review. Only after a certified review by all agencies and departments that the government chooses did we publish the book you're now reading.

During that review process, government bureaucrats from nine separate agencies and departments attempted to stop me. They delayed publication for almost eight months (stretching out a process that normally takes three to four months) to edit minor parts of ten paragraphs. Only after I filed a federal lawsuit against the government did the Department of Defense (DoD) magically finish its work and "release" my manuscript.

During the review process, the government often demands unnecessary redactions under the pretext of protecting classified information and—get this—"unclassified information that may lead to the compromise of classified information." As you will see in this book, abusing the classification system is a common tactic government gangsters use to cover their tracks and bury their own corruption. They used this maneuver to redact some of the material in these pages.

I could have fought again in court to remove the unnecessary redactions, but at the cost of delaying publication even longer. It was more important to get the truth out as soon as possible, even if I couldn't expose every last detail.

Special thanks to Christopher Mills for taking the fight to federal court.

This book was not easy to publish. It's the book the Deep State doesn't want you to read. But they failed. I will not—and will never—let government gangsters stop me from putting the Mission First.

To Mummie & Pappa,
for daring to cross the Earth in search of the American Dream, for
providing us with that Dream, and for letting us create our own
Dreams. And for everything else, this book is for you, JSK.

K$H

CONTENTS

Part V: January 6th

The Deep State and Its Discontents

Sometimes I wonder how, for the past seven years of my life, I have been on the front lines of every major national security and political battle against what has become known as the Deep State.

I'm just a guy from Queens and Long Island with the same story as so many others. I didn't have some special upbringing or education. My parents aren't rich or famous. They're just a couple of working-class immigrants from India. Hell, my biggest memories as a kid are going to Disney World and hockey games—pretty much as milquetoast Americana as it can get. Yet somehow I found myself right in the eye of an extended shitstorm that probably did more than anything to rip off the mask of our elites and reveal the rank corruption behind their façade. I guess it all started when I ended up breaking open the biggest criminal conspiracy by government officials since Watergate—Russia Gate.

Russia Gate was as dangerous to our country as it was convoluted: Agents from the Democrat Party hired a foreign asset to cook up false rumors about the presidential nominee of the Republican Party. Then, crazed partisans hijacked the law enforcement apparatus using those rumors, repeatedly lying to a federal court in order to unlawfully surveil the Republican nominee and rig the election. Targeted disinformation campaigns by government operatives and the jackals in the fake news mafia fueled a "scandal" leading to a witch hunt investigation that consumed years of the nominee-turned-president's term. I don't know if a spy novelist could have come up with something more outrageous and tragic. How that scandal came to light—and my part in it—comes later. But that's only a small piece of this book.

Ultimately, this isn't a story about one scandal, or even an exposé on the famous cast of malicious characters in Washington, DC (though trust me, I have a lot to say about them). This is a story about how the American people—myself included—slowly came to realize the truth about those who run our country; how the problems we face are not just the result of our leaders' incompetence but more so their malice; how the media is not just one-sided but liars; and most of all how what became known as the Deep State isn't some crazy conspiracy but a real force—and the most dangerous threat to our democracy.

The Trump era was, more than anything else, an apocalypse in the truest sense of the word. It was an unveiling. It was a time when suddenly we came to see that unaccountable elites in Washington armed with the powers of the state believe that anything is justified—absolutely anything—to preserve their power. This book is about how we discovered that truth and what we should do now that we know what we're up against.

For years as a public defender, a federal prosecutor, a congressional staffer, and finally a top aide to President Trump, I was able to observe our elites firsthand and see how the system worked. I fought battle after battle against the spiteful mandarins who continually attempted to subvert the orders of the duly elected president to achieve their own political ends. I made enemies of the most powerful names in the imperial city. Through it all, I refused to play the part of the always-losing loyal opposition. Instead, I learned how to win with the truth, exposing their corruption—and the Deep State has never forgiven me for it.

What exactly is this "Deep State" that I speak of? Some of the characters in this book are elected leaders. Others are yellow journalists in the media who serve as peddlers of propaganda and disinformation at the behest of the ruling elites. Still others are Big Tech tycoons and actors affiliated with non-governmental organizations, who carry water for the Democrat Party and the radical left. But my most dogged opponents were officials within the executive branch itself—members of the unelected federal bureaucracy who think they have the right to rule America, not Congress or the president. Altogether, these actors have come to be known as the Deep State. A few years ago, most Americans had never heard the term "Deep State," and those who had would have thought that the idea of some murky shadow government operating behind the curtains in Washington, DC, was just a little too outlandish—something that may exist in other countries but certainly not in the United States in the twenty-first century.

Today, it is impossible to deny: America simply doesn't work the way we were told in *Schoolhouse Rock!*. All sides of the political spectrum can acknowledge that the people are not the sole sovereigns of America acting through their representatives in Congress and in the White House. The people and their wishes are not even the primary deference point for power in our government. Instead, there are groups of people at the highest levels of government, business, and culture who operate independently of elections and of the people. They aren't mentioned in the Constitution, and they have their own rules, priorities, interests, and sources of power. As I confronted them time and again, I caught them manipulating the national security apparatus and failing to put our government's no-fail mission first—the mission to keep the American people safe and secure. Not only that, but they would abuse their power to subvert what the people voted for, twisting reality according to their own purposes and shredding the foundations of our constitutional republic in the process.

At first glance, they can seem to be everywhere and nowhere all at the same time. Here we see a politicized investigation, and there we see the absence of a needed and legitimate investigation, coupled with failure of oversight, accountability, or even interest from Congress or the press. Here we see a selective leak of classified information to damage a certain political movement or actor, with the establishment media acting in unison—often using the exact same language and phrases—to reinforce the Deep State's narrative. There we see a seemingly coordinated cover-up where the truth seems to always remain hidden, or even blocked from dissemination by Big Tech. Taken in isolation, every little event is able to be explained away. "It was a bad apple." "It was an oversight." "It was a single abuse of authority." But taken together, a picture emerges of a coordinated, ideologically rigid force independent from the people that manipulates the levers of politics and justice for its own gain and self-preservation. This group is the Deep State.

It is worthwhile to be very clear who we are talking about. Because the Deep State likes to operate in the shadows using arcane bureaucracy, opaque legal minutia, hidden levers of power, and insider political gamesmanship largely unfamiliar to the American public, it is easy to believe that the Deep State has more power than it really does.

But the Deep State is not some highly organized international league with regular meetings at Davos, the UN, or the WHO where they plot global domination. Nor is it limited to single bad officers or bad actors within the vast federal government who make wrong decisions that undermine the public trust. Really, the Deep State is the politicization of core American institutions and the federal governmental apparatus by a significant number of high-level cultural leaders and officials who, acting through networks of networks, disregard objectivity, weaponize the law, spread disinformation, spurn fairness, or even violate their oaths of office for political and personal gain, all at the expense of equal justice and American national security. Within the government, they operate at the highest levels of almost every agency, from the Federal Bureau of Investigation (FBI) to the intelligence community to the Department of Defense (DoD). In many ways, this bureaucratic wing of the Deep State is the most dangerous.

The existence of an independent, unelected, politicized bureaucracy is not new. It has been operating and growing within our government for decades. President Eisenhower warned about it when he spoke of "an immense military establishment and a large arms industry [that] is new in the American experience," which he dubbed the "military-industrial complex." Eisenhower warned in his farewell address that "in the councils of government, we must guard against the acquisition of unwarranted influence…by the military industrial complex. The potential for the disastrous rise of misplaced power exists and will persist."[1]

Eisenhower wasn't the only one to bristle against independent actors within his own government. President Nixon also faced recurring trouble as bureaucrats continually attempted to stymie his initiatives. Almost every Republican president has come across the Deep State within the government in less obvious ways when the bureaucracy that is supposed to be under presidential authority slow-walks directs orders, leaks false information designed to damage the administration, or presents the president with restricted options on key questions that fit into the box the bureaucrats have already designed. In the most extreme circumstances, corrupt bureaucrats imagine a crime and then manufacture the evidence to pin on their opponents. They are thugs in suits, nothing more than government gangsters who act like they are righteous.

For the most part, this politicized bureaucracy hampers Republicans and supports Democrats. There are many reasons for that. The bureaucracy is centralized in DC, one of the most liberal places in America. Staff is uniformly left wing, and not at all moderate. By its nature, it is made up of pro-government people who are all "educated" at left-wing universities. Not to mention, the left tends to fetishize government power while the right sees the government sometimes as a tool and other times as a barrier to human flourishing. Because of this, Republicans have traditionally been skeptical of, and sometimes even hostile to, the politicized federal bureaucracy while Democrats have supported it. It's a simple rule that is almost always the case: Democrats and the Deep State are on the same team.

But for the Democrats, this is a devil's bargain. Shortly before Donald Trump took office, an unlikely person laid out the threat. Senate Democrat Chuck Schumer warned Trump against crossing a key member of the Deep State—the intelligence community. "You take on the intelligence community?" Schumer said. "They have six ways from Sunday of getting back at you."

Senator Schumer said this with obvious glee. His words were a threat that Trump should watch himself. But when you embolden and unleash a power you can't control, it's only a matter of time before that power turns on you. Right now, the Democrats and the Deep State are on the same team. Only a fool could imagine that their interests will align forever. But even if Democrats get most every policy they want with the help of the Deep State, will it be worth the cost? The price of rule by the Deep State is high—nothing less than the end of self-government in America.

That is not hyperbole. Our battle with the Deep State isn't just another theater in the fight between Democrats and Republicans. At the root, this isn't partisan at all. It's about the nature of our government. The Deep State is a cabal of unelected tyrants who think they should determine who the American people can and cannot elect as president, who think they get to decide what the president can and cannot do, and who believe they have the right to choose what the American people can and cannot know.

This is a battle between the people and the corrupt ruling class. It's a choice between whether America decides its policies and direction by vote, or whether we are ruled by the whims, egos, greed, and power struggles of a small body of incestuous, power-hungry, unelected oligarchs in Washington who hate us and play by their own made-up rules. If they win, we don't have a democracy, a republic, or a sovereign people anymore. We have a tyranny that has arrogated for itself the right to wield absolute control over the American people.

So while Democrats might enjoy watching the Deep State do battle against President Trump and the America First movement, they—and all Americans—should be very afraid. The shocking and terrible details of what the Deep State has already done to increase its power fill this book. Suffice to say, there are no depths to which the Deep State will not descend, crimes they will not commit, or lives they will not destroy to get their way. But that doesn't mean they are invincible.

I have confronted the Deep State as a public defender in Miami and a federal prosecutor at the National Security Department in the

Department of Justice (DoJ). I uncovered their inner workings as the lead investigator of the Russia Gate hoax while serving as a staffer in the House of Representatives. And I continued to fight the Deep State as the senior White House counterterrorism official in the Trump administration, the principal deputy to the acting director of national intelligence, and the chief of staff for the Department of Defense. In these pages, I will take you through every stage of my journey, how I battled the agents of the Deep State leviathan, what I did to win, and how we can defeat them for good.

We have no time to lose. The survival of the American Republic is at stake.

PART I

THE DEPARTMENT OF JUSTICE

CHAPTER 1

Reckless DoJ

I wasn't always a committed warrior against the corrupt permanent bureaucracy in Washington, DC. But looking back, what I learned when I was young—and what I saw throughout my career—led me to become one of the Deep State's most dogged opponents. In many ways, it was the normalcy of my life that has made me so disgusted with the abnormality of the Deep State. Like so many regular, honest people, I found it hard to believe that anyone in real life could be as treacherous and evil as the villains portrayed in books and movies. Yet my eyes were opened. Let me explain.

Like most Americans who grew up in the '80s and '90s, I was pretty trustful of public officials, if I ever thought of them. Truth be told, I was much more focused on other things. Our home was always busy with my siblings, my parents, my dad's eight brothers and sisters, and me all living in the same house. But beside the tight quarters, overall it was a pretty milquetoast Americana upbringing. I grew up watching the New York Islanders and playing hockey, a passion I still have today. One of my favorite memories as a kid was when my extended family would take an annual pilgrimage (fifteen-cars-deep) from our home in Queens to Disney World.

Like a lot of immigrant parents, my mom and dad urged me to focus on my studies and be mindful of religion and my heritage. Because of that, I've always had a very deep connection with India. As I was raised Hindu, my family went to temple and prayed at home in our shrine room, making sure to celebrate big holidays like Diwali and Navratri. I remember going to Indian weddings as a kid that were unlike any other party I had been to before—or since. Five hundred people celebrating for a full week was considered a small affair. But some of my favorite memories were more personal. Because my mom didn't want any meat in the home and preferred to serve vegetarian meals, my dad and I would have to sneak away to get our fix. Every time we wanted some butter chicken, we'd head out to Jackson Heights in Queens over to Little India on 72nd Street. I can still remember all the smells and flavors and how wonderful it was to spend time with my dad. Of course, we weren't really that sneaky. My mom knew exactly what we were doing and gave us a little wink and nod. Going out for butter chicken became a weekly ritual for me and my dad.

While I am very close to my parents, growing up we didn't talk much about philosophy or first principles or anything like that. But my whole childhood was infused with a sort of dispositional conservatism: my family is proud to be American, we value hard work, we cherish fairness, we believe in personal responsibility, and we don't think anyone has a right to special favors or special treatment. The vast majority of the American people share these values, and we expect those around us, especially our leaders, to do the same.

PUBLIC DEFENDER

Acting like a stereotypical Indian American, I grew up wanting to be a doctor. Two things disabused me of this idea. First, a guidance counselor in college sat me down and laid out what the next eight years of my life would be like if I decided to pursue medicine. "You know, it's going to be a lot of hard work," she told me. "After graduating, you have to apply for medical schools. If you get in, then you have to study again for even more years before you apply to residency. Then if you actually get into a residency program, you do that for a few years before you can finally get out and start your career in your thirties."

I am very thankful for doctors. That doesn't mean I want to be one. I took one look at the med school program and said, "Nope, I'm out."

The second reason I dropped the idea of being a doctor was because I had another career path unexpectedly planted in my head. In high school, I used to caddy at the Garden City Country Club in Long Island. There were a lot of very wealthy members and important New Yorkers who hit the links there, but a few guys in particular always caught my attention. It was a group of defense lawyers. Of course, when they got on the course, they always talked business, and they had some of the most interesting (and sometimes terrifying) stories about their clients and the high drama of the courtroom. I didn't understand exactly what they did, but being a lawyer seemed interesting.

After listening to them and deciding against the medical school route, I figured law school was a perfect option. But truth be told, I didn't exactly want to be a defense lawyer like those guys on the golf course. In a trial, everyone deserves a lawyer—even criminals. But in my mind, I saw law school as a perfect way to climb the economic ladder. Instead of being a first-generation immigrant golf caddy, I could be a first-generation immigrant lawyer at a white shoe firm making a ton of money. Of course, the image was all the more appealing considering the amount of debt I'd have graduating from law school.

With that, off to law school I went. Problem was that my dreams of the sky-high salary at the prestige firm never quite materialized. In fact, after all my applications, nobody would hire me. It was certainly humbling, but I think the universe was planning something much better by pushing me in a different direction.

So why did I eventually end up as a public defender? I enjoyed a class on trial litigation in law school, and the defense lawyers back at the Garden City Country Club were certainly some fascinating characters. I decided it could be worth a shot. On the advice of a buddy of mine, I headed out to Miami to interview as a public defender. Only later did I learn that the public defender office in Miami-Dade, Florida, was the number one defense office in the country. Surprisingly, I got the job, and I would be learning from the very best. So much for the high-rise legal world.

While I was very excited to start, it was admittedly a strange fit. As I mentioned, I grew up pretty apolitical. Through my college years, I started to move more and more to the right politically. But public defenders are left-wing. Actually, they're not just left-wing. They are to the far left of the left wing. These are the types of people who often don't mind letting criminals off the hook because they had a bad upbringing, or because they didn't hurt the victims *that* badly. In fact, they are the types of people who usually see criminals as the true victims and American society as the real bad actor (unless, of course, the alleged criminal is a right-winger who participated in the January 6th protest in Washington; public defenders have no kind words for them).

All that being said, I couldn't be happier that I became a public defender. Yes, some of my colleagues were crazy. But me, I always cared about justice and wanted those who did good to be rewarded and wrongdoers to be punished. As a public defender, I saw firsthand that results like that don't just happen. The most effective way to reach the right results in each and every case is to have the right process—to have *due* process—and public defenders are essential to achieve due process.

Lawyers, like a lot of professionals, often try to make things overly complicated to prove how smart they are. But for all its complexity in the legal field, the basis of due process is very simple: every single person accused of a crime is presumed innocent until proven beyond a reasonable doubt that he is guilty, and the evidence to prove that guilt has to be laid out openly and fairly in a court of law. Over the centuries, the British and then Americans built upon their experience to create safeguards that would guarantee a fair outcome, developing what we now call due process. For example, in law, like in any field, people can be corrupt or biased. In a court case, a corrupt or biased person serving as the judge can send the wrong person to jail, or worse. To help fix that, our forefathers created the jury system so that no single person's faults would improperly condemn the accused. Similarly, if innocence is always presumed, then if the federal government is prosecuting someone, and the prosecutor discovers evidence that supports the innocence of the defendant, the prosecutor is obligated to share that with the defense. Imagine you're accused of robbing a bank, but the person prosecuting you finds video surveillance showing you at a Subway down the street at the same time. This rule means that the prosecutor can't hide that information in order to secure a conviction. In America, we call that the Brady rule, named after a 1963 US Supreme Court decision.

All of these procedures are supposed to act as guarantees that innocent people don't get locked up for crimes they didn't commit—and to be 100 percent sure that the people who are punished by the law deserve it. Public defenders are a vital part of this system because the average person accused of a crime will have no training in the intricacies of the law and probably can't afford a high-dollar private defense attorney.

All that theory aside, I did learn pretty early on that while left-wing public defenders often grandstand about due process and the rights of the accused, they frequently act like hypocrites. The people I worked with in the public defender's office were totally comfortable representing some criminals, like robbers or murderers. But when it came to more seedy crimes like sexual assault or crimes with children, nobody volunteered. They claimed to believe everyone being prosecuted has a right to a lawyer, but they never actually wanted to personally be that lawyer. I knew that if I was going to be a public defender, I wasn't going to half-ass it. I figured that if due process is the right of *all* people in *all* criminal cases, then that applies to the worst of the worst as well. If my client was guilty and deserved punishment, I completely agreed with the conviction. But at a bare minimum, the prosecutors had to *prove* guilt beyond a reasonable doubt with all the evidence on the table. With that in mind, I volunteered to represent those whom nobody else wanted to.

Putting my colleagues' hypocrisy aside, the lawyers I worked with did teach me an extremely valuable lesson: in order to be a good public defender, I needed to be able to walk into a court of law, look a law enforcement officer or a federal prosecutor in the eye, and call him a liar to his face, if the evidence warranted it. Too often, people are afraid to contradict those in authority positions. And of course, the vast majority of law enforcement personnel and federal prosecutors are good people. But some aren't—and some have absolutely no problem lying or twisting evidence in order to secure a conviction.

Ultimately, this taught me a lot about human nature, including lessons that helped me during my battles against the Deep State in Washington. I learned that when people think they are in the right, then they can always find a way to make the ends justify the means. If they have to lie, leak, cover up, or twist the truth to accomplish their mission, it often doesn't matter as long as they are convinced that their mission is righteous. I also learned that if people in authority face no consequences when they break the rules, then they will break the rules. Worse, when people are encouraged to break the rules, they will break them again and again. The lack of accountability breeds contempt for the law and incentivizes bad behavior. Frequently, people with power won't do what is right when nobody is looking.

This is exactly how I saw the Deep State operate in its attempt to take down President Trump. Ruling class elites determined that Trump was evil and that they were good, so in their attempts to take him out, nothing was out of bounds. Yet even long before Trump's election in 2016, these lessons about human nature were hammered home to me in one of my biggest cases as a public defender, a case focused on a Colombian drug cartel.

BRADY VIOLATION

There is something different about people who spend their lives working for the federal government. There are many great, dedicated federal employees out there. I worked with loads of them in the Trump administration. But there is something about Washington that gives people an air of haughty self-righteousness. In the Department of Justice, it seems the closer one gets to the top, the more shameless and self-righteous one becomes. But even in the lower levels, many federal employees have a chip on their shoulder. That was certainly the case with some federal prosecutors.

I was a public defender first for Miami-Dade and then in the Southern District of Florida for nearly nine years. As a federal public defender, I regularly stood toe-to-toe in the courtroom against federal prosecutors. Honestly, I can't tell you how many times I caught the feds abusing due process or lying on the witness stand. The worst instance I ever experienced came in 2013 when I was representing Jose Luis Buitrago, a Colombian national accused of drug smuggling. It was all part of one of the biggest narco-trafficking cases in the history of the US Southern District of Florida.

Based on everything I had learned during my years as a public defender up to that point, I knew that even if my client was guilty in some way, it was wrong for me to just assume that he was guilty of *everything* the government asserted. Prosecutors commonly pump up their accusations to the highest degree possible knowing that if they have a lot of claims, they can secure a heavier conviction. It's not a bad tactic—as long as your claims can be supported with evidence. Speaking of evidence, by that point, I had also learned that evidence of wrongdoing or of innocence doesn't just appear out of nowhere. It has to be found—and that takes a lot of legwork. So for this case I got myself on a plane and flew to Colombia. Part of the federal prosecutor's case hinged on Colombian cops who had caught the alleged drug traffickers before they were brought before the court in Florida, so I wanted to talk to those cops.

After searching out some witnesses in the less-than-glamorous neighborhoods surrounding Bogota, I discovered some bombshell evidence: the Colombian cops who had caught my client and others had their salaries paid by the US government through the US Drug Enforcement Administration (DEA). Not only did the federal prosecutor on the case fail to disclose that these payments had happened when she was explicitly asked, she even denied having known about the payments at all when we caught her. But the Colombian cops I spoke with had clear-as-day testimony. They were paid by the US federal government, they proactively worked with the federal government to entrap my client, and they had discussed this openly with the federal prosecutor on the case.

Big trials like this take a long time. You have to gather evidence, review a massive amount of documents, interview witnesses, set court dates, and so much more. Over that time, I showed the federal prosecutor how I caught her lying through her teeth. I gave her my witness testimony showing that she was withholding exculpatory evidence about my client—a direct Brady violation that was clearly unconstitutional. As the months and months went on preparing for the trial date, I gave the prosecutor every single out possible, telling her that all she had to do was come clean and admit that they had withheld the information, and we could move on. Truth be told, the prosecutor could have made her case even if she openly acknowledged that the feds had paid the Colombian police. But for some reason the prosecutor just couldn't admit the truth. Government officials at the DoJ are used to prosecuting those who violate the law. They are not used to being caught violating the law themselves—and when they are, they *never* like to admit it.

With that, I had no choice but to represent my client to the absolute best of my ability in accordance with the law. On the first day of the trial, through cross examination of the first witness the government called, I showed the evidence to the judge demonstrating undeniably that the federal prosecutor had lied and committed a Brady violation, a cardinal sin for a prosecutor. The judge was absolutely livid, berated the prosecutor for violating the law, and effectively forced the government to dismiss the case, releasing the client with a sentence of time served. It was a major embarrassment for the federal prosecutor and the Department of Justice. In the end, the DoJ threw out one of the biggest drug prosecutions in history all because they were too proud to admit they were wrong and too self-righteous to follow the rules of due process. True to DC form, the prosecutor was not held responsible or fired for what she did. Sadly, it wasn't the last time I would catch federal law enforcement trying to bury exculpatory evidence without facing consequences. Soon enough, I would see the failings of the DoJ from the inside.

CHAPTER 2

In the Belly of the Beast

W hen high-level members of the federal bureaucracy like Sally Yates or James Comey actively undermined President Trump, one of the media's most common defenses was that these civil officials were defending their institutions—like the DoJ or the FBI—against political manipulation. The truth is that most of these people don't give a damn about the institutions they are supposed to serve. They only care about themselves. I experienced this personally at the DoJ. After my years as a public defender, I was hired by the National Security Division in DoJ headquarters (commonly referred to as Main Justice) in Washington, DC, as a terrorism prosecutor. I had enjoyed my time as a public defender, and I did a lot of good in Florida. But after nine years, I wanted to help convict terrorists the right way. And then there's the fact that a job as a federal prosecutor at Main Justice is a dream job for a young and ambitious lawyer.

TAJIKISTAN

I started the job in the winter of 2013 to 2014 just as ISIS was beginning to emerge as an international threat. With terrorist attacks continuing around the world, my new job gave me the opportunity to save lives through my prosecutions and make a name for myself within the DoJ.

Yet while I was trying to do my best to serve my country and accomplish the mission of the DoJ, I soon realized that my bosses at HQ didn't have my back. Ultimately, they were more concerned with politics and optics than with defending those who wanted to serve the institution. This hard lesson came after I was unjustly thrown out of a court by a rogue judge. The case involved a man named Omar Faraj Saeed al-Hardan, whom we were prosecuting for working with ISIS. He was in contact with Syrian bomb makers, and we uncovered plans that he was going to attempt to blow up American shopping malls.

After a yearlong investigation, we finally took the case to the grand jury and received an indictment, formally charging al-Hardan with terrorism-related offenses. After this point, there was a quick arraignment, which I held in Texas (where the case was charged), and then a lengthy recess before we were due back in court. In the meantime, I had other cases I was working and headed to Tajikistan, a Muslim majority country that borders Afghanistan, to track down witnesses as part of my work to take down the ISIS emir of special operations. Out of nowhere, the judge in Texas on the al-Hardan bomb maker case decided to schedule a hearing. The local US prosecutor wasn't able to handle it because he didn't do terrorism cases, so Main Justice called me and told me I had to get to the hearing, which was set for less than twenty-four hours from when I got their phone call. It didn't matter that I was in Dushanbe, Tajikistan, about as far away from the continental United States as it is possible to get. What mattered was that the mission came first, which meant I needed to get stateside *fast*. So I ran to the airport, hopped on a plane, and barely made it, rushing from the airport to the courtroom with my lead FBI agent providing transport.

I didn't have time to prepare. When I travelled to Tajikistan, I had slacks and a blazer, but I left all my suits at home. Tajikistan isn't exactly a place filled with western wool suits and ties. When I got off the airplane, I didn't have anything else suitable for court, so I showed up to the judge's chambers in what I was wearing: pants, a button down, and a blazer. The judge in Houston was having none of it. He started berating me, telling me I had no purpose there, asking why the taxpayers had to waste money to fly me around, and condemning me for coming in without a tie. He demanded to check my passport to ensure I wasn't lying to him about where I was, as if I wanted to show up without a full suit before a judge who was known to be rather cuckoo. It didn't matter that all these problems stemmed from my work to peg an ISIS terrorist. The judge had it out for me from the get-go, and the local prosecutors were abject failures to the mission. They didn't say a word in my defense.

I put on a perfect face answering with, "Yes, your honor," and, "No, your honor," in all the right places, the whole time refusing to let him get under my skin. He eventually threw me out of his chambers. Throughout the entire experience, all I could think was to not blow up or do anything stupid. I wasn't going to let a hothead judge ruin our case against terrorists. I had to put the mission first. It was way more important to secure a guilty verdict against a criminal than it was to push back against a judge who let his position go to his head.

Back at Main Justice, folks read the transcript of what happened. I even have emails from Sally Yates—the woman who would later have to be removed by President Trump as the acting attorney general after she infamously refused to enforce travel restrictions on terrorist hotspots—who expressed to me that the judge was in the wrong. Senior leadership at the Justice Department told me they were furious about what the judge did to me and praised me for keeping my cool. In fact, years later the transcript of that conversation was still used to train federal prosecutors on how to avoid being provoked.

The problem was, all those officials like Sally Yates refused to say any of that publicly, and the media would report whatever they wanted to. In this case, they had the judge's side of the story and that was it, so they ran with it and dragged my name through the mud. It was far from the last time the media would slander me. Meanwhile, my superiors at the Justice Department did nothing, effectively letting the judge loudmouth about my allegedly disrespectful conduct while the DoJ was restricted from sharing our side of the story. It all came down to a calculation: they didn't want to stick their necks out to defend one of their own because they didn't want to risk bad press or getting in a spat that might tarnish their reputations. Senior DoJ leaders had no problem covering for the rotten federal prosecutor who violated the Constitution in the Colombian narco-trafficking case. That's because their opponents were an accused drug runner and a lowly public defender. Yet when their own prosecutor was actually in the right, they refused to step up to the plate because their opponent was a federal judge, and nobody wanted to be seen contradicting a federal judge. Cowards.

For too many at the highest levels of the DoJ, optics, not justice or any consideration of right and wrong, governs decision-making. As I soon experienced, those optics never matter more than when it came to DoJ officials defending their Democrat political allies—especially Hillary Clinton.

PROSECUTING THE BENGHAZI TERRORISTS

The September 11, 2012, attack in Benghazi, Libya, that killed four Americans—Ambassador Christopher Stevens, Foreign Service Officer Sean Smith, and two former Navy SEALs named Glen Doherty and Tyrone Woods—was a complete tragedy. It was also completely avoidable. A large group of terrorists associated with al-Qaeda descended on our diplomatic compound and a nearby CIA facility nearby over the course of the night as a result of massive and scandalous intelligence failures and security lapses. Leadership in the State Department, the CIA, and the Obama administration was caught completely unaware.

The American people were justifiably outraged. How could terrorists kill an American ambassador eleven years after 9/11? What the hell were our leaders doing—or not doing—that allowed this to happen?

Back in the States, it was clear President Obama thought he had a much bigger problem than the murder of Ambassador Stevens on his watch. He was in the final months of his reelection campaign, and one of his campaign's core messages was that he had terrorism under control. In fact, he was running on the slogan "bin Laden is dead, and General Motors is alive." Benghazi blew that narrative to pieces. The terrorist attack was also a massive embarrassment for then secretary of state Hillary Clinton, who, as the head of the State Department, was ultimately responsible for the safety of her diplomats.

Both Obama and Clinton had to take some of the blame for what happened in Benghazi. But it's what they did afterward that turned a tragedy into one of the most shameful displays of politicking our nation has ever seen. In order to deflect criticism away from themselves, the Obama administration engaged in a ludicrous disinformation campaign to spread the lie that the Benghazi attack happened because of an anti-Muslim video in another part of the world. How those things were connected they never did say and never could prove. The point was to find some excuse—any excuse—instead of what was obvious: that they failed to provide enough security for their ambassador and that President Obama and Hillary Clinton did not have a handle on terrorism. Ultimately, they lied about what caused the death of four brave Americans for the sake of political expediency.

In the end, it worked. President Obama won reelection against the Republicans' very weak candidate, Mitt Romney. Meanwhile, several government entities were still investigating what exactly had happened in Libya. At the Department of Justice, I was part of the team conducting the criminal investigation into the Benghazi attack. This wasn't the same thing as a congressional inquiry designed to have public hearings and produce a report. This was a real-deal national security investigation created to assemble mountains of evidence in order to prosecute the terrorists who murdered four Americans.

It was no small task. After I started at the DoJ, I was embedded with America's top special operations teams, through the US Special Operations Command (SOCOM), to help manage special military operations and maximize impact. As a representative from the DoJ, I was there to help manage the legal side of special operations. For example, if we found a terrorist, I was one of the stakeholders looking at the evidence, helping determine recommendations for what to do next, whether it was a drone strike, a Special Forces raid, or even attempting to capture the terrorist to bring him back to America for prosecution.

Another important job of the DoJ liaison at SOCOM was to help find evidence in active conflict zones. We called it captured enemy material (CEM). It could be anything from witness testimony to surveillance footage to laptops and hard drives. The point was if we needed to prosecute a terrorist up to the American standards of justice, we needed to line up all of this material and turn it into evidence that was usable in a court of law in America, which was a monster lift. Not every piece of material can be used as evidence. American courts require strict rules to ensure faulty evidence is not used to prosecute anyone, though this cuts against us sometimes in national security prosecutions. One limitation in these prosecutions is that we can't have our ███████████ Special Forces officers marching into an open US court hearing, ███████████████. So we have to get creative and abide by due process at the same time. ██ ███.

Captured enemy material was exactly the type of on-the-ground evidence we were using in the Benghazi prosecution. By the time the DoJ was moving in full force to compile evidence and bring prosecutions against the Benghazi terrorists, I was leading the prosecution's efforts at Main Justice in Washington, DC. The Benghazi prosecution was a monumental effort involving multiple teams at the department. My job was to help coordinate the efforts, working with the US attorney who would actually go to trial to get search warrants, approve indictments, and do all the necessary background work that has to take place long before a trial ever starts, including turning CEM into usable evidence.

While at Main Justice, I got a much closer view of the senior leadership of the department and other big names in Washington—people like Obama's attorney general, Eric Holder, and his successor, Loretta Lynch, as well as other personalities who would soon become household names in America, like FBI Director James Comey and his deputy, Andrew McCabe. When it came to the Benghazi investigation, I saw that these leaders were nothing more than political gangsters, frauds, and hypocrites.

Despite the fact that we had reams of evidence against dozens of terrorists in the Benghazi attack, Eric Holder's Justice Department decided to only prosecute one of the attackers. Rank and file lawyers in the DoJ, like myself, told our leadership that we had the evidence to win against all of these terrorists, but they ignored us and only brought the cases that they deemed "fit."

Knowing their decision to go soft on terrorists would cause a lot of grumbling, both in the department and among the American people, DoJ leadership then attempted to act tough against the one terrorist we were prosecuting by charging him with crimes that we didn't have the evidence to support. Because of that decision, when Main Justice asked me if I'd be willing to move to the trial team, I declined. I told them explicitly that I didn't trust the prosecutorial decisions they were making. I ended up being proven right. On the entire second set of charges where I informed DoJ leadership that we didn't have enough evidence, the Benghazi terrorist was acquitted on all such counts.

But it wasn't just DoJ leadership making bad decisions. It was also the FBI, a sub-agency under the authority of the DoJ. While the DoJ may prosecute cases, the FBI is the entity tasked with collecting evidence. That means outside of the DoJ, the only people who knew the strength and breadth of the evidence we had against dozens and dozens of Benghazi terrorists were the investigators at the FBI. But when Holder's Justice Department decided not to prosecute, the FBI said nothing. It was easily within the power of people like Comey and McCabe to call up the Department of Justice, lay out the facts of the case, and say that they stood by the FBI's work and that we had more than enough evidence to lock these terrorists up. But they didn't. They let the evidence that their agents spent untold numbers of years collecting and processing sit and gather dust while terrorists avoided American justice.

And it's not like senior leadership at the FBI was averse to pushing their preferred prosecutorial decisions. Within a few short years, Comey would go on national television and tell the world that he recommended no charges be brought against then presidential candidate Hillary Clinton for her unlawful mishandling of classified information on her private email servers. His actions totally hijacked the role of the DoJ—which has sole discretion to make the decision whether or not to press charges—and politicized the Clinton investigation in an election year. It was not his call to make, but he didn't seem to care.

So why was Comey so adamant to publicly and improperly influence the prosecutorial decision-making against Hillary Clinton but deathly silent, even on legitimate internal channels, when it came to Benghazi? Why did the Obama Justice Department decline to prosecute the rest of the Benghazi terrorists and then permit Comey to bandy about on the national stage, doing their political dirty work for them as America's top cop? Comey's political grandstanding revealed his true aversion to justice and exposed just how massive an ego he has. It wouldn't be the last time he'd put on such a display.

As I sat there in the Department of Justice looking at all the information before me, I could only come to one conclusion: whether it was Eric Holder or James Comey or anyone else with a high-level leadership position in the federal bureaucracy, all of their decisions were 100 percent political. Obama may have won reelection despite the Benghazi scandal, but by the time we were prosecuting some of the terrorists who committed the attack in 2014, Hillary Clinton was preparing her run to succeed Obama and become the next president. A high-profile court case that reviewed all the details of the Benghazi fiasco would hinder Hillary's political chances, so the Obama administration and their FBI allies beat it all back.

This was the complete opposite of what I observed in other, less politically charged cases. I served as the lead DoJ prosecutor for the 2010 World Cup bombing in Uganda, which killed an American. The case was a perfect example of the US government and international partners working together to get things done. I had a personal stake in this one too. My father is from Uganda, so I was able to visit his home under police escort while visiting the country. The police escort was necessary because literally the night before the trial started, the lead Ugandan prosecutor on the case was assassinated in front of her children. Despite the grave danger in this case and continued threats from the terrorists, we tracked down every person responsible for the attack and for the assassination of the prosecutor. We were able to prosecute every single one of them. That's how it's supposed to be done. But when it came to Benghazi, political leaders at the top kept our hands tied.

Ultimately, when it came to Benghazi, the Obama administration, the FBI, and the DoJ wanted to seem tough on terrorism, so they kept minimal prosecutions open and brought up big sounding charges that we couldn't support. But what they wanted most of all wasn't justice. It was political power. And in an attempt to keep political power, they threw out American justice, and terrorists went free on their watch.

CHAPTER 3

When Politics Obstructs Justice

The federal bureaucracy is rotten at the top because senior leadership thinks government exists for the glorification of their own egos and forgets government service exists for the benefit of the American people. The Deep State is really just a collection of unaccountable bad actors at the highest levels of the federal bureaucracy, the media, elected office, corporations, and cultural institutions, who abuse the power they have been given and the institutions they were hired to serve in order to protect themselves and manipulate politics in their favor. And they are aided and abetted by staff in the government who are either in on the game or too afraid to speak up. I regularly used to tell people that the fastest way to move up in the government is to just screw up, and the bigger the screwup, the bigger the promotion. Every person implicated in your mistakes has an interest in covering up what they did, so they will promote you. That means the people at the very top are usually the most immoral, unethical people in the entire agency. As I learned, this corruption has been present within the DoJ for years. But recently, it reached unbelievable levels.

When we understand exactly how the rot has spread and manifested itself, we can craft reforms that address the particular problems within the DoJ. Our goal is not to destroy federal law enforcement. It's to stop federal law enforcement powers from being abused for corrupt ends. When we do that, we get one step closer to restoring a government that serves the people as the ultimate sovereign in our nation.

ENDEMIC CORRUPTION IN THE DOJ

One of the main sins of a politicized DoJ is selective prosecutions. For example, in 2021 the Department of Justice charged former Trump advisor Steven Bannon with criminal contempt of Congress for refusing to go along with the Democrat's sham January 6th committee.[2] Meanwhile, former Obama CIA director John Brennan lied to Congress about the CIA's efforts to spy on congressional staffers, and former Obama director of national intelligence James Clapper likewise lied to Congress saying there were no National Security Agency (NSA) programs collecting data on Americans. Neither of them has ever been charged for perjury, and they probably never will be. Welcome to the two-tier system of justice in modern-day America. I never thought I'd see it, but as I discovered, now it operates everywhere.

Similarly, the Department of Justice has thus far refused to bring charges against President Biden's son, Hunter Biden, despite his well-documented influence peddling deals with nefarious foreign governments, not to mention his illegal possession of drugs and guns. Yet January 6th protestors are locked up, denied bail, and kept in disgusting conditions, often while being charged with minor criminal offenses. This has now gone on for two years. What we are witnessing is the total corruption of due process. How is it that illegal aliens coming into the country can commit heinous acts of violence and immediately be given bond, but Americans who entered the Capitol on January 6th are denied the same? For our Deep State regime, justice is clearly no longer blind. Prosecutorial decisions are now political decisions.

And frequently enemies of the Deep State are targeted even if they didn't commit any crimes at all. The media—fed lies by government leakers—reported that I *could have* been under investigation for improperly disclosing classified information. The source of this attack was shameless Deep State mouthpiece David Ignatius, a columnist for the *Washington Post*. His original article on the purported "scandal" surrounding me was the definition of disinformation. His sources were two possible anonymous individuals who refused to give their names because they knew they were spouting lies. Meanwhile, Ignatius's article was written with carefully crafted verbiage—a perceptive reader would see that Ignatius made no actual definitive fact claims but was really just spreading rumors in official sounding language. Only a close reader would see that the "investigation" was really just a theoretical claim. Everyone else would just read the headlines shouting, "Kash Patel under investigation," and presume the worst.

In a later piece, Ignatius followed up his original smear, reaching out to me for comment about the status of the "investigation." I told him that he could write the truth—that he made it up out of whole cloth and that the so-called investigation never began. Of course, he didn't write that. That wouldn't have helped his narrative. Instead of correcting the record, he allowed the disinformation campaign he started to spread.

The truth is there was no investigation into my handling of classified documents because I did everything by the book while in Washington. Not only that, but if such an investigation really did exist, it would be a clear example of the two-tiered justice system in America, because the Justice Department did absolutely NOTHING to prosecute the near daily leakers of classified information in the Trump administration—leakers that not only damaged the Trump presidency but harmed American national security. Regardless, the Ignatius piece worked exactly as planned. The rest of the fake news media mafia, ultimately fed by Deep State anonymous rubes, smeared my name relentlessly without any consequences.

Why did they target me? Because, as I'll discuss in the next section, I successfully uncovered the corruption of the FBI and DoJ when I led the Russia Gate investigation on the Hill. I learned that when you go after government corruption, you must be prepared to have your reputation destroyed by the fake news mafia and the corrupt Deep Staters in government. They will do anything to stop you. But I don't bend the knee. Too bad for them.

I'm not the only law-abiding person the Department of Justice has turned on. In an effort to demonize the over seventy million Americans who voted for Donald Trump in 2020, President Biden has repeatedly slandered our own citizens as white supremacists and racists. The Department of Justice took that one step further. Under President Biden, the Justice Department targeted parents who are pushing back against programs to teach their children vile and hateful critical race theory. The DoJ justified its threatening campaign against parents in a memo that labelled these law-abiding citizens as "domestic terrorists."[3] I literally used to prosecute actual domestic terrorists, and now they put parents in the same category because they disagreed with the education platform the Biden administration was forcing on our youth.

It's increasingly clear that while leadership at the Department of Justice had no problem letting al-Qaeda affiliated terrorists off the hook, they consider American citizens the real terrorists and enemies.

REFORMING THE DOJ

When presented with such monumental levels of corruption within the federal government, it's tempting to want to just tear it all down. However satisfying that might be, it would also do more harm than good. We can see this clearly at the DoJ. America needs a Department of Justice. The government should have a team of lawyers that can prosecute people who violate federal law and bring them to justice, whether that's drug traffickers, terrorists, or corrupt federal officials who abuse their power. But the DoJ also needs a massive overhaul.

The problem isn't that we have a Department of Justice. It's not even necessarily that the laws we have are bad (though some certainly are). The biggest problem is that the law is selectively applied. When it comes to political allies, left-wing radicals at the DoJ play with kid gloves, refusing to prosecute or even proactively trying to absolve their friends of crimes. Yet their political opponents are prosecuted and harassed to the greatest extent of the law and even far beyond the law—even when they've done nothing wrong.

The DoJ desperately needs a comprehensive housecleaning, and that starts at the top. First, we need an attorney general who will take on his own staff and put an end to abuses of prosecutorial discretion. Laws should be applied fairly and equally to all. Right now, they are applied selectively based heavily on politics.

Hillary Clinton is proactively absolved from prosecution while President Trump is hounded for years by the illegitimate Mueller Special Counsel based on fabricated claims. Antifa terrorists who lay siege to a federal courthouse in Portland are ignored or let go with a slap on the wrist. Staffers for TV personality Steven Colbert were arrested while trespassing at the Capitol, yet the DoJ gave them a total pass. Meanwhile otherwise law-abiding Americans who walked through the halls of the Capitol on January 6th and did nothing else wrong—violating the same laws that Colbert staffers did—are harassed and prosecuted. These flagrantly unequal applications of justice are not only unfair but completely erode public trust in the DoJ. Those specific prosecutors, and division within the department, that selectively apply the law should be removed and brought to heel. At the same time, a reform-minded attorney general should set clear, objective standards that will help federal prosecutors determine who should and should not be prosecuted. For example, anyone caught trespassing in the Capitol, no matter the political affiliation, should be prosecuted. These clear and specific standards will deprive politicized prosecutors from unequal decision-making.

This is an easy change to make. All it requires is the attorney general modifying the *Justice Manual*, formerly known as the *United States Attorneys' Manual*—the guidebook that all federal prosecutors must follow. Any attorney general can change these absurd rules, but none have because they don't want to undermine the institution by changing tradition—a farcical excuse in an institution with rapidly diminishing credibility. As a result of these fears, the DoJ hasn't made any major changes to these rules since Eric Holder was in office under President Obama; this despite the fact that gross abuses and misconduct have been uncovered during and since that time.

Amending the *Justice Manual* can fix a wide variety of problems even beyond establishing equal prosecutorial standards. For example, the manual can be changed to ban FBI agents and DoJ prosecutors from conducting midnight raids on non-violent offenders, like they did with Roger Stone. It can forbid the jailing of political dissidents without bond. Whenever actors at the DoJ or FBI step out of bounds, there's a decent chance that a change to the *Justice Manual* could help fix the problem.

Another problem with selective application of the law is that leadership within the Department of Justice, like many of the most powerful people in Washington, has this disgusting view that if a person has reached a high enough level of government while being a member of the Democrat Party, then that person is absolved from following the law. Whether that person is Hillary Clinton, John Brennan, James Clapper, James Comey, Andrew McCabe, or even other bad actors (like Lois Lerner, who targeted conservative groups at the IRS, or former Obama national security advisor Susan Rice, who lied about unmasking the identities of Trump officials to spy on them), Democrats in power are not held accountable for their crimes. The DoJ must return to its role of prosecuting those who commit federal crimes. That doesn't just include those at the highest level of government, it *especially* means those at the highest level of government. When federal officials are given a position of a public trust, they should be held to an even higher standard than the average American citizen. The only way to restore faith in our justice system is to actually hold the elites who break American laws accountable. If we fail to do so, the frustrations and anger currently tearing American society apart at the seams will only get worse. People will lose their faith in the law, which is the one safeguard we have against violence and societal breakdown. Americans cannot have faith in a system of justice that only looks outwards, investigating the public it serves. There must be internal accountability pursued just as rigorously, if not more so, than the outward application of the law.

Senior Democrat government officials aren't the only ones currently free from being prosecuted. Leakers against Republican administrations also get a free pass. From the very first day, the Trump administration experienced a deluge of leaks, including the release of classified materials and private calls with foreign leaders. These leaks didn't just damage American foreign policy. They are also criminal. It is flagrantly illegal to leak classified information, yet for years the Democrats and liberal DoJ lawyers gave it a pass because the leaks were harming a president they didn't like.

The only way to stop leaks is to prosecute leakers. This isn't as hard as it may seem. For any classified document, there are only a handful of people who have access to it. That and classified documents are almost always viewed within government office space or on secure government computer systems. Every single government device is monitored, so discovering who sent what document to whom is not terribly difficult. Yet even for those better at covering their tracks, the Department of Justice and the FBI have forensic ways to discover who sent and received information. That is literally a main part of their job. Armed with that information, the Department of Justice needs to bring down the hammer hard. Every single leaker needs to be outed and prosecuted. Every. Single. One. And the leakers of sham classified "investigations" against political targets must be hunted down and prosecuted as well. It is the only way to shore up American national security and restore the professionalism of our government, which should always put the safety and security of our nation above scoring cheap political points against opponents.

An additional way the DoJ has covered for its political allies is by either hiding or leaking the existence of important investigations into public figures. For example, during the 2020 campaign the Department of Justice was investigating Hunter Biden's corrupt multimillion-dollar deals in places like Ukraine and China—deals that enriched the Biden family and even implicate President Biden himself. Yet the existence of those investigations was hidden until after the election so that it wouldn't hurt Joe Biden's electoral chances. Not only that, but the Deep State in the FBI was leveraging their relationships with their allies in Big Tech to squelch the Biden laptop story even before it broke. Years after the election, Facebook chief Mark Zuckerberg revealed that the FBI approached Facebook to warn them to be wary of Russian disinformation that would soon drop, a clear effort to sway Facebook's judgment against the bombshell story. Altogether, this was a monumental rig job, especially considering that at the time the Biden campaign and the media were running a coordinated smear campaign trying to discredit the Hunter Biden accusations. It didn't matter that the primary source proving Biden family corruption wasn't some anonymous source of selective government leak but that it was Hunter's own laptop.

While the DoJ and FBI were doing their best to hide and spin the Biden corruption scandal, other members of the Deep State from the intelligence community were also running political interference. Fifty-one intelligence officials, including four former cabinet secretaries from the Department of Defense, the Central Intelligence Agency, and the National Security Agency issued a public letter declaring that the Hunter Biden laptop "has all the classic earmarks of a Russian information operation"[4]—an absurd falsehood that the intel officials manufactured after admitting they had not even looked at the laptop themselves. Of course, these officials knew the media would run with headlines designed to convince the people that the laptop was some sort of Russian plant. When later confronted (sadly, after the election) with their lies, not a single one of them apologized. In fact, many have stated that they are proud they helped take down Trump.

If the DoJ had informed the public of its investigation, it would have shattered the Deep State and fake news media narrative that the Hunter laptop was Russian disinformation. The DoJ hid the truth, so the intelligence community's actual disinformation was able to spread unobstructed. Meanwhile, every time President Trump or one of his family members was ever under an investigation, that information was either announced or leaked, undoubtedly in an attempt to tarnish his reputation and imply that Trump and those around him were obviously guilty of something.

The Department of Justice should end this unequal practice by adopting a single, uniform standard: If anyone of public interest is under investigation, they should announce that investigation immediately and publicly, unless the attorney general and FBI director decide based on operational necessity that they are unable to do so. If they are not able to inform the public, then they must notify the Gang of Eight in Congress—senior members privy to high-level classified information—of the target and their reasoning for keeping it hidden from the American public. This policy should cover broadly all public figures, including political appointees, members of Congress, or one of their family members. Of course, all people are presumed innocent until proven guilty, so the mere existence of an investigation doesn't mean that the person being investigated is going to prison. But at a bare minimum, this puts both parties on an equal playing field. The Department of Justice can no longer use the announcement of investigations to damage Republicans while waiting to announce investigations into Democrats until the announcement will do the least political harm.

The DoJ has other policies that do grave harm to the American public that must be reformed. One of them is the use of a backdoor way to effectively implement "laws" through guidance and memos rather than through the people's elected representatives in Congress. The way it works is that lawyers within the Department of Justice—especially within the Civil Rights Division—will send out some sort of public letter saying how they interpret the law. For example, in 2016 the Obama Justice Department along with the Department of Education said that in their opinion, civil rights law demanded that schools allow men to access and use girls' bathrooms and locker rooms. It didn't matter that civil rights law says no such thing, that Congress never passed a law to allow men to enter women's restrooms, or that there are many schools opposed to this policy. All that mattered was that unelected DoJ lawyers said they thought the law should be applied to force schools to let men into girls' bathrooms, and that was that. As a result, schools started changing their bathroom policies because they feared getting prosecuted by the Department of Justice. Effectively, the DoJ changed the law by threatening public schools with lawsuits if they didn't do what they were told.

This is a completely undemocratic and un-American way to enforce the law. Laws are supposed to be passed by a vote, not by the threat of lawsuits over novel interpretations from left-wing Deep State lawyers. The Department of Justice should completely do away with the use of memoranda and guidance to implement and interpret the laws. It is the job of the judicial branch, not lawyers in the executive branch, to interpret the law. And it is the job of Congress to write laws more specifically and with clear instruction. If anybody thinks that laws passed by Congress are unclear, they can file a lawsuit and take it to court, not just reinterpret the law from some DoJ office in DC.

Speaking of DC, a final reform that would vastly improve the operations of the Department of Justice would be to drastically curb the practice of prosecuting trials within the District of Columbia. In 2020, Washington, DC, voted 92 percent for Joe Biden and less than 6 percent for Donald Trump. Obviously, the jury pool available for DC courts will be woefully biased in politically charged cases. Yet time and again, left-wing leadership at the DoJ chooses to prosecute their cases in perhaps the most liberal jurisdiction in America. Not to mention, DC doesn't even have the most experienced national security practice at the DoJ, so bringing up such cases uses less qualified lawyers in a biased jurisdiction. The results are infuriating but totally foreseeable—and easily remedied.

For example, at the end of the Trump administration, prosecutor John Durham was tasked with investigating the roots of the Russia collusion hoax. Durham has indicted several people for their illegal actions that led to the Obama FBI proactively spying on its political opponent, Donald Trump. Yet one of those indictments against Clinton lawyer Michael Sussmann, who in the 2016 election covered up his connections to the Democrats while claiming to the FBI that the Trump campaign had secret back-channel communications to Russia, was nullified by a biased jury. There is no doubt that Sussmann lied to the FBI. I actually took Sussmann's deposition during the probe into Russia Gate that would later prove he was willfully misleading federal authorities. But to a slanted jury, that didn't matter.

I bet if you polled the residents of Washington, DC, large numbers of them would say they actually believe the insane conspiracy that President Trump was a Russian agent. Yet those same people were asked to serve on a jury to judge Sussmann, one of the original authors of that conspiracy. There was little chance they were ever going to decide the case fairly. Don't believe me. Just listen to the jurors' own words. After the trial, the jury forewoman told left-wing outlet NPR that the whole trial was a waste of time, saying, "I think we have better time or resources to use or spend to other things that affect the nation as a whole…We could spend that time more wisely."[5] Really, that means they never even looked at the black-and-white evidence—and the evidence was clear as day. It was as if a bank robber were being prosecuted, and we had a video of the robbery with the perp's face flawlessly visible. The only way you don't convict is if you close your eyes. In the Sussmann trial, the jury was closing its eyes.

This practice of choosing exclusively from liberal jury pools needs to end. The Department of Justice should prosecute criminals where there will be a fair trial, not just where the courthouse is closest to the DoJ main headquarters. Washington, DC, may have a lot of lawyers, but it is far from the only place that is qualified to adjudicate violations of federal law. When lawbreakers commit crimes that influence the entire country, the jury shouldn't just be liberal residents of Washington.

***

The Department of Justice is not beyond reform. Perhaps more than any other corrupt federal bureaucracy in the Deep State, the DoJ can be fixed through a strong attorney general and tough lieutenants who are willing to take on the swamp and implement these reforms. Fixing the DoJ is our only hope to reestablish equal justice under the law in America.

PART II

THE FEDERAL BUREAU OF INVESTIGATION AND RUSSIA GATE

CHAPTER 4
Objective Medusa

One of the most cunning and powerful arms of the Deep State is the Federal Bureau of Investigation (FBI), the primary investigatory agency within the executive branch, which operates under the authority of the DoJ. The Central Intelligence Agency (CIA) may have a greater air of mystery around it (and it's certainly the subject of many more spy thrillers), but in many ways a hyperpoliticized FBI is a much greater threat to American freedom and self-government. That's because while the CIA has the power and authority to collect intelligence and operate in clandestine manners overseas, the FBI focuses inside of the United States. We have legal and procedural safeguards in place in order to prevent abuses, but as the nation has learned, those safeguards are not even close to being enough. The FBI is now the prime functionary of the Deep State. The politicized leadership at the very top has turned it into a tool of surveillance and suppression of American citizens.

The power of the FBI has been abused before. Government skeptics everywhere know about the infamous case of Martin Luther King Jr. being under FBI surveillance for over a decade before his assassination.[6] But however unjust and unwarranted it was for the FBI to invade MLK's privacy, the abuses of today are orders of magnitude larger—and more dangerous. Nothing reveals more how the government gangsters at the FBI operate than the Russia Gate scandal—a coordinated disinformation campaign conducted by the FBI, the Clinton campaign, the fake news mafia, and elected Democrats to take down the Republican nominee for president through false claims that he was a Russian agent. These disinformation campaign attacks against Donald Trump were unlawful. But the exposure of the Russia Gate scandal also revealed the inner workings of the politicized national security establishment that turned the most powerful tools of the federal government against innocent American citizens.

Unlike previous scandals, from the Bay of Pigs to Watergate, the press was totally unwilling to investigate the truth behind Russia Gate. Worse than that, they were actively spreading lies and publishing disinformation disseminated by the FBI itself, running cover for the corrupt government officials whom it is their duty to hold accountable. With the press serving as a functionary of the Deep State, few others were capable of discovering the truth. So the fact that this scandal was even exposed is a bit of a miracle. I know because I'm the one who exposed it.

HOUSE STAFFER

After President Trump's earth-shattering victory in 2016, many people were vying for spots in the incoming Trump administration. One of my friends was trying to get a job, and another friend of mine put me in touch with the chairman of the House Permanent Select Committee on Intelligence (HPSCI), Devin Nunes, with the hopes that maybe he could help my job-searching friend out. As I sat down with Devin, we got along right off the bat. Russian collusion stories were all over the news at the time. Over the course of the campaign, reports were swirling around that President Trump—or at least his campaign—was somehow compromised or colluding with the Russians to "steal" the election. Some even went so far as to argue that the incoming president was himself a Russian agent. Devin knew that his committee would have to investigate what happened and find the facts—and my background intrigued him. He had been asking about my experience with investigations as a public defender and federal prosecutor, and when I was embedded with Special

Forces at SOCOM. Knowing I had all these years of experience, he asked me how I would handle something like an investigation into Russian interference.

I gave him a basic outline, telling him that the best way to start would be to gather the paper trail and gather documents, because documents don't lie but witnesses do. Only after building a case and gathering information through documents would I recommend interviewing witnesses to test the veracity of his findings. As we continued talking, Devin offered me a job to run the whole Russia investigation. I told him absolutely no. Both Devin and I figured the outlandish claims about Trump and Russia would eventually pass over, and in the end the committee would issue some boring report on ordinary Russian cyber activity that very few people would ever care about or read. It didn't seem like the most appealing job, not to mention, I NEVER wanted to work on the Hill.

But Devin is a persuasive guy. We continued talking, and within a couple months, Devin told me that if I helped him with all the grunt work required for an honest investigation, then he would give my resume to the White House and do everything he could to get me a job at the National Security Council (NSC)—a dream job of mine. When all was said and done, he estimated the investigation would take just a year.

It seemed like a good opportunity not just to get my foot in the door at the NSC, but also to help clear the air around the 2016 election and give Americans an accurate picture of what had happened and if Russia was involved. So I told Devin yes but on one condition. I was going to follow the facts wherever they led, and at the end of the day, we would share what I found with the American public. I told him I wasn't there to pursue a partisan con job. I had never met, spoken to, or exchanged messages with Donald Trump. I hadn't worked on his campaign or donated a single dollar. I was a career federal prosecutor and public defender. I knew the only way to have true accountability was to uncover and publish the entire truth. If Congress was going to play its legitimate role conducting oversight, those were the terms. Everything would get put out for the world to read. Nunes agreed immediately, and I accepted. Now I was a staffer at the HPSCI, a position that would change my life—and change America—forever.

SPYING ON THE TRUMP CAMPAIGN

The first thing I did on the HPSCI team was to take a look at the Foreign Intelligence Surveillance Act (FISA) application the FBI used in order to obtain a warrant to surveil a one-time Trump campaign official by the name of Carter Page. I had worked FISA warrant applications at the DoJ while running terrorism investigations, so I knew the standards of evidence and proof that had to be met for the judge to approve this invasive surveillance, especially of an American citizen. If the Trump campaign really did "collude" with Russia, whatever that means ("collusion" after all is not a legal term but something that was conjured up by the media), then the FBI's extremely invasive decision to effectively wiretap an aide to a presidential candidate seemed like a good place to start to find the evidence.

To put the Carter Page FISA warrant into perspective, this wasn't just routine police work. By getting a FISA warrant on Carter Page, the FBI effectively had the ability to spy on most, if not all, of the Trump campaign communications, including messages from Donald Trump himself. That's because these warrants don't just let the FBI observe the subject of the warrant but also people one or even two degrees removed from the subject. That means the entire Trump campaign could have been in the FBI dragnet. The FBI launched Russia Gate while Trump was a leading candidate for the presidency, meaning there was a decently strong likelihood that he could be the next commander in chief.

I told Devin we had to get all the documents. What I didn't realize is that this would become a monumental lift, often obstructed by President Trump's own appointees at the DoJ and FBI. But after some time and effort, we were able to get at least some access and see the Carter Page FISA warrant. Before reviewing the FISA documents, I assumed that the FBI must have had some extremely thorough and damaging evidence against Page. But as I read the warrant application, something didn't make sense. Almost everywhere I looked, the FBI based its work on a dossier filled with wildly outlandish claims about Trump. The document came from a British former MI6 agent turned FBI source named Christopher Steele.

Throughout 2016, members of the press had been sitting on the dossier. Someone within the government had leaked it, presumably with the hope that it would be published to demolish Donald Trump. But the press delayed publishing it because nobody could substantiate the ridiculous claims in the document. Then, very early on in 2017, before President Trump had even assumed office, BuzzFeed did what no other outlet was willing to do and put the dossier online, claiming Americans had a right to know because it was the source of investigations.[7] As I would soon learn, the Deep State would commonly use the existence of investigations as a tool to farm out to the media damaging information on their political opponent, or even false accusations, through selective leaks. The rest of the press soon followed suit and began discussing the dossier openly.

Anybody with half a brain who wasn't totally deranged by hatred of Trump could tell that the dossier was a total fiction. Russian hookers. Pee tapes. Secret trips to Prague. Intimations that Trump—an extremely public businessman and reality TV star—had been "cultivated" by Russian intelligence for years and that he was "handled" by Russian President Vladimir Putin directly. It even had basic factual information totally wrong, such as saying that certain people were present in certain countries at specific times when flight records and other evidence showed the person was nowhere near there. Basic gumshoe reporting 101 should have taught any self-respecting journalist how to spot these obvious flaws and inaccuracies. But the mainstream media had already long ago jettisoned journalistic integrity in their mission to destroy Trump.

At the time, the document was labelled by the media as the "Trump Dossier." After reading it, I told Devin that it didn't make sense to call something filled with easily falsifiable information and scandalous, unfounded accusations against President Trump the "Trump Dossier." Instead, we should start calling it the "Steele Dossier" so that Steele's name, not Trump's, would forever be attached to his own BS reporting. We did, and it worked.

While the Steele Dossier was being spread all over the media, it didn't come out of nowhere. Former British spies don't just make up a bunch of lies about a presidential candidate and feed it to the FBI as a big joke. Somebody had to have paid for it. As I learned in the DoJ man-hunting terrorists, the best way to find out who did something wrong was to follow the money. Every transaction has documents attached to it, and every bank account has a person associated with it. Witnesses can lie, and communications can obscure the truth. But money doesn't lie. I started digging deeper and found out Steele was employed by an American firm called Fusion GPS. Whoever paid for the dossier would have sent money to Fusion GPS, so I was convinced that we needed to get ahold of Fusion GPS's bank records. The only way to do that was to issue a congressional subpoena.

When I presented all of this to Devin, his first reaction was, "No." He was convinced by my work. But he was hesitant to take this leap because, in the entire history of the House before this point, the HPSCI had only ever issued one subpoena. As a committee chairman, Devin had the right to issue a subpoena, but he would have to get the permission of Speaker Paul Ryan, and Devin was very skeptical that Ryan would approve a subpoena for financial records based on the hunch of some new committee staffer.

Week after week, any chance I got, I kept making my case to Devin. Every summer, Devin, as chairman, would visit different regions around the world to improve our intelligence community. That summer, he invited me to come along. At the end of each day, Devin and I would sit down for what he dubbed "the final," a cocktail to recap the day. At the end of one of these long days, I made another plea. We were sitting in the town square of the majestic five-hundred-year-old town of Vicenza, Italy, clock tower and all, sipping negronis. I laid it out for him again. The only way to break open this case was to follow the money. I was so confident that I told him if I was wrong, he could fire me right on the spot.

Devin knew I was right, and he had already stuck his neck out more than any other congressman to find the truth. We had to keep going. So he gave the thumbs-up. Back stateside, he promised that he would ask Speaker Ryan for the subpoena. Speaker Ryan was hesitant at first and not willing to give the green light. He was averse to doing anything that might rock the boat too much. But Devin kept on him. It took months, but after Devin and Speaker Ryan shared a couple beers on the Speaker's Balcony at the Capitol Building, Ryan finally agreed to give Devin the subpoena I had been pressing for.

The moment we issued the subpoena, Fusion GPS brought the heat. I knew we had hit signal jackpot—a military term for when you accomplish a determined objective. Their obstruction was the best indicator yet that we were onto the truth. Fusion GPS took the case all the way to federal court, but we were completely within our rights. After a monthslong battle, and a recusal from a federal judge whom we had figured out worked for Clinton World in her past as a lawyer, we got the court order we knew was coming. When we finally got the bank records, it was a bombshell. Pay dirt. The money directly came from the Hillary Clinton campaign and the Democrat National Committee (DNC). They sent millions through their law firm, Perkins Coie, to pay Fusion GPS for the Steele Dossier and more. That meant the Trump campaign was spied on based upon opposition research paid for by the Democrats to the tune of millions of dollars.

UNDER OATH

What if I told you back in 2016 America that one of the two major political parties would buy their way into the intelligence and law enforcement communities and hijack the FBI and CIA to use against their political opponent? Then those federal offices would work in concert with a secret court and the mainstream media to implement the largest criminal conspiracy in US history by illegally spying on a president and his campaign—all in attempt to take down a president based on completely false and fabricated information. Would you believe it? In America? I wouldn't either.

Nothing like this had ever happened in history. Under normal circumstances, this scandal would have shattered every American's faith in the FBI. But since the target was Trump, the fake news built an entire false and destructive narrative about President Trump to help the Democrat machine, manipulating roughly half the nation to believe a lie. But the truth was the truth, and we had to get it out—and uncover the rest of the story.

By linking the Steele Dossier to the Clinton campaign and the DNC, we revealed that the Russia collusion hoax was nothing more than a political hit job. But how did the Steele Dossier find its way into the hands of federal law enforcement in the first place? The more questions I asked, the less the Department of Justice was willing to cooperate. After a lot of back and forth, the DoJ reluctantly allowed two people of Chairman Nunes's choosing to go to the DoJ and review their records in person without being allowed to take any notes or copies of what was there. The FBI was doing everything to cover its tracks, and, as we soon learned, they would commonly mark documents as "classified" even if they weren't classified in an effort to hide their corrupt conduct from the public.

Devin sent me to go see the records, and using the Justice Department's and FBI's own documents, I started to piece together the biggest political scandal in American history. I was still trying to work out the details, but back on the Hill, I told Devin that we weren't dealing with one bad actor or even a one-off event. We were facing the full-scale politicization of the national security apparatus. It was like the ancient Greek myth of Medusa. Medusa was just one monster, but on her head there were dozens and dozens of individual snakes. To defeat Medusa, you couldn't just kill a single snake. You had to cut off her whole head. So as we expanded our probe, I dubbed it Objective Medusa.

As I was sifting through all the documents, including FBI reports, FISA warrants, and bank documents, the committee reached the next phase of our investigation: sworn witness testimony. I was starting to stitch together the full story, but I wanted to get the main actors on the record, including FBI Director James Comey, Deputy Director Andrew McCabe, and everyone else who had or could have had a part in the scheme. To ensure we did it right, I decided to ask every single witness the same exact set of questions: "Have you personally seen evidence that the Trump campaign or Trump conspired, colluded, or coordinated with the Russians?" I labelled my tactic the "Three Cs."

The evidence was telling me that the national security state was spying on Trump based on an easily debunkable dossier and fabricated "intelligence." So when I confronted the witnesses with my Three Cs, they all answered as expected. I would ask my questions, and they told me they heard x, y, or z, repeating a rumor here or something from the dossier there. They told me that Trump was a billionaire who did business all over the world, so he certainly did business in Russia. OK, but what evidence have you seen of collusion? They'd say that Trump had famously asked, "Putin, are you listening?" at a rally. OK, but what evidence have you seen of coordination? They would say that Trump seemed oddly reluctant to go along with the Russia interference narrative and that he was hostile to investigations, and why was he worried if he had nothing to hide? Yet again, I would say, "OK, but have you personally seen evidence that Trump or his campaign conspired, colluded, or coordinated with the Russians?" Under oath every single one of the over sixty witnesses I interviewed answered, "No." The documents we had compiled were proving the case that the Russian collusion narrative was a Democrat-funded, government-perpetrated crime of historic proportions. The testimony we gathered sealed it. And with that, any last remaining faith I had in the DoJ or the FBI to act fairly and with respect for the law was gone.

BRIEFING STAKEHOLDERS—AND FACING ROADBLOCKS

All the Republican staff on the House Permanent Select Committee on Intelligence prepared our reports meticulously, knowing that we were about to put some people to the fire who had never been held accountable before. The report was called the Nunes Memo but internally soon became known as the Kash-Gowdy memo after myself and Representative Trey Gowdy, a leading member of the Intelligence Committee. I was happy Devin recognized our work. But I was more happy that we had proven my friend Trey Gowdy wrong—something I know now would put a grin on his face. You see, when I first met Trey at the beginning of the investigation, we were in a sensitive compartmented information facility (SCIF) in the basement of the Capitol where it's possible to view classified documents safely. He came up to me and said, "Well, I hear you are going to be running our Russia investigation. I hope you know Congress is where righteous investigations go to die." I could tell he was half-kidding—but also half-serious. Trey had just finished his tenure as the chair of the Benghazi Select Committee while I was coincidentally the Main Justice lead Benghazi prosecutor for two years. We both had uncovered a lot of damning details about Benghazi, but we both also saw the political establishment do everything in their power to bury it. With Russia Gate, we were determined to not let the same thing happen. This time the establishment lost, and the truth won out.

With the report near completion, my next duty was to brief interested parties who had a right to be in the know before our findings went public. An easy way to destroy a relationship is to have someone find out information in the press instead of from you personally. Plus, we needed all fronts pushing out the truth, not fighting for political preeminence on TV.

One of the most important groups who needed to be in the know were members of Congress. Per orders we received from the Speaker's Office, I had to personally brief every single member of the Republican conference not only on the entire Nunes Memo but also on all of the underlying documents. This was no small task—especially considering that much of what we found was classified, meaning members of Congress had to sign a non-disclosure agreement before viewing the report. So there I am, sitting in a SCIF in the basement of the Capitol, informing members of Congress of the biggest bombshell political scandal in American history. Then, as they're leaving, I have to remind these people who make a living giving speeches and going on TV that they can't tell anything to anyone. Congress is not exactly used to that. In one instance Congressmen Jim Jordan, Mark Meadows, and Matt Gaetz were all together in one group that I briefed. As soon as they each finished the memo, they looked up and said, "We have to get this out." I knew we had it right.

Amid the congressional briefings, I also had sit-downs with the Department of Justice, along with other staff on the HPSCI. By this time we were only a few weeks out from being done with the memo, and the DoJ was shitting bricks. The FBI is under their authority, and they knew that if the public found out what we knew, they would be in the middle of a firestorm. Up to that point, we had been making document requests to the DoJ in writing and asked that they respond in writing as well. When you put things down on paper (or in this case, on email) people can't hide behind claims that there was miscommunication or that they never received the request. There was very little they could do behind the scenes to hold us up because our request, timestamp and all, was there for everyone to see.

In that context, Deputy Attorney General Rod Rosenstein issued a threat. He said if we were going to act like litigators by demanding documentation, the DoJ was filled with litigators, and they could do the same—by subpoenaing the committee's records and emails, meaning *my* records and emails. In effect, the nation's top lawyer (when it came to the Russia investigation at least) was threatening to use the law enforcement powers of the United States government to threaten a House staffer conducting oversight on his department, likely because he did not like the corruption I was about to expose. It was a direct and personal threat against me and against Congress's rightful oversight authority, and I wasn't going to let it scare me.

I went to Speaker Ryan's senior staff to tell them how Hot Rod (as we called Rosenstein because of his explosive temper) and other officers of the executive branch were outright threatening a Hill staffer, their employee, for conducting congressional oversight they had requested—one of the core functions of a co-equal branch of government. The

Speaker's Office flatly refused to have my back. It was very reminiscent of the time when the DoJ refused to stand up for me after being attacked by the unstable judge in Houston on my way back from Tajikistan. The lesson is the same: it doesn't matter what branch of government it is, in Washington the vast majority of people watch out for themselves and have no interest in defending what's right or protecting the integrity of the institutions they serve.

The Speaker's Office refused to stand up for me, so I pulled from the Washington playbook they had written and went to the press, giving the story to a Fox News reporter named Catherine Herridge. She is one of the few reporters out there who isn't in the tank for the Deep State. One way or another, the public needed to know that the executive branch was threatening to use underhanded tactics to stop a legitimate investigation into their crimes. After the story broke, Speaker Ryan was not pleased. During a full session of Congress when members and staff were rushing around the floor of the House for voting and speeches, Speaker Ryan grabbed me and asked me not to leak to the press. When the Speaker "asks" you something, there's a lot of weight behind that. I told him absolutely. I would have no problem doing that the moment he, as the Speaker of the House, started having the backs of people falsely attacked for their work on behalf of the House. Let's just say Speaker Ryan was a media darling for a reason. He was a total failure and a coward. He would have let the corruption we exposed be buried on his watch if we hadn't pushed so hard to get it out.

Hot Rod's threat fell flat, but the Deep State wasn't quite done trying to prevent the release of the memo. In one last attempt to stop our work, Christopher Wray, the new FBI chief, asked me to meet with some of his top people and discuss the memo before its release. I, of course, agreed to a sit-down with the FBI's top counterintelligence agent, Bill Priestap, along with another FBI employee named Sally Moyer (both of whom ended up being bounced for their involvement in Russia Gate). My partner in the investigation and I went to the FBI headquarters in downtown Washington and sat in a SCIF the size of a jail cell. There we waited and waited until the agents finally showed up. When they sat down, I asked them one single question: "Was any single fact that we produced in the memo wrong?" They didn't answer, giving the typical bureau response that we needed to delay, ostensibly so they could take more time to review the memo.

So I told them, "No. I am here because your boss, Director Wray, asked me to meet with his two head people. Are you telling me you didn't review the memo before we showed up?" With that, they had to answer that they did read it. So I asked again. "Is anything incorrect?" Reluctantly they had to answer no, but they still requested that they have more time. I told them that wasn't their decision to make, and the meeting was over. They already spent two years running this bullshit op. It was time for the world to see their corruption.

With all the different equities briefed (or fought off), the moment of truth had come. It was time to tell the public what we knew. True to my word, I went to Devin and said, "OK, now we've got to tell the world." He didn't hesitate for one second. He agreed, and what we released rocked the nation.

CHAPTER 5
The Nunes Memo

T he Russia Gate scandal offers a never-before-seen glimpse into how the government gangsters in the FBI operate, using methods of entrapment and extortion that would make the mafia proud. As such, it's worth reviewing in detail the facts we uncovered in the Nunes Memo in the HPSCI and through subsequent declassifications I worked on in the Trump administration.

THE STEELE DOSSIER AND THE FOUR FISA WARRANTS

As detailed earlier, the root of Russia Gate is the Steele Dossier paid for by the Hillary Clinton for President Campaign and the DNC. They spent millions to conjure up lies in order to stage false attacks against their opponent, Donald Trump. Politicians paying for dirt on their political opponents is par for the course in American elections, and if that were the whole story, nobody would be concerned. The real scandal is how the bogus Steele Dossier got hijacked by the intelligence community and law enforcement agencies to carry out an elaborate disinformation campaign. That story reveals a dark web of corruption at the highest levels and deepest reaches of government.

As we uncovered in our report, Steele, the author of the memo, was also a paid FBI informant and had multiple meetings and payments from the FBI leading into the 2016 election. Steele was eventually caught leaking a story to David Corn at *Mother Jones*. It was one of the first stories to mention the Steele Dossier (long before it got that name), and it helped kick off the disinformation that Trump was a Russian agent. After that story published, Steele also delivered a copy of his dossier to FBI General Counsel James Baker.[8]

FBI sources are strictly prohibited from speaking to the media, so when he was outed, Steele was technically fired. But instead of issuing a burn notice on Steele, the FBI kept using him as a source through a back channel in a way that had never been done before. They used a senior-level DoJ lawyer who had a relationship with Steele as their cutout. The FBI's new source was still Steele, but on paper it was a DoJ employee named Bruce Ohr.

Ohr worked as director of the Organized Crime Drug Enforcement Task Force in the DoJ and served as associate deputy attorney general, right below the number two in the department. His wife, Nellie, was a former CIA employee. Nellie had also been hired by Fusion GPS to collect dirt on Trump while Ohr was acting as an FBI cutout, so Steele and Nellie's disinformation was funneled through Bruce Ohr back to the FBI. The FBI is a sub-agency within the Department of Justice, and other offices within the DoJ work with the FBI all the time. However, it is hardly the job of a DoJ employee like Ohr to funnel political smears masquerading as intel to the FBI; all the while his wife is getting paid by Fusion GPS, which Steele worked for and which was bankrolled by the Hillary campaign and DNC. The Ohrs and Steele were working together as early as January 2016, and the FBI never revealed the biased way this information was collected to the FISA Court.

During the House investigation, I visited Deputy Attorney General Rosenstein's office with Devin and Trey and told him directly that his associate deputy was a cutout for Steele. Hot Rod blew up and told me that it was absolutely not the case. I told him not to believe me; it was all documented in the Woods files, a collection of documents—a catalogue if you will—that states with specificity the predicates for each fact in applications for surveillance before the Foreign Intelligence Surveillance

Court. Incredibly Rosenstein, the number two at the DoJ, had no idea what a Woods file was. I was shocked, but I dropped it. I wasn't about to embarrass Rosenstein further in front of his staff during an active investigation. I had to keep the mission first, even though he deserved to be taken down a peg.

So I told him in front of his staff, Devin Nunes, and Trey Gowdy to have someone get the FBI's Bruce Ohr 302s—the documents detailing FBI operations and meetings. With that request in the presence of the deputy attorney general, the obstructionists at the DoJ were caught in a corner and had to produce. Not only did we show Bruce Ohr's name as Steele's middleman, the next day I was called back to Main Justice where they pulled out pages and pages of Bruce Ohr's 302s that our counterparts at the DoJ had actively hidden from us by never disclosing their existence.

We had proven that Ohr was a cutout. Yet at the same time Steele was feeding information through Ohr to the FBI, he also appeared to be leaking information to the press to drum up stories about Trump-Russian collusion—stories the FBI would use as a rationale to feed the investigative machine. In effect, Steele was part of an FBI circular reporting ring. Steele would leak information, then the FBI would use the media reports planted by their own source to bolster its investigations.

One particular story went to Michael Isikoff at *Yahoo News*, which discussed how Trump campaign aide Carter Page travelled to Moscow and met with what I dubbed the two Igors—Igor Diveykin, Putin's deputy chief for internal policy, and Igor Sechin, the CEO of Rosneft, Russia's multibillion-dollar state-run oil company—both close Putin allies. The insinuation was that Page was working out a deal to trade access to Trump for personal gain, meaning the Trump campaign and Russia would be in some sort of cahoots.

The FBI used this leaked story—a story that they, the DNC, and the Hillary Clinton campaign paid for—in order to justify part of their FISA warrant application on Carter Page. Steele and the FBI chose Carter Page not because he was the true subject they wanted to spy on. He was just the easiest to dirty up with probable cause. Because he had travelled to

Moscow and rumors about him were more easily laundered through the press, he was a much easier target than Donald Trump for the FBI. But anyone who could do basic math could see that accusations against Page were ludicrous.

Specifically, the Steele Dossier alleged that Page traded access to Trump for a nearly 20 percent stake in Rosneft. Well, do the math. Rosneft is worth over $50 billion. So that means Page's agreement, if real, would have been worth around $10 billion. What the hell would the Russians be thinking forking over $10 billion to a low-level aid working on a campaign that the wider world all thought was going to lose? Even if you took the claim seriously, where was Page going to put all that money? How could he possibly launder it all while avoiding authorities? Every premise of the scheme is insane and untrue. But the FBI pretended to believe this easy-to-disprove line of intelligence because it would gain them access to spy on Trump.

As I mentioned earlier, the FBI didn't need to spy on Donald Trump personally because a single surveillance warrant on one person in the campaign would give them the ability to do all the spying they could need on effectively any person in the campaign, including the candidate himself. That broad reaching surveillance would help them accomplish their real goal, which wasn't to nab Carter Page or to stop Russian collusion—something they had to have known was completely fabricated by Steele—but instead to cast a wide net as they searched for absolutely anything incriminating that they could pin on Trump.

Later the FBI would, by all appearances, leak that Carter Page was under investigation, a patently unlawful dissemination of classified intelligence, as all FISA warrants and their underlying intelligence are classified. Yet again, the FBI was creating a circular reporting ring to attack opponents. First, the FBI or their political allies manufacture "news" stories based on lies and unverifiable hearsay, in this circumstance by claiming Page was trying to secure a deal with Rosneft. The FBI then uses their own planted story to justify investigations of the political opponent. The FBI then leaks the fact that they are investigating the political opponent to the press, which runs stories smearing the political opponent as a subject of federal investigation based on anonymous sources. Those stories would then be used by the FBI to corroborate their "amazing" source reporting and permit their unlawful investigation and surveillance. This manifest corruption of due process by the FBI damaged the very foundations of American democracy.

I've had similar media operations conducted against me. As I mentioned previously, in 2021 *Washington Post* columnist David Ignatius ran a hit piece on me, painting me as some sort of wild conspiracy theorist for standing against the Deep State (which he assured his readers doesn't exist). In the piece, he insinuated that I was under Justice Department investigation for leaking classified documents all based on false anonymous reports. Despite the fact that this was a bald-faced lie, these types of Deep State cronies never stop. In 2022, Ignatius ran yet another hit piece on me, trashing my efforts to declassify documents for the public to see and calling me a "Zelig figure"—an insult based on an old Woody Allen movie meant to say that I weakly take on the personalities of those around me to please them. The Deep State and their media allies' obsession with me, a mere government staffer, only makes sense because I helped release the truth, and nothing scares them more than the truth that exposes their corruption.

When it came to the spying warrant on Carter Page, it was the FBI, not Carter, that acted criminally. Not only was the FISA application based on a Democrat-funded dossier, but the author of that dossier was also infected with Trump Derangement Syndrome. As the Nunes Memo reported, Steele told Bruce Ohr that he "was desperate that Donald Trump not get elected and was passionate about him not being president."[9] The FBI knew about Steele's bias and that the Clinton campaign and the DNC had paid for the dossier at the time they submitted their FISA warrant application to spy on Carter Page, but they never told the FISA judge either of these facts, as was required by law. They knew that if they told the judge the full truth, the judge would laugh them out of the courtroom and reject their request to spy on Carter Page and Trump.

Additionally, I later discovered from our sworn interrogation of Andrew McCabe, the deputy director of the FBI, that the FISA warrant on Page would have never been granted without the Steele Dossier. The fake dossier was the lynchpin for the whole operation. This was yet another detail the Deep State tried to hide when Obama's former director of national intelligence James Clapper went on to CNN and said that the dossier was not used to start the investigation.[10] It was a flat-out lie, but it did serve Clapper's true purpose, which was to help his Deep State allies at the FBI.

Lest anyone think that this gambit to spy on the incoming president of the United States was perpetrated by rogue actors in the FBI, it's worth noting how the FISA application process works. For every single FISA application, the director of the FBI as well as the attorney general, deputy attorney general, or the assistant deputy attorney general for national security at the DoJ have to personally approve each one, verifying that the applications are accurate and true. That means the most senior members of the FBI and DoJ are implicated by attesting that these patently fraudulent applications were accurate. Altogether, there were four FISA applications in Russia Gate. As a result of our investigation, the inspector general for the Department of Justice ultimately found that all four warrants would have never been granted if judges had been told the truth, and the Foreign Intelligence Surveillance Court (FISC), also known as the FISA Court, rescinded two of the warrants in their entirety based on our investigation.

SHORING UP THE FISA APPLICATION

Folks at the FBI knew that the dossier was a farce. Regardless, they were able to intentionally lie to the FISC to get a warrant. Anyone with the temerity to start poking around and asking questions could show that their entire investigation was built on a Democrat smear campaign. Their arrogance was their downfall. They never thought they would ever be caught, let alone by some random Hill staffer.

Even so, the FBI knew that sourcing everything to one fake dossier was a dangerous move. So they launched an effort to hide the fact that the Steele Dossier was all they had, coming up with their infamous "insurance policy" (at least what I'm able to say about it, as the heart of the matter still remains classified and sequestered by DoJ). The "insurance policy" was first discussed by Peter Strzok. Strzok was formerly the deputy assistant director of the FBI's Counterintelligence Division and the man who formally opened up the Russia collusion investigation, which the FBI dubbed Crossfire Hurricane. He texted his mistress Lisa Page (no relation to Carter Page) that they needed an "insurance policy" in case Trump was elected.

As we uncovered in the Nunes Memo, both Strzok and Lisa Page, like Steele, had a documented hatred of Donald Trump. Their texts reveal that they were prepared to do anything to stop him from becoming president. Many of these texts we were able to reveal during the Russia Gate investigation, but not all. The rest would come when I worked on declassification in the Trump administration. While I was working for the HPSCI, the vast majority were marked classified despite being sent on government cell phones which, by definition, could not be classified. Classifying incriminating information to cover up crimes is a classic game the Deep State plays, and it was only when I worked in the Trump administration that I was able to help declassify the bulk of these text messages.

Based on public reporting of the texts, part of Strzok and Lisa Page's "insurance policy" was to send FBI informant Stefan Halper to spy on Carter Page and see if he couldn't drum up anything incriminating—or at least another excuse the FBI could use to continue surveillance on Trump even after the election. The lovebirds discussed this plan even though Strzok later acknowledged that there was "no big there there" in the Trump-Russia collusion case.[11]

Halper's surreptitious interviews with Carter Page came up with nothing. That should have been a big sign to the FBI that they needed to stop their unjustified spying on the Trump campaign and put an end to their illegal activities. Instead, they do what corrupt government gangsters always do. They doubled down. It was government arrogance at its height. The FBI doctored Page's comments to make him look like a criminal and hid exculpatory evidence from the FISA Court, such as the fact that Page totally denied being a Russian asset and that, quite to the contrary, he had a history of helping the CIA—information demonstrating that Page is far from a Russian spy but actually a faithful citizen. Just think: the FBI intentionally altered their own documents and lied to a federal court in 2017 America.

With their search for incriminating evidence on Page himself coming up empty, the FBI was desperate to bolster support for their warrant against the Trump campaign. So they turned to a new target. On top of Carter Page, they added another Trump advisor, George Papadopoulos, to the mix. The FBI hoped to increase the credibility of their unprecedented operations against Trump by telling the FISA Court there were multiple possible Trump campaign links to Russia and that the FBI was pursuing reports of these links not just because of one dossier but because of reports from multiple sources.

Amazingly enough, the evidence used on Papadopoulos in the FBI's FISA warrants was just as ginned up as what they used on Carter Page. The "evidence" the FBI used came in from Australia's ambassador to the United Kingdom, Alexander Downer, who had had a conversation with George Papadopoulos weeks before in a bar in London while drinking, in which Papadopoulos allegedly said that it could be suggested by someone that Russians could suggest they had dirt on Hillary Clinton that one might suggest the Trump campaign could receive. If that sentence sounds ridiculous to you, that's not far off from the actual original report. The original report noted (in redacted form) that it was written "concerning statements Mr. Papadopoulos made about suggestions from the Russians" and alleged that "Mr. Papadopoulos…also suggested that the Trump team had received some kind of suggestion from Russia" that it could assist them.[12] The report went on to note that "it was unclear whether he or the Russians were referring to material acquired publicly" and that "it was also unclear how Mr. Trump's team reacted to the offer." "Suggested." "Unclear." The rampant use of qualifiers alone proves that Downer's reported conversation meant nothing.

The FBI desperately hoped this report was true because, under Title 52, eliciting help from a foreign source to influence a presidential campaign is illegal.[13] The implication of the alleged conversation was that Papadopoulos was trying to get damaging information that the Russians had hacked the Clinton email server so that he could use it in the 2016 campaign, which certainly would have been a problem.

That is, if it actually happened. Not only did Papadopoulos state that he had absolutely no recollection of mentioning Russian dirt on Clinton in his conversation with Downer, the Australian envoy reported the conversation weeks after the fact and did it outside of the formal channels our nations have erected for vital intelligence sharing. America has intelligence sharing agreements with Australia, Canada, New Zealand, and the United Kingdom in an arrangement known as Five Eyes. If it was legitimate intel, it should have been shared through the Five Eyes channels with all its standards in place to verify credibility and confirm sources. The Australian envoy subverted that process and merely told the information to an employee at the US embassy in London because it was all hearsay and wouldn't have passed muster under the Five Eyes agreement. And if this wasn't enough to cast doubt on the matter, the counterpart Downer passed the information along to was an American foreign officer named Elizabeth Dibble, a woman who previously worked as Hillary Clinton's principal deputy assistant for Near East affairs at the State Department when Benghazi happened. Not exactly an apolitical operative.

Most damning of all, the Australian envoy was just as much of a partisan as Christopher Steele and the FBI agents running the case. Downer had previously pledged $25 million to the Clinton Foundation, the nongovernmental organization the Clintons had been using to grease relationships and trade favors abroad. Yet again, the FBI was basing its spying operations on political hit jobs, drunken bar room banter, and from people tied to the Democrat Party and the Clintons.

To add another layer of intrigue, the FBI is unable to conduct investigations on foreign soil unless they have permission from a host nation. For the FBI to get this information, they had to get approval. How do they get that? Through the CIA operation in the region. A senior CIA officer at that time was Gina Haspel, a woman who would soon go on to be President Trump's CIA director where she would repeatedly obstruct our investigation. Haspel may be a quintessential swamp creature, but she's not stupid. It is almost certain that she knew the FBI investigation was BS, which is why she worked so hard to keep roughly 40 percent of the Russia Gate documents that Devin and I worked so hard to declassify from being released to the public. Haspel is one of the main reasons why so many damning documents related to Russia Gate remain under lock and key. Where are those documents now? They should be in the hands of the public.

All these Deep State operators cover for each other in a creepy, incestuous relationship. And that extends even outside of government. When Gina Haspel eventually left the Trump administration, she was hired by a law firm named King & Spalding, where one of the partners is none other than Rod Rosenstein, the deputy attorney general who threatened to use the prosecutorial powers of the DoJ against me personally to stop the Russia Gate investigation. And who was a former partner at King & Spalding? Current FBI director Chris Wray. These corrupt officials are all in bed with each other and always have been.

On top of all of this, when the FBI used their informant Stefan Halper to try and get Papadopoulos to say that Trump was colluding with the Russians to hack the DNC, Papadopoulos said he would not engage in "this type of activity because at the end of the day it's...illegal," adding, "this is a form of treason."[14] With those words, Papadopoulos was rejecting outright the very crime that he was being accused of. Just as they did with Carter Page, the FBI excluded known exculpatory information about Papadopoulos from their FISA warrant application and hid it from the FISC judge.

A supreme irony behind all of this was that the FBI was investigating someone who had allegedly *talked* about Hillary Clinton's emails just before FBI Director James Comey publicly and illegitimately declared that the Department of Justice should not bring charges against Hillary Clinton for her *actual* mishandling of classified information on those same email servers. Papadopoulos allegedly spoke about Hillary's emails, and he and the Trump campaign were spied on for it. Hillary Clinton actually committed a crime through her handling of classified emails and was preemptively exonerated—a two-tiered justice system.

Papadopoulos later pleaded guilty not to conspiring with Russia or any shady foreign dealings, but to lying to the FBI after the FBI set him up in a perjury trap. Papadopoulos had told the FBI that he believed a professor he was talking to in 2016 didn't have high-level contacts in the Russian government. The government said that it believed he did know that the professor had high-level contacts. The fact that the professor himself told the *Washington Post* that he had "absolutely no contact with the Russian government" didn't matter.[15] The FBI claimed Papadopoulos intentionally made false statements that negatively impacted their investigation. There was every reason to believe the young staffer was telling the truth, but DoJ lawyers weren't looking for the truth. They wanted the scalp of a Trump staffer.

DESPERATION

In my opinion, the FBI agents behind Crossfire Hurricane must have been getting nervous as the 2016 campaign came to a close. They launched a FISA warrant based on the Democrat Steele Dossier, sicced an FBI informant on a Trump campaign official, doctored evidence, hid exculpatory information, spied on the Trump campaign, and buttressed their case with drunken tavern talk. Yet despite all that, the FBI's investigation was coming up with nothing. Nobody in the Trump campaign was found coordinating with the Russians. No proof outside of Steele's crazed musings came to light to show that Donald Trump was a cultivated Russian agent. There was nothing to be found because there was nothing there. The ultimate plan was working insofar as their investigation was damaging candidate Trump. But the FBI never actually uncovered anything illegal to help justify their spying in the first place.

In an effort to manufacture an explanation for how the Trump campaign could be evading the FBI dragnet, Clinton lawyer Michael Sussmann came up with the crackpot idea that Trump was secretly talking with the Russians through a secure communication link set up by a financial institution called Alfa-Bank. This claim was yet another parallel operation next to the Steele Dossier to take down Trump.

Sussmann didn't invent this Alfa-Bank idea out of nowhere. He was one of the over sixty witnesses I interviewed during the Russia investigation, and I asked him explicitly if he went to the FBI on his own volition or on behalf of a client. Under oath, he said he went on behalf of a client, meaning the Clintons. Yet again the Clintons were feeding lies to the FBI to fuel illegal investigations against President Trump. Meanwhile, Sussmann never mentioned to the FBI that he was sending them this information on behalf of Donald Trump's opponent. Sussmann sent a text to the FBI's general counsel, James Baker, the night before their meeting effectively saying that he was meeting with them as a Good Samaritan. He wrote that he was "coming on my own—not on behalf of a client or company—want to help the Bureau."[16] In my deposition of Sussmann during the Russia Gate investigation, I asked him if a client directed him to have conversations with the FBI, to which he replied, "Yes." Sussmann had told the FBI an outright, documented lie, and he did it with intent—which is exactly what a skewed DC jury failed to convict him of during his trial after this whole story was exposed.

Making it even more clear that he was working on behalf of the Clintons, Sussmann arrived at the FBI with a thumb drive filled with his Alfa-Bank fantasy. Later investigations revealed that Michael Sussmann bought that thumb drive at a Staples around the corner from his law office in Washington, DC. The name of his law office? Perkins Coie, the same firm that paid for the Steele Dossier on behalf of the Clintons and the DNC. He then billed his purchase of the thumb drive to the Hillary Clinton campaign.

Even before the election, the *Financial Times* threw cold water on the Clinton team's latest assault, reporting that the alleged communications between the Russians and Trump were probably something like spam or marketing emails. The fiction was never reasonable. But that didn't stop it from being spread.

THE EVOLVING CONSPIRACY

Donald Trump was smeared by the Democrats, mocked and slandered by the media, and derided by just about every cultural influencer and institution under the sun. At the same time, the Nunes Memo and HPSCI documents later revealed that the Deep State conducted an unprecedented spying operation against the Trump campaign in an apparent effort to tarnish Trump's reputation and derail his election. Despite having every force against him, Trump shocked the world and was elected president of the United States.

With that, the Deep State moved into full-scale panic mode. The man they had done everything possible to defeat was now going to be president. Not only had they failed, they also had to worry about something else: What if he and the nation found out what they did?

Meanwhile, with the FBI unwilling to admit its wrongdoing, the Russia collusion conspiracy soon grew out of hand, beyond even the Deep State's control. Gullible people in the media and beyond seemed to actually believe the lies they were peddling. It's possible even people in the FBI started to believe their own disinformation. Whatever the facts were, by the time Trump was elected, the Deep State couldn't control the narrative they manufactured, even if they wanted to (which they didn't).

So Donald Trump's political opponents came up with a two-pronged tactic to cover up their crimes. First, they would continue Russia Gate. The FBI had found nothing, and every single lead they did have came up short because they had falsely ginned up their entire investigation from the jump. But if they found something, anything, that could possibly link Trump and his associates to Russia, then they could justify everything they had done so far. Second, they moved swiftly to hide their activities, cover their tracks, and defame those who would investigate them.

The Nunes Memo was set to shatter their false narrative and show the American people a big piece of the truth. To the Deep State, that was unforgivable. As payback for even thinking to question them, they rained hell on us.

CHAPTER 6

The Snakes Bite Back

The Nunes Memo was a rare actual bombshell report. After it dropped, the arrogant Deep State was in shell shock. We hit them right where it hurt, all based 100 percent on facts. Even though a lot of our report had to be kept classified—including the over sixty interviews we did under oath where not a single person investigating the Russia hoax said that they had evidence of the Trump team conspiring, colluding, or coordinating with Russia—the full scope of what we were able to uncover and prove was staggering. To the politicized federal bureaucracy and their allies in the Democrat Party and the media, Devin Nunes and the HPSCI team committed an unforgivable sin in Washington: we held powerful people accountable by proving their corruption. As a result, we were public enemy number one. They did everything in their power to take us down—and haven't stopped targeting us ever since for it.

POLITICAL HACKS TRY TO UNDERMINE THE MEMO

Even before the Nunes Memo was released, we could tell the Deep State and their allies were sweating. They started planting attacks in the press, shouting breathlessly (and without a shred of evidence) that the memo would undermine national security and reveal intelligence sources, putting them at risk. The media organs pushing all of these attacks had never seen the memo, so they were just parroting whatever their FBI anonymous sources leaked to them or whatever Democrat members (like the HPSCI's ranking member, Adam Schiff, his hapless sidekick Eric Swalwell, and others) of the HPSCI told them to say. The media never mentioned the fact that our memo was entirely based on documents produced by the DoJ and the FBI and the sworn testimony of their employees. If there was anything damaging in there, it was the people who did it who caused the damage, not the HPSCI for making it public.

As we were conducting our investigation, frequently the Democrat staffers under Schiff would deride the Republicans on the staff as immature and childish, saying we were acting like Disney characters chasing imaginary bad guys. The Republicans on the House staff worked in the same secure space as the Democrat staff—think of it like a big cube farm. So the Democrats had ample opportunity to mock us. Soon, they really dug into the Disney theme and started saying that my team and I were conducting a Mickey Mouse operation like the *Mickey Mouse Clubhouse*, an old TV show for little kids where Mickey, Daffy Duck, and other Disney characters tried to solve all sorts of problems. We turned the joke on them, and I bought our office a giant, plush *Mickey Mouse Clubhouse* rug that stared at the Democrat staffers every time they walked through the door of our office. Our team started proudly calling ourselves the Mickey Mouse Clubhouse.

Of course, the joke was on the Democrat staffers in the end: it was the Mickey Mouse Clubhouse that blew open the biggest political conspiracy in American history. Some of those guys I worked with on the HPSCI to expose Russia Gate now work with me at Truth Social, the immensely popular social media platform President Trump founded and where I serve on the board of directors. To honor them and all of our work together, I bought us another Mickey Mouse rug that sits prominently as the centerpiece of the Truth Social HQ office.

But however bad the Democrat staffers were, their boss, shifty Adam Schiff, was from the inner circle of Dante's *Inferno*. This man is the definition of a corrupt politician. There is no depth he will not descend to in order to elevate himself and destroy his political opponents at the expense of a nation he purports to serve. He is a man without a single shred of decency or self-respect. I don't know if I've ever seen him do a single honest thing in all the years I worked near him. He even lies about lying.

Case in point, during the investigation Devin and I would give regular updates behind closed doors to committee members. I would write on a large white board to brief the members weekly, and the members loved it. In the end the white board became a sort of joke. So we carried it in every time to the briefing room and back to our office at the end. We'd often bring it back to the cube farm filled with made-up nonsense on it, knowing that the Democrats would look at it when they walked by our desks and try to decipher what we were doing. We never revealed anything, however, because the briefings were completely classified. Of course, Devin would give updates to the press, but he was always extremely careful to never reveal classified information while always telling as much of the truth as possible. Schiff, on the other hand, used the veil of classification to launch an all-out disinformation campaign against our investigation and President Trump. Like a modern-day Senator McCarthy, he would walk out in front of the press and tell the world that he had evidence not just that President Trump was compromised by the Russians, but that he was actually a Russian agent himself! Then, when anybody would ask him what that evidence was, he would immediately respond that he could not say what because it was all classified.

Devin and the entire Republican HPSCI team knew that Schiff was full of it. The facts proved that Trump was obviously *not* a Russian asset. That was a lie made up by the Democrats. Yet even as Schiff went on the air spreading this lie, we couldn't do a thing. We had proof that Schiff was lying, but since it was classified and we were committed to following the law, not leaking, and doing the investigation the right way, we just had to sit there and watch him lead the people astray. That is, until we released the Nunes Memo and later our HPSCI report of our entire investigation. The Nunes Memo disproved all of the lies Schiff had been telling for months. But he never apologized and was never questioned by the press.

In the end, we did get him back in a small way. Since we reported the facts, the only way the Democrats could fight back was with lies. So my plan was to goad Schiff into writing his own memo. Schiff will do anything for publicity, so he took the bait. He wrote his own memo, and the Republicans on the committee were more than happy to vote unanimously to make it public. It was filled with all sorts of falsehoods and disinformation that we were able to contradict with the facts as soon as the truth was finally presented to the public, laying waste to the Democrats' made-up narrative.

But besides publicly embarrassing him by shoving his own lies back in his face, Adam Schiff was never held accountable. He was made the chairman of the HPSCI. Like so many in Washington, his personal failings, scandals, and lies didn't get him fired; they got him a promotion.

PERSONAL ATTACKS

The Deep State, the Democrats, and the media were hardly satisfied just trying to undermine the memo itself. The ruling class wanted to send a clear message that exposing their lies and unlawful actions came with consequences, and they wanted that message to be personal.

It started with attacks against Chairman Devin Nunes. Billboards started rising up in his district back in California depicting him as a Russian stooge beholden to Vladimir Putin. Misleading political ads are normal enough, but things started to get weird when a story surfaced attempting to link Devin to a cocaine-infused, prostitute-filled yacht party. The story was so strange and a clear attempt to slander him that Devin filed a lawsuit against the media group behind the attack—of course, only after the media plastered the story everywhere.

Soon, the attackers crossed a line. Devin started to receive anonymous death threats, and his wife even received threats at the elementary school where she worked. The Deep State forces we were exposing have no moral compass and have no problem attempting to destroy the lives of innocent people to protect themselves. They even falsely attacked his grandmother.

The ruling elites started coming after me as well. As a member of Congress, Devin expected attacks, even if death threats and targeting his family clearly were never acceptable. For the media to come after a Hill staffer though? That was unprecedented. Up to this point, Hill staffers were off limits. Attacks on us just didn't happen. That the media with Schiff and Co. crossed that line showed just how much our work threatened permanent Washington.

The first attack came from the *Daily Beast*, which outed me as the head of the Russia investigation and quoted some anonymous source calling me Devin's "Torquemada"—the name of a dictatorial friar who helped kick off the Spanish Inquisition, murdering thousands along the way. The irony here is that I am the son of a man who fled an actual genocidal dictator, Idi Amin of Uganda, and lawfully immigrated to the United States to live the American Dream. My family is a living testament against violent repression. The Torquemada smear wasn't just a lie, it was an insult.

Before long, the *New York Times* launched another attack. I was travelling to England with another colleague on an unrelated intelligence matter, conducting the business our committee used to routinely do before Russia Gate. But our investigation never had time for a pause, so we always capitalized on opportunities. We decided while we were in town to stop by the office of the lawyer who represented Christopher Steele. By this time, Steele had been sued in the UK for defamation based on his bogus dossier, and his lawyer's information was on the public pleadings filed before the British courts. The lawyer wasn't there, so, in the presence of a witness, I left my card and told the office that our committee would like to speak with their client if he would be willing to sit down with us. My colleague and I then enjoyed a full English breakfast, got on the plane, and headed home.

By the time I got off the plane back in the States and turned on my phone, my inbox was flooded, and I had a pile of missed calls. Adam Goldman, the *New York Times* "reporter" who wrongfully won a Pulitzer Prize for spreading the fake Russia collusion conspiracy, was particularly aggressive, calling me the moment I got off the plane. He wasn't the only one. Apparently, the lawyers for Fusion GPS in America were in constant contact with Steele's attorneys in London. They had leaked to the press that we had come by, and the media was running with this wild, incorrect story that I had flown to London in an attempt to ambush and confront Steele in his countryside retreat. We did everything by the book, attempting to reach Steele through his designated legal representative and leaving immediately after we were told that he was unavailable. But the story still is circulating to this day that I executed a stealth incursion across the Atlantic to ambush Steele.

Two *New York Times* reporters, Katie Rogers and Matthew Rosenberg, went so far as to imply that I was so mindlessly obsessed with the president that I was part of a group called the Dons—a name that they believed referred to the 45th president. The big hole in their story, though, was the fact that I am part of a hockey team called Dons Hockey, which existed long before Donald Trump ever announced he was running for president. We had actually named our team after Don Cherry, a legendary and flamboyant Canadian hockey announcer beloved by hockey fans everywhere. Any kid who ever spent his winters with a hockey stick in hand could have told the reporters that we were paying our respects to *Rock'em, Sock'em, Hockey* (Don Cherry's videos), not Donald Trump. But the truth is, Rogers and Rosenberg didn't even need to ask a hockey fan. They could have just looked it up on the internet. Instead, like all the media liars, they pushed a fake news story because it fit their narrative.

Just like what happened with Devin, media attacks were only the beginning. During my time on the HPSCI and afterward, I received multiple death threats. Hill staffers don't exactly get security details, so now I am forced to live my life watching behind my back in case any of those crazies are serious. This is how far the Deep State will go to cover up their crimes.

Everyone on our team knew the media and the whole corrupt cabal of entrenched interests in Washington were trying to make an example of me. The message was that if you dare to stand up and call the Deep State out, then get ready to have the media start sifting through your life, following you around, and twisting your words and actions to try to take you out. But the media machine didn't know who they were messing with. They wanted a fight? Fine. Game on. All their attacks only convinced me that we were on to something big. Who knows, maybe if they didn't attack me so hard I wouldn't have had such certainty about the case or pursued it so fervently. Regardless, they didn't take me or Devin down. The media may hate me, but the American people were thankful to finally have access to the truth.

"13 ANGRY DEMOCRATS"

Throughout much of the time we were running our investigation, the Deep State had formed a completely unaccountable and corrupt strike team of Democrat lawyers armed with the power of the Justice Department to keep the Russian collusion narrative alive and to continue the FBI campaign to find something, anything, they could possibly pin on Trump as a way to force him out of office. That strike team was called the Mueller Special Counsel probe.

After President Trump fired the corrupt James Comey from the FBI, the Deep State started to scramble. His number two, Andrew McCabe, was just as bad. McCabe had overseen the Clinton email "investigation" at the FBI as well as the spying operation on the Trump campaign. He signed one of the FISA warrants on the Trump campaign that was later revoked after our investigation. While running the Clinton investigation, he leaked sensitive information to the media to create a false narrative, an abuse he was later fired for. Not only did he have a demonstrable hatred of President Trump, McCabe's wife also received $675,000 from close Clinton allies during her unsuccessful run for the Virginia State Senate. The McCabes were in bed with the Clintons and the permanent Washington establishment, so it was obvious to everyone that Trump wouldn't tap him to head the FBI. The Deep State feared that if an honest person actually got the job, they would expose the truth about Russia Gate.

The politicized bureaucrats at the FBI and DoJ desperately needed some way to hide what they did. The best way to hide what they did was to pin something on Trump. So they chose a special counsel as a tool that would be vested with the power of the Department of Justice to call witnesses, subpoena documents, and even indict people for crimes.

The media helped with a massive public pressure campaign pushing for a special counsel. Unfortunately, the leaders at the Department of Justice were too weak to put a stop to the witch hunt then and there. Attorney General Jeff Sessions recused himself, and Deputy Attorney General Rod Rosenstein didn't have the backbone to call BS and end the madness. Meanwhile, disgraced former FBI head James Comey worked overtime to get a special counsel appointed. Comey gave his memos, including documents of his meetings with President Trump, to a professor at Columbia Law School, telling his friend to leak it to the press, which he promptly did. As if that weren't bad enough, the memos contained classified information. Just like how he exonerated Hillary Clinton for her illegal handling of classified information, Comey lived by the same standard for himself. Leaking classified information was considered completely acceptable if the Deep State itself did it.

Comey's memos added fuel to the fire, and Rosenstein caved. He named Robert Mueller—an utter swamp creature, former director of the FBI, and colleague of James Comey and Andrew McCabe—as the special counsel. With that, the Democrats and the Deep State got exactly what they wanted: a state-funded fishing expedition with large amounts of power and no time limit.

When Mueller was named special counsel, the HPSCI had yet to expose to the public the full extent of the FBI and DoJ fraud that was the Russia Gate conspiracy. But while the world still hadn't learned the truth about the depths of corruption at the FBI and DoJ, Mueller and his team could have easily contacted us to see what we had already found. Even though Mueller didn't, he still did have access to the same documents, and more, than we had at the HPSCI. He could see how the FISA warrants were almost entirely based on the Steele Dossier. He could read the dossier and know that it didn't pass the smell test. He could find out, just like we did, that the dossier was paid for by Donald Trump's political opponents then laundered into the FBI through partisan Democrats. He would be able to find out that Carter Page vehemently denied being a Russian spy and that he actually had helped the CIA in the past. He would also be able to look over the months and months of spying the

FBI had already conducted on the Trump campaign and White House to see that the FBI had found *nothing* so far. Knowing all of this, what the hell was Mueller doing for two years? It was a taxpayer-funded hit job from a group of government gangsters hired not because of any qualifications they had, but because of their shared hatred of Donald Trump.

For the Deep State, the best part about the special counsel was that if Trump ever tried to end this ridiculous injustice and artificially manufactured assault on his presidency, he would be accused of obstruction of justice. Of course, the media kept tossing around that charge of "obstruction of justice" every single time President Trump said something bad about Mueller. But what none of the media mentioned was how the president could be obstructing justice by criticizing a multiyear-long probe into an innocent man. You can only obstruct justice if you prevent an investigation into an actual crime. It is not obstruction of justice to publicly disapprove of an investigation designed to manufacture a crime that they can pin on you.

In fact, documents released years later showed that the DoJ's Office of Legal Counsel urged Attorney General Barr to say publicly what they knew—that President Trump never obstructed justice. Unconscionably, Barr shielded that conclusion from disclosure, though a federal court ultimately forced the DoJ's hand.[17] The wasn't the only time Barr undermined President Trump. Later, after working in the administration for some time, President Trump considered making me the deputy director of the FBI to help clean up the mess I uncovered there. Incredibly, Barr threatened to resign as attorney general if Trump made the appointment, claiming I didn't have the ability or the qualifications. That was rich. By that point I had been in the government fifteen years and was forty-one years old— exactly the same age Barr was when he was first appointed attorney general in 1991.

But I digress. Despite the fact that Trump did not commit a crime and did not obstruct justice, Mueller kept the Russia hoax alive for years past its expiration date. He gathered a partisan team that President Trump dubbed the 13 Angry Democrats. The lawyers Mueller hired were all partisans. Some of them were viciously anti-Trump. Another even attended Clinton's election night party in 2016. Many of them had donated thousands to Democrats, including to Hillary Clinton and President Obama. But even with unlimited resources and a team of hardcore Democrats, the Mueller probe came up with a laughable report. Despite being released *after* the Nunes Memo had blown open the whole story, the Mueller report fails to mention Fusion GPS, contains numerous factual errors, and doesn't even discuss Stefan Halper's fraudulent involvement at the behest of the FBI, among other glaring issues.

Worst of all, Mueller went far beyond the traditional role of a federal prosecutor—ultimately the job of a special counsel—to declare that his report "does not exonerate" Trump. This is a complete bastardization of due process. In America, you are innocent until proven guilty. It is not the job of a prosecutor to declare somebody innocent. You either charge them with a crime or you don't. If you don't charge them, you move on to the next case. Mueller's "no exoneration" game was a complete breach of prosecutorial ethics and DoJ standards.

The end of the Mueller investigation put a formal nail in the coffin of the Russia witch hunt. Of course, the Russia collusion conspiracy theory lives on to this day. But no reasonable and well-informed person can believe the lies anymore. In the end, the corruption at the FBI did untold damage to our nation and undermined the people's duly elected president. America is still dealing with the fallout of the greatest political scandal in American history. But there is a silver lining. Perhaps more than any event, Russia Gate took the mask off the Deep State. Before 2016, if you went around claiming that the FBI uses manufactured evidence and doctored testimony in order to spy on the political opponents of the ruling class and take down a sitting president, people would have thought you were a nut job. Many people would have thought that even if the FBI wanted to do such a thing, they would have never had the power to do it. Now, the veil has been taken off. As we will see, in scandal after scandal surrounding the Deep State, all roads begin and end with Russia Gate and the crimes, abuses, and tactics we uncovered there.

The Deep State is real—and if we want to save our country, we have to fight back.

CHAPTER 7

Crossing the Rubicon: The Raid on Mar-a-Lago

The rot at the core of the FBI isn't just scandalous, it's an existential threat to our republican form of government. The most powerful law enforcement agency in the world, bloated with billions of dollars of taxpayer money every year and empowered with the most invasive tools of espionage and spy craft, is being used as a weapon against political opponents and to deprive people of their ability to democratically choose the leaders they want. Sadly, these abuses have hardly stopped with Russia Gate. That's because nobody has been held accountable.

James Comey, who should be a disgraced former head of the FBI, is instead getting multimillion-dollar book deals *after leaking classified intelligence to the media.* Andrew McCabe, Comey's Clinton-loving deputy who signed off on numerous Russia Gate abuses, was fired from the FBI for lying about leaking to the press. Yet unlike George Papadopoulos, McCabe was never charged for his lies. Not only that, he was rewarded with lucrative media contracts. Peter Strzok, the man who formally launched the Crossfire Hurricane investigation that spied on President Trump on the basis of bogus intel, worked for years at the FBI after we caught his corruption. John Carlin, my former boss and the man who ran the National Security Division at the DoJ when this fraudulent collusion investigation was launched, has been promoted to be the number three person at the DoJ in the Biden administration. His former number two, Mary McCord, now holds a prestigious position as the executive director for Georgetown Law's Institute for Constitutional Advocacy and Protection. Lisa Monaco, who was Carlin's superior at the DoJ, is now the number two at the DoJ. Robert Mueller, despite running a two-year witch hunt against the president of the United States that they knew from the very beginning was based on Democrat-funded and FBI-perpetuated lies, is regarded by the media and the elite class as a sort of elder statesman. Again and again and again the innocent have had their reputations destroyed while the people who did it are rewarded. That is how a corrupt government functions.

When malicious political hacks manipulate the powers of the DoJ and the FBI for evil purposes and end up sometimes better off than they were before, that only incentivizes more corruption. Sadly, the political jackals at the FBI have been emboldened to commit even more abuses of power in their mission to solidify the two-tiered system of justice they helped create.

THE HUNTER BIDEN COVER-UP

One egregious wrong perpetrated by the FBI occurred in the final months of the tumultuous 2020 campaign centered on the Hunter Biden laptop. Democrat presidential candidate Joe Biden's son, Hunter Biden, left his laptop at a repair shop. After the lapse of many months, the laptop became the property of the repair shop owner. The laptop contained mountains of incriminating evidence—not just photographs and videos of Hunter's illegal drug use and hiring of prostitutes, but also documents and communications revealing the Biden family's corrupt and enriching business deals with countries like Ukraine and Russia. The laptop revealed that Joe Biden, who was running for president as a self-proclaimed paragon of moral decency, had actually enriched himself at America's expense by taking cuts of his family's multimillion-dollar deals with foreign entities, including some closely tied to the Chinese Communist Party.

The Hunter Biden laptop story should have changed everything in the 2020 campaign. Few Americans are comfortable electing a man to the presidency who has been bought and paid for by the Chinese. But the media and Big Tech companies, all brimming with partisan Democrats, took unprecedented steps to squelch the story, doing everything they could to ban it from being shared online and hide it from the American people. According to a whistleblower, the FBI had already refused to investigate the Hunter Biden laptop as far back as 2019 for fear that it would damage Biden. Local FBI leaders reportedly told their employees, "You will not look at that Hunter Biden laptop," because they feared finding the truth would mean that the FBI could "change the outcome of the election."[18] Senators Chuck Grassley and Ron Johnson later revealed that the FBI whistleblower who brought this scandal to light was suspended without pay—an act that smacks of reprisal.[19] But that's not all the FBI has done to cover their ass. When the truth about Hunter Biden could no longer be buried, the FBI created a back channel with Facebook weeks before the Hunter Biden news story broke in order to prepare a defensive disinformation campaign.[20] Yes, a government agency essentially partnered with the world's largest social media company to rig an election.

It was the biggest cover-up in American history, and it changed the nature of the campaign. Later studies revealed that if Biden voters in swing states had known the truth about the Biden family corruption before the election, a large number of them would have never voted for Sleepy Joe—enough, in fact, to change the results of the election, meaning the election was rigged.[21] Public opinion agrees with these findings. An overwhelming 79 percent of Americans say that if voters had known the truth about the Biden family and Hunter Biden's laptop before the election, then President Trump would have been reelected.[22]

Amid all of this, corrupt leadership at the FBI worked with the media and social media tech giants to try and bury the Biden family scandal to sway the election against Trump. According to FBI whistleblowers who came to Iowa Senator Chuck Grassley, the FBI falsely labelled the salacious information that came from Hunter Biden's own laptop as Russian "disinformation."[23] This happened even before Big Tech giants shut down the accounts of the *New York Post*, which broke the story, and crushed how widely the story could be shared online.

The FBI was made aware of the Biden family corruption as early as August 2020, two months before the *New York Post* bombshell, yet an FBI analyst named Brian Auten allegedly tried to discredit any derogatory information about Hunter Biden by falsely claiming that none of it was true. Auten was another player in the Crossfire Hurricane investigation into Russian collusion who, according to the Department of Justice inspector general, knew that there were lies within the Steele Dossier but moved forward with the corrupt spying operation on the Trump campaign anyway. He also personally pushed for the very FISA warrants against Carter Page that excluded exculpatory evidence. Not only that, but Auten even interviewed Steele's primary source, a man by the name of Igor Danchenko, who told him that large portions of the Steele Dossier were inaccurate, false, and bore no resemblance to reality.[24] Auten and his co-conspirators at the FBI by all accounts hid this damning indictment of the Steele Dossier as they used the dossier to spy on the Trump campaign—just like how he later worked to hide damning information about the Biden family and rig the election. Durham would later indict Danchenko himself during his investigation, revealing just how pervasive the corruption was and is. Meanwhile, Auten is also under investigation by Durham.

Of course, Auten didn't act alone. He worked under Comey, McCabe, Strzok, Priestap, and the whole cabal at the FBI. The fact that we only learned Auten's name years later proved that the corruption of the FBI and the Deep State in general extends far deeper than just the big personalities and well-known names we uncovered during the Russia Gate probe.

Yet just like his superiors, Auten has faced no real accountability in light of these findings. The fact that Auten was not fired from the FBI and prosecuted for his part in the Russia Gate conspiracy is a national embarrassment. The fact that he was then reportedly allowed to meddle in the Hunter Biden investigation reveals, without a doubt, that the FBI remains utterly corrupt and without remorse for the damage it has done to America.

THE FBI RAID ON MAR-A-LAGO

After spying on the Trump campaign and on a sitting president, it seemed like the FBI had no more lines it could cross. Then, in August 2022, the FBI did something it had never done before. They raided the home of a former president of the United States and a man who could well run for the presidency again. I know better than anyone just how deeply the FBI has been politicized and corrupted. But even so, the Mar-a-Lago raid shocked me.

The raid was approved by none other than Attorney General Merrick Garland himself. The White House publicly denied having any involvement, but that's not how these things work in Washington—and it's certainly not possible in this case. There is absolutely no way that the White House Counsel wasn't fully engaged beforehand with the FBI and DoJ about raiding the home of the president's former and potentially future opponent. In fact, not only did they know, but subsequent reporting on uncovered documents showed that the Biden White House authorized the recission of executive privilege so that presidential documents protected by this longstanding privilege could be grabbed by the FBI.[25] In fact, the White House Counsel's office was proactively emailing the National Archives and Records Administration, along with other government officials, who were engaging with the FBI and DoJ to prepare for the raid.

The Mar-a-Lago raid makes Watergate look like the teacup ride at Disney World. Instead of the sitting president having political cronies break into the offices of his opponent, his administration had the taxpayer-funded FBI violate longstanding precedent, which protected the constitutional privileges of the executive branch, by busting into the personal residence of his predecessor and political opponent.

Amazingly, the FBI and the DoJ at first made no attempt to explain themselves. Days after the raid, Attorney General Merrick Garland finally held a press conference, arriving an hour late while looking like he was in a hostage video. In his remarks, he didn't acknowledge that vast swaths of the American people—Republicans, Independents, and even many Democrats—felt like the FBI had crossed the Rubicon. Instead, he attacked people who criticized the FBI and the DoJ. It's as if he had no ability to understand why anybody would doubt the motives of federal law enforcement, despite everything he, his predecessors, and other senior leaders in the bureaucracy had done over recent years to completely undermine public trust in our institutions.

Attorney General Garland's message was clear: They weren't wrong for committing an egregious and unprecedented mafia-style mob invasion against their political opponent. *We* were in the wrong for questioning them. It was just like how they attacked us during Russia Gate. Ultimately, it was a threat. He was attempting to disqualify President Trump from ever running again while sending a message to the American people that if they can do this to a former president, they can do it to anybody, so you'd better shut up and get in line.

The alleged rationale for the Mar-a-Lago raid was that President Trump had boxes of documents that were "marked classified." Only later did the corrupt authorities and media shills start to say that Trump had "extremely sensitive" intelligence. If that's the case, why did they wait nearly two years to get the documents? Additionally, the judge signed the search warrant on a Friday, but the FBI took a holiday over the weekend until Monday to execute. How could they possibly wait those extra days if the materials were "extremely sensitive?" This is not how an apolitical investigation works. All of this was another excuse to implement a two-tiered system of justice.

The truth is that Trump was the most transparent president in history. Toward the end of his term he declassified whole sets of documents, including every single document relating to Russia Gate and to the Hillary Clinton email scandal. In fact, as president he had the unilateral authority to declassify absolutely anything he wanted. When a president says something is declassified, it is declassified. That's it. The Supreme Court even ruled that the president has this authority in the 1988 case *Navy v. Egan.* That is why I believe the FBI should come up with double zeros on this raid.

In fact, the legal precedent and federal case law is overwhelming that the president has the power to declassify and/or keep records at will. When former president Bill Clinton was caught hiding recordings from his presidency in his sock drawer, a watchdog group filed a lawsuit to force the National Archives to retrieve the recordings. In that case, a US district judge ruled that the archives had no authority to seize such records and that "the decision to segregate personal materials from Presidential records is made by the President, during the President's term and in his sole discretion." The judge went on saying that attempting to seize records directly from a former president is "unfounded, contrary to the [Presidential Records Act's] express terms, and contrary to traditional principles of administrative law." [26] Clinton still has his recordings to this day, for all we know sitting in the same sock drawer. Why hasn't the DoJ applied this legal standard to Trump? It is a two-tiered system of justice.

Further, Trump isn't even hiding the documents he held at Mar-a-Lago. Before the raid, Trump let the Department of Justice in to see the records. In June 2022—two months before the raid—government agents came in to look at the boxes and asked that the president put an extra lock on the room where they were kept. President Trump personally met those agents at Mar-a-Lago, showed them the documents, and complied with their request to add another lock. Ironically, that was the very same lock the FBI went on to break during their raid.

Few details provide more proof that this was a politically motivated raid than the fact that the Justice Department had to go judge shopping in order to find an extremely partisan magistrate who would approve the search warrant. Jurisdiction, as is justice, in all cases is supposed to be blind. The magistrate judges who have the authority to approve such warrants work in rotation. Yet the Department of Justice waited until one particular judge was reviewing cases in order to request their warrant—a judge by the name of Bruce E. Reinhart, whose last day on rotation was the very Friday the FBI phoned it in. I mean that literally. The FBI couldn't even be bothered to show up to court. Instead, in an egregious violation of protocol, they used Zuckerberg's WhatsApp to phone in their warrant request, possibly transmitting classified and confidential information using the platform.

The FBI selected Reinhart on purpose. Judge Reinhart is an Obama donor. Before he was a judge, he represented infamous pedophile Jeffrey Epstein's pilots and his scheduler. And just weeks before approving the search warrant, the judge had to recuse himself in Trump's lawsuit against Hillary Clinton for spreading the Russia collusion hoax.[27] It is a violation of impartiality that this judge wouldn't recuse himself when it came to the search warrant. He is a partisan, and the DoJ knew that before they asked him to approve the raid.

Purposefully choosing a biased magistrate wasn't the only partisan action the FBI took. Mar-a-Lago is in Florida. If the FBI had legitimate concerns, they would have used FBI agents from the local jurisdiction to conduct their operations. Yet FBI bigwigs didn't choose a local FBI raid party. Instead, they chose a corrupt and politicized Washington-based team, just like they have in every major FBI scandal in recent memory. How corrupt? It's the same crew of DoJ officials and FBI agents that ran Russia Gate, the same officials conducting the faux investigation of Hunter Biden, the same officials involved in the January 6th inquiry, the same officials mixed up in the FBI-driven plan to kidnap Michigan governor Gretchen Whitmer, and the same officials who work in the very division under investigation by Special Counsel John Durham for political bias, corruption, and abuses of power.

To name just a couple connections specifically, Brian Auten, the FBI agent who reportedly ran cover for the Bidens by falsely labelling the Hunter Biden laptop as disinformation and who hid exculpatory evidence from the FISA Court on the Trump spying operation, is a supervisor in the division that handled the Mar-a-Lago raid. Timothy Thibault, who worked with Auten at the FBI on the Hunter Biden disinformation campaign, was also central in the Washington field office. Thibault travelled with none other than Bruce and Nellie Ohr—the DoJ director and Fusion GPS employee who were central nodes of the Russia Gate conspiracy—to the Czech Republic in 2016 as part of their anti-Trump campaign. FBI Director Wray knew his presence on the Mar-a-Lago raid team would be so embarrassing that he reassigned Thibault only days before the raid so that the rabid partisan wouldn't be on the team during the operation itself—only during the preparation.[28] When Thibault's presence and history was made known, he was forced to resign in embarrassment and was walked out of the FBI building. All said and done, the agents who planned and conducted the Mar-a-Lago raid are literally the FBI's political government gangsters armed with guns and badges.

Ultimately, the same DoJ and FBI officials who committed Russia Gate used judge shopping and highly politicized agents and lawyers in order to implement a two-tiered system of justice. But it's not just the dishonesty of these corrupt bureaucrats that matters. It's also who they fail to investigate. The Mar-a-Lago raid was spurred after the National Archives and Records Administration (NARA), the agency that keeps presidential records, referred their concerns about Trump's handling of allegedly classified documents to the Department of Justice.

The same then head of the NARA when the decision was made to refer Trump to the DoJ, a Hillary supporter, never referred Hillary Clinton to the DoJ for her verifiably proven mishandling of classified documents. In fact, when it came to Hillary Clinton intentionally moving classified information (in explicit violation of federal statute, I would add), James Comey essentially changed the law by saying they wouldn't prosecute her. In fact, the FBI let Clinton's lawyer keep a thumb drive with the classified material in his office and approved of the safe the lawyers used to store the information.[29] Despite that precedent, the FBI raided Trump's home, presumably with plans to gain evidence to prosecute him. Adding insult to injury, after James Comey illegitimately exonerated Clinton for her unlawful handling of classified information, he publicly admitted to leaking classified documents to the press. So where are the raids on Clinton's home? Where's the prosecution of Comey? I hate to be a broken record, but it bears repeating: it's all a two-tiered system of justice.

At the root, the Mar-a-Lago raid wasn't solely about classified documents. It was another show. Undoubtedly knowing that the public would be aghast at what they did, the FBI ran a January 6th committee-style disinformation campaign, mobilizing Hollywood, allies in Congress like Adam Schiff, and the media to gin up ridiculous fears about Trump, like he was secretly hiding the nuclear codes. In the end, the political establishment wanted the image of doors being knocked down, guns blazing, and leaked photo splashes from the DoJ with "top secret" cover sheets strewn across the floor so that the American public would think to themselves, "Wow, Trump must have really done something terrible to be raided by the FBI."

Their big show was just another attempt to craft a political narrative to discredit Trump and prevent him and the America First movement he represents from having power ever again. In that, the raid was just like every other attack the Deep State has conducted on Trump. The FBI spied on the Trump campaign not because it was colluding with Russia, but because opening an FBI investigation would tarnish Trump's reputation. The investigation was meant to sow doubt in people's minds: if the FBI thought President Trump needed to be spied on, maybe he really was *that bad*. The same thing happened with the two impeachments of Trump. Democrats knew that Trump didn't do anything worthy of impeachment. They knew they didn't have the votes to actually convict him and that it was all a huge disinformation campaign, just like Hunter's laptop. They did it all so that they can say that Trump has been impeached twice, so it would be illegitimate to ever vote for him again.

While the political hit job was one of the goals of the raid, there was a more sinister purpose as well. When President Trump declassified all documents related to Russia Gate and Hillary's email scandal, the FBI collectively shit itself. Only about 60 percent of the documents that Devin and I discovered have been released to the public, and the ones that haven't are even worse than people could imagine. I know, because I've read them all. Yet after Trump left office, the federal bureaucracy kept throwing up roadblocks to stop the release of these documents, claiming incorrectly that the executive is bound by ever-changing rules and regulations invented by the executive bureaucracy. This is an example of Deep State insubordination at its finest—in their minds, everyone, even the president, is supposed to be subservient to unelected bureaucrats. They violated the very chain of command they swore to uphold to prevent accountability from happening.

I believe that, fearing that their roadblocks might fail, the FBI conducted the Mar-a-Lago raid in part to get those Russia Gate documents and other materials back under lock and key. By raiding Mar-a-Lago, the FBI can now use one of their old plays and claim that everything taken is now part of an active investigation, including the Russia Gate docs. That means they will refuse to release to the public what the president explicitly ordered to be released when he was in office. Just like the Mueller Special Counsel, the Mar-a-Lago raid is another way the DoJ and FBI are trying desperately to cover their corrupt actions.

If you need any more proof of this, look at what happened after the raid. The DoJ released the affidavit the FBI used to get the search warrant. That affidavit was so heavily redacted that only two names appeared in it: Donald Trump and the lead investigator for Russia Gate—me. It's effectively impossible to read the affidavit they released because they redacted so much information. Yet they made sure not to redact my name so that I would be smeared in public. Worse, as a result of their selective, politicized release, I yet again received death threats. The people who executed the Russia Gate scandal were taking their revenge on one of the main people who exposed their lies in an attempt to scare me and anyone else who would dare to contradict them. But it won't work. The truth will get out. We won't stop fighting. The House has a lot of work to do now that the gavels have flipped.

BURNING THE HOUSE DOWN

In all of these overtly political and unlawful actions, dishonest bureaucrats and lying government gangsters are leveraging and abusing the reputations of institutions they did not create. They are destroying the American people's faith in their own government and tearing our country apart, all in an attempt to stop Trump and retain their own positions and privileges. They are civilizational arsonists. For all their talk about wanting to defend democracy and protect America, they are burning it all down through their lust for power. To put it another way, they are inverting what America is supposed to be. Lincoln famously proclaimed that America has government of, by, and for the people. We know that our government is designed to serve us. But the Deep State wields power so that the American people can be made to serve them, their egos, and their bank accounts.

The Deep State thinks that the Mar-a-Lago raid was just another play in their long-running campaign to destroy the America First movement. But it's much more than that. Using the organs of the people's government to raid the home of President Trump is a national tragedy. The Mar-a-Lago raid will go down in history as a sign of the destruction of our once great institutions of equal justice and fairness. Even scarier, it's only a matter of time before they execute their next op.

CHAPTER 8

Overhauling the FBI

T hings are bad. There's no denying it. The FBI has gravely abused its power, threatening not only the rule of law, but the very foundations of self-government at the root of our democracy. But this isn't the end of the story. Change is possible at the FBI and desperately needed. The fact is that we need a federal agency that investigates federal crimes, and that agency will always be at risk of having its powers abused. So we must be constantly on guard, instituting reforms, removing wrongdoers, and erecting guardrails to stop the politicization of the FBI. Enacting these reforms won't be easy, but curbing the rise of government tyranny never is. We must always remember that no matter how much corrupt actors have twisted our government, America is ruled by the people— and we have the authority and obligation to take our country back.

THE NECESSITY OF CONGRESSIONAL OVERSIGHT

It all starts with extremely aggressive congressional oversight, just like what Devin and I did during Russia Gate. The FBI must be brought back under the control, direction, and accountability of elected officials and have its vast power curtailed. Congress has a vital role to play. They must liberally exercise their subpoena power to expose every single bit of filth and corruption at the FBI and DoJ. The agents and lawyers who think they can hide in the shadows while abusing their positions will be put on immediate notice. If they do wrong, they will be exposed, they will be dragged before Congress, and the American public will know exactly who they are. Then, when Republicans retake the White House, those people must be held accountable. The next president must fire the top ranks of the FBI. Then, all those who manipulated evidence, hid exculpatory information, or in any way abused their authority for political ends must be prosecuted to the fullest extent of the law. The only way to stop the corruption is to make it abundantly clear that corruption has consequences.

A major feature of accountability is demanding the release of documents that the criminals in government arrogantly created detailing their malfeasance. When the Deep State resists, Congress must force their hand. We did this during Russia Gate. FBI Director Wray and Deputy Attorney General Rosenstein received numerous subpoenas from Congress for documents, yet they repeatedly refused to cooperate. After continued obstruction, Devin and I finally convinced Speaker Ryan to use a tactic called "fencing." That means Congress withholds a portion of funding for a certain bureaucracy until the documents come in. The moment we announced that the DoJ and FBI might have some of their precious tax dollars withheld, they started playing ball. The next morning, we had a thousand documents on our doorstep. The strategy worked wonders, but Ryan was too weak to let us use it more than once. Now that Republicans have retaken the House in the 2022 midterms, they need to step up to the plate and use tactics like fencing the money to get documents. They need to force corrupt officials like Director Wray to testify publicly without time limits, and not permit him to use a government-funded jet to fly to his summer lake house in upstate New York and cut short his testimony, like he did in August 2022. Congress has ample authority. It's time they use it.

Of course, the Deep State's allies in the Democrat Party and the fake news mafia will not go quietly. They will claim we are endangering national security, undermining the integrity of federal law enforcement, and politicizing the DoJ and the FBI. This is a strategy that used to work, but not anymore. They did the same thing to us during Russia Gate. They screamed bloody murder that if we exposed their corruption and unlawful conduct, then America as a whole would suffer irreversible damage. Wray and Rosenstein publicly stated that Devin and I would cause the death of sources, destruction of relationships, and demise of our law enforcement community. We knew that was BS. After we released the Nunes Memo and piles of other documents, not a single source died, no relationships were ruined, and our national security was actually strengthened because a large portion of America was freed from the insane belief that our president was actually a foreign agent. What did happen, on the other hand, was that federal law enforcement lost its integrity. But that wasn't because we exposed their corruption. It's because they committed the crimes and the cover-ups in the first place.

The next president and his top deputies, including the attorney general, must be immune to these attacks. The Deep State will leak embarrassing information. They will start fraudulent investigations. They will try to hide their activities with false labels of classification. We know their playbook, and we shouldn't believe their lies. When they come at us, we must hit them back harder, calling them out for the grave damage they have done to our nation, all for the glorification of their massive egos.

President Trump has proven that if you don't bend the knee to the left's disinformation attacks, you can win. In fact, as Devin Nunes and I learned during the Russia Gate probe, when they attack us, it's because we are, as a friend once told me, "over the target." Their attacks got louder and more desperate the closer we got to the truth. So we must stay the course. The more we expose of their machinations and lies, the more the American people will understand the truth and demand reform. That is how public officials keep the mission first, that is how they deliver accountability, and that is how they honor their duty to serve the American people they work for.

FIXING SPECIAL COUNSELS

When it comes to special counsels, we must institute a complete structural overhaul. Special counsels are supposed to be appointed when there is a complete conflict of interest within the Department of Justice, meaning that the leadership within the DoJ and FBI effectively recuses itself from the investigation and tells the entire department to stand down while the special counsel does the work for them in an apolitical way, at least in theory. But ironically, the special counsel still reports to the head of the Department of Justice—the exact organization that admitted by appointing a special counsel that it could not investigate the case. Mueller reporting to Rosenstein is a case in point. Rosenstein himself authorized the corrupt warrants against Carter Page only to then outline the parameters of Mueller's probe, delineating what Mueller could and could not investigate. Do you think Rosenstein had a motive to hide his own wrongdoing and stop Mueller from going there? Damn straight. That's just a small part of what made the Mueller probe a farce. It was just an illusion for the mainstream media to sell to the public.

Worse, now Special Counsel John Durham, charged with investigating the origins of Russia Gate, reports to the biggest political puppet to sit as attorney general, Merrick Garland. Garland is the man who personally approved the Mar-a-Lago raid and has been running cover for the Democrats on the Hunter Biden laptop investigation. Of course he's going to try and stymie any real investigation into the origins of Russia Gate.

There is no perfect solution, but one reform would be to remove special counsels from DC altogether and to mandate that special counsels are no longer allowed to use DC grand juries. Along with that, rules should be implemented that ensure only associate US attorney generals are able to serve as staff on special counsel investigations—attorneys from Main Justice in Washington should not be considered. Finally, the scope of special counsel investigations must be specifically limited to a single purpose in order to stop the sort of meandering investigation conducted by Robert Mueller. We cannot allow a prosecutor with a grudge to be given carte blanche.

REFORMS AT THE ROOT

The FBI needs structural reforms as well. Even if we fix special counsels and have the most rigorous congressional oversight possible, the FBI has become so thoroughly compromised that it will remain a threat to the people unless drastic measures are taken.

Most importantly, we need to get the FBI the hell out of Washington, DC. There is no reason for the nation's law enforcement agency to be centralized in the swamp. Keeping the FBI in its behemoth Washington HQ building only allows for institutional capture and incentivizes senior leadership in the FBI to lose focus on their mission and learn how to play political games instead, currying favor with politicians and cultivating relationships with the press to advance their career. Ambitious FBI agents are forced to swim in this environment. Right now, every agent is taught in field offices across the country that if you want to rise through the ranks, then you have to do a tour in Washington.

These perverse incentives must be eliminated. FBI agents should be in the field investigating crimes, not covering for their swamp masters to get their next title. Kissing ass in Washington, DC, has nothing to do with solving federal crimes, which occur throughout the United States. And as we've seen in the most highly politicized cases in FBI history from Russia Gate to the Hunter Biden "investigation" to the Mar-a-Lago raid, it's always the same corrupt agents quarterbacking the entire op from Washington. Moving the FBI out of the capital will break up the corrupt networks and politicized strike forces the FBI uses to attack political opponents. Not to mention it will put federal law enforcement agents where they belong, in everyday America rooting out crime and securing our communities.

This can be accomplished in a variety of ways. Congress can remove funding from the Washington, DC, headquarters and instead reassign FBI funding—and therefore FBI personnel—throughout the United States, putting field-level agents back in the field. If Congress wanted to, it could reduce the FBI behemoth in Washington, DC, to just a single field office dedicated to investigating crimes within the district and place the headquarters anywhere else in America. They could even go so far as to have senior FBI leadership run the circuit, as it were, managing the affairs of the bureau from different branches and moving after a set period of time to reduce the chances of entrenched interests and political relationships being formed. Yet even if Congress doesn't alter funding, the president and a reform-minded FBI director can internally reassign agents outside of Washington, emptying out the DC HQ in order to put agents back in the field. A new FBI director could also change the rules dictating that FBI agents must do a tour of duty in DC before getting a promotion, instead focusing on promoting those with the most experience and success in the field.

The FBI and DoJ should also be banned from jurisdiction shopping, and policies should be instituted to ensure truly blind jurisdiction choices. Judge shopping has led to grossly political outcomes that undermine faith in our institutions and make a mockery of the idea of equality under the law. This, and many other reforms, can be done through revising the *Justice Manual*. I've already discussed how revising the manual can be used to curb selective prosecutions. The manual should also be altered so that attorneys are required to bring cases in jurisdictions that are not biased for either the defendant or for the DoJ but are neutral. Likewise, the manual demands that every high-profile case be funneled through political bureaucrats for approval. A revised *Justice Manual* can set new standards for field-level operators to take charge, not just DC.

Additionally, the scope of the FBI's authority must be dramatically limited and refocused. The original purpose of the FBI was to pursue real, physical threats, not to conduct ideological witch hunts. Congressional and presidential oversight must hold the FBI to its true purpose by using the budgeting purse strings to demand obedience to the oath of office every agent takes. Part of the way Congress can do this is through fencing, the tactic Devin and I used during the Russia Gate probe where Congress withholds budgeted funds to agencies until they cooperate. We know who the bad actors are. We must rein them in.

Practically, one important reform that can be implemented to accomplish this goal is to reduce the size of the FBI's General Counsel office. This is one of the top offices within the FBI that is involved in the most important investigations at the bureau. Today, the General Counsel's office has far exceeded its authority. Instead of operating as a purely investigatory body, the General Counsel office has taken on prosecutorial decision-making. In effect, they are centralizing power to both investigate and prosecute crimes, even though it is the job of the Department of Justice alone to prosecute crimes. There is a reason two separate agencies exist—one to investigate, another to prosecute. That's because prosecutors should only prosecute real crimes, not find evidence for "crimes" they want to prosecute. That line has all been blurred, and cowardly leadership at the DoJ has genuflected to the whims of the FBI brass while they manipulate the DoJ's core mission. This has led to costly failures and a destruction of the chain of command in law enforcement. Remember, the FBI reports to the DoJ, not the other way around.

FIXING FISA

This centralization of authority is a recipe for abuse. For example, the FBI General Counsel office certified the FISA warrants (that were later invalidated) to spy on the Trump campaign. That should have never been their decision as investigators. If, in the course of their investigation, the FBI determines it could be aided by a warrant, the bureau should be required to submit their information and request to the DoJ, where a trained lawyer and prosecutor can determine whether or not to take the prosecutorial step of requesting a search warrant. Currently, prosecutors are only brought in at the end of the process. This reform will force the FBI to actually put all its cards down on the table and reveal their evidence. When the FBI gets to decide without accountability to investigate whatever they want, whether the activity is criminal or not, we end up with fishing expeditions like Crossfire Hurricane.

In fact, the moment an FBI agent opens up an investigation, it should be done with the assent of a DoJ prosecutor. This is an extremely powerful way to curb the overreach of the FBI since FBI agents will only be able to investigate what DoJ lawyers allow them to investigate, not whatever they feel like looking into. DoJ prosecutors are actually trained to know what evidence matters and what doesn't. They know that you can't just go around searching for evidence to manufacture a crime (and you certainly can't manufacture evidence in order to justify warrants). Instead, the agency should be investigating *crimes* to find evidence of wrongdoing based on real probable cause.

That being said, I know from personal experience that involving federal prosecutors does not guarantee that we will end corruption. Some DoJ prosecutors are compromised as well, and similar to how the FBI shopped for a magistrate judge guaranteed to approve their warrant for the Mar-a-Lago raid, shady FBI agents could certainly shop around for DoJ prosecutors who they know will help them conduct their political witch hunts.

That is why we need decisive reforms to the FISA Court, the FISC. There are many out there who want to get rid of the FISA Court altogether. It has clearly been abused. But as a terrorism prosecutor, I also have seen numerous times how the FISA Court can be used as one of the best manhunting tools on planet Earth. I used it to track down terrorists all over the world, including members of al-Qaeda and ISIS. Without it, we would lose a critical surveillance tool not just for the DoJ, but for the Department of Defense, the intelligence community, and all other parts of the national security apparatus.

Thankfully, the FISA Court, too, can be reformed. It is part and parcel of the outlined reforms above. This starts with FISA Court judges themselves. Currently, the chief justice of the Supreme Court chooses judges to serve on the FISA Court for short, one-month terms in rotation. That means every month a new judge walks in who has no background on the cases before them and sometimes little to no knowledge of national security or counterterrorism law. When these judges lack the requisite background knowledge, they are at the mercy of the FBI or whatever other prosecutor is there pushing for a warrant, since those are the only people in the room who have knowledge of the case. As a result, the vast majority (often over 99 percent) of warrants are approved with a literal rubber stamp.[30]

After installing properly trained, long-term judges to the FISA Court, we must institute ways to hold those demanding warrants accountable. As I learned from the early days of my career, nothing holds a federal prosecutor to task better than a public defender. The FISA Court should have standing public defenders who act as advocates for the accused, picking apart the prosecution's case, demanding to see the source evidence, and confronting the prosecutor for any Brady violations where they willfully withhold exculpatory evidence. The presence of a public defender-like role at the FISC could have prevented many, if not all, of the unlawful search warrants approved to spy on the Trump campaign, because somebody would have been there to poke holes in the Steele Dossier and call the FBI out on their bull.

Lastly, and most stunningly, there is no court reporter at the FISC. Unlike what you see in every single criminal and civil proceeding in every single court across this country, at FISC there is nobody typing away as those in the court speak, immediately putting to paper every word uttered. Without that record, nobody knows what was said during FISC proceedings. This must change overnight. Every single hearing must be transcribed to the written record during the proceedings. How else are we supposed to correct the wrongs of the past if we don't even know what happened? When Devin and I wrote the FISC to address their grave abuses during Russia Gate, they told us in their response that we should talk to the DoJ, not them, because they have no formal records of any kind to release. This is the destruction of due process. Requiring a court reporter in the FISA Court may be the single most important and easiest of reforms suggested in these pages.

As a final layer of protection, search warrants need to be randomly checked by a team of seasoned, experienced, nonpartisan national security lawyers who report directly to the White House or the attorney general. Anybody who has donated to political candidates, engaged in electioneering, or worked in any other partisan fashion is immediately disqualified. These lawyers will serve for short terms to prevent institutional capture, and their job will be simple: they will review search warrants and ask questions. Why was this warrant allowed and not this one? What is the source evidence for this claim? Did you hide any exculpatory evidence? What is the verification for the source, as well as his or her bias and political leanings? With these reforms, any agency pursuing a FISA warrant will then know that their work will be checked not just by some newbie judge alone but by a seasoned judge, a dedicated defense attorney, and an independent team of auditors. If we truly care about the equal application of the law in all circumstances, we should consider applying these reforms to every federal court when it comes to applications for searches and seizures, not just the FISC.

***

The FBI was created for a noble purpose. It was designed to conduct investigations for crimes that crossed state borders and to protect our homeland. Today, it is frequently being directed against the political opponents of the ruling class. By removing this central node of corruption in DC and reorienting the FBI to accomplish its original mission, the FBI can regain the trust of the American people and fulfill their oaths of office, serving the interest of the American people and not their own. When we do that, the FBI will no longer be used as a tool to undermine the will of the people, and we will have taken a major step toward restoring self-government in America.

PART III

THE NATIONAL SECURITY COUNCIL AND THE INTELLIGENCE COMMUNITY

CHAPTER 9
Manufactured Impeachment

From my years as a public defender and federal prosecutor to the time I spent as the lead investigator of the Russia Gate hoax, I had gotten a first-person view into how the Deep State operates within the Department of Justice and Federal Bureau of Investigation. I had seen their lies, cover-ups, rampant abuses, and overblown egos destroy the lives of innocent people and tear the fabric of our nation at the stitch line. I had watched as they undermined our democratic institutions and tried to subvert the will of the people. I had uncovered enough corruption to last a lifetime and fill the pages of innumerable books. Little did I know that this was just the beginning or that I would later actually write a book about it.

The DoJ and FBI are particularly bad actors in the politicized bureaucratic cabal undermining our nation. But they are far from the only ones. Unintentionally, the next steps in my career led me into direct confrontation with the Deep State in the national security apparatus and the intelligence community—the two main forces who would pick up where the DoJ and FBI left off and launch the next machination to try and overthrow the people's president.

HIRED AT THE WHITE HOUSE

With the Nunes Memo published and the Mueller witch hunt ending, my work at the HPSCI was coming to an end. Additionally, by the fall of 2018, the Democrats had just won enough seats to retake the House, so the scumbag Adam Schiff was poised to become the chairman of the HPSCI. If there was ever a time for me to leave the House, it was then. That winter I asked Devin to uphold his end of the bargain that he had made two years before. I was asked to investigate Russian interference. I had uncovered an FBI and DoJ corruption scandal few ever could have dreamed of. Now, I wanted to get back to the counterterrorism work I had been doing, but this time at the White House on the president's National Security Council (NSC).

Devin, true to his word, spoke with the president—and told him that I had saved his presidency by revealing the unprecedented political hit job designed to take him down. When President Trump learned who I was and what I did, he told his chief of staff to hire me immediately onto the NSC. But Trump's national security advisor at the time, John Bolton, was an arrogant control freak who resisted following the orders of the president he served if it didn't suit his interests. Presumably Bolton didn't want anybody working for him who the president personally requested and who had no special loyalty to Bolton himself (resisting the constitutional authority of elected leaders is a prime sign of the Deep State). So Bolton threw up roadblock after bureaucratic roadblock to prevent me from being hired.

Bolton held up my appointment for months. When Devin called the president again to tell him that the NSC had refused to implement his order to hire me, Trump was having none of it. He told Bolton to cut the crap and offer me a job. Like a bitter teenager finally forced to do his chores, Bolton followed orders but did so reluctantly. Instead of hiring me in my area of expertise, counterterrorism, he instead offered me a job to manage the "international organizations" portfolio, hoping that I would balk and turn down the job. But good things come to those who wait. One of my rules is that if you want to do anything, you have to show up. I took my chance to get in, and I accepted the job. Other senior aides who didn't share Bolton's immediate dislike for me said that I could expect a promotion soon to my dream job as the senior director for counterterrorism—the role that runs all counterterrorism for the White House.

Even more important than the title or a plumb post at the NSC, I earned something else that White House staffers covet: access to the president. While it would take me a while to establish a real personal relationship with President Trump (remember I still had not met or spoken with him), the president knew that by doggedly standing for the truth, I had put the mission first—not for him but for the country. Like him, I knew that the truth only mattered in politics if you were willing to stand up for it against repeated assaults by the media.

The president and I would soon meet in person in the Oval Office. In those first meetings, I was quickly starstruck and could not remember what happened. Thankfully that would wear off, and soon I had an extraordinary relationship with the president far beyond what would be expected. It certainly helped me accomplish my job. But it also made me the target of backbiting and suspicion among my colleagues on the NSC, including Bolton himself. Thanks to their petty suspicions and drive to advance false conspiracies, I was thrown right into the middle of the Deep State's next plot to take down President Trump.

A PERFECT PHONE CALL

While the Russia collusion hoax continues to have true believers in certain corners of the media and the left-wing conspiracy internet, Mueller's reluctant declaration that there was no collusion between Trump and Russia in the 2016 election meant that the Deep State had to look for another vehicle to take out the president. So only two days after the Mueller investigation ended, the Deep State came up with a new bogeyman.[31] Instead of Trump colluding with Russia to take down Hillary Clinton, they manufactured the story that Trump was *actually* colluding with Ukraine to take down Biden. All they did was swap the name of the country and the Democrat politician. The Deep State has a lot of

95

power and hatred, but they don't have a lot of imagination. The strategy of every ginned up Deep State fantasy is the same: make something up, get the fake news mafia to carry your water, and leak classified intel to falsely attack Trump. When they eventually find that the narrative blows up when faced with facts, they turn to Hollywood to make it a spectacle instead of a legal battle. Rinse, repeat, rinse, repeat.

This latest attack started with a disgruntled NSC staffer named Eric Ciaramella, who formerly had worked under Vice President Biden during the Obama administration. Investigative reporter Lee Smith put together every detail of what happened before I got my job at the White House in his groundbreaking book *The Permanent Coup.*

As a career civil servant detailed to the NSC from the CIA, Ciaramella found himself with a job under President Trump despite being a bitter partisan Democrat. The first shot Ciaramella took at the president missed. After he noticed that the president had had a (completely standard) meeting with the Russian foreign minister and ambassador a few days before he decided to fire Comey, Ciaramella made a massive jump in logic and reportedly concluded that Trump must have had his actions directed by Vladimir Putin.[32] According to Smith, Ciaramella's accusations provided cover for then acting director of the FBI Andrew McCabe to launch yet another investigation against Trump when Comey was fired. That investigation quickly came up with zero.

This embarrassing failure didn't stop Ciaramella, though. The next year in 2019, Ciaramella filed a whistleblower report based on unnamed sources that Trump was influencing foreign governments to meddle in the 2020 election—an unironic repeat of the 2016 attacks on Trump that claimed he asked the Russians to find damaging information against Hillary Clinton. Ciaramella claimed that Trump withheld foreign aid from Ukraine in order to push them to start an investigation against the Biden family.

Ciaramella had some experience with putting political pressure on foreign governments. He started working at the NSC in 2015 under Vice President Biden where he handled Ukrainian and Russian policy. Coincidentally, this was around the same time that Joe Biden *actually* threatened to withhold foreign aid to Ukraine—something he later bragged about publicly—in order to make them stop an investigation into his son Hunter Biden's corrupt dealings with Ukraine energy giant Burisma. With some slight alterations, Ciaramella was accusing Trump of doing exactly what Biden had actually done in Ukraine *while Ciaramella was working on Biden's Ukraine policy.* These people have no shame.

Just like the Steele Dossier, Ciaramella had no proof of his accusations. He appeared to get all of his information secondhand from a swamp creature with a deep-seated hatred of the president named Alexander Vindman, then the director of Ukraine policy at NSC. Using Vindman's gossip, Ciaramella filed a whistleblower report—and he was promptly laughed out of the room. The intelligence community inspector general and the DoJ both said that the so-called whistleblower report failed to meet their standards and dismissed it.[33]

So, just like the FBI did with their Russian collusion investigation, the Deep State rebirthed their slander outside of official channels with the press, which dutifully began publishing stories about how unnamed officials said Trump had called Ukraine's president and bullied him to meddle in the 2020 election by investigating the Biden family. Adam Schiff, as the new chairman of the House Permanent Select Committee on Intelligence, immediately took up the new disinformation narrative and began an investigation, subpoenaing Ciaramella's faulty whistleblower report. With that, Ciaramella and Vindman's lies were released to the public and touted as fact, even after being dismissed by the federal government.[34]

Then, Trump did something that the Deep State, the media, and the Democrats didn't expect: he released the transcript of his call with the Ukrainian president. It was a perfect call. He didn't threaten to withhold foreign aid if Ukraine didn't investigate the Bidens. He said that Europe wasn't doing enough to support Ukraine considering how much America sends. In fact, getting Europe to pull their own weight in their region and fund NATO according to their obligations was a core part of Trump's campaign platform. So the Deep State was trying to take out

President Trump not for collusion but for fulfilling his campaign promise of making Europe contribute to their own national security.

It didn't matter. Speaker of the House Nancy Pelosi immediately launched an impeachment inquiry, and the Democrats started searching for something besides Trump's call with the president of Ukraine to prove their new foreign collusion hoax. With the impeachment train running at full speed, the Deep State landed on their new "proof": me. The Deep State strategy restarted with another lie, and the rest of the stages were coming. Rinse, repeat, rinse, repeat.

THE BACK CHANNEL THAT NEVER EXISTED

The Trump-haters in Washington had already convinced themselves that Trump *must have* meddled with Ukraine, despite there being zero evidence and despite the fact that the Trump-Ukraine call that was supposed to prove collusion in fact exonerated him. But if Trump hadn't colluded with Ukraine via phone call, how did he do it? Within weeks, they came up with a new story. Trump was working on corrupt deals with Ukraine through a secret back channel—and that back channel was Kash Patel.

It was a patently false and ludicrous claim. By that time I was the NSC senior director of counterterrorism. I had nothing to do with Ukraine or Ukraine policy. During my entire time in the White House, I never even spoke with the president about Ukraine. Yet here I was, being dragged right into the middle of the fraudulent Trump impeachment craze. Why? It all happened because anti-Trump Bolton staffers wanted to at least take me out, even if they couldn't overthrow President Trump. They hated Trump for actually doing what he promised and reorienting our nation's foreign policy by putting America first. And they hated me for exposing the truth about Russia Gate and for actually implementing the president's agenda.

So when Bolton staffers saw me leaving the Oval Office where I had been speaking to the president without Bolton's approval (something that was certainly not required), they started building up grand conspiracy theories in their heads, imagining that I was secretly meeting with

Trump to serve as his Ukraine back channel. The fact that, even during an impeachment hoax, the president might still care enough about hunting down terrorists to talk with his top counterterrorism advisor never seemed to cross these Bolton staffers' minds. Or better yet, it probably did; they just didn't care. They placed politics and their egos over national security.

Soon enough, the *New York Times* published a piece co-authored by Adam Goldman—the same "reporter" who ambushed me after I tried to reach out to Christopher Steele's lawyers in London—saying that White House officials suspected I was Trump's Ukraine back channel. The article smeared me for my role in exposing the Russia Gate hoax and then went on to report how Fiona Hill, a former NSC staffer, claimed I was improperly involved in Ukraine policy running a "shadow effort on Ukraine." CNN, Politico, and others piled on as well, repeating the gossip without any concern for the truth.

Even while dragging my name through the mud, the media failed to mention a much more nefarious and real connection. Fiona Hill used to work at the Brookings Institution. While there, she was the person who introduced Christopher Steele to Club FBI. If that's not politicizing national security enough, Fiona Hill also hired an employee at Brookings by the name of Igor Danchenko—the very same Igor Danchenko who served as the primary source for the Steele Dossier (and who later told the FBI that the dossier was riddled with falsehoods, information the FBI hid). Incredibly, the FBI didn't cut ties with Danchenko after the Steele Dossier fiasco—they actually put him on the FBI payroll as a confidential human source from 2017 to 2020, one imagines so he could continue to make up more fake dirt on the government's dime.[35] This was also presumably done as a tactic to shield Danchenko from congressional inquiry or other investigations. If they could claim Danchenko was a valuable informant, then they could also claim that any attempts to question or subpoena him would jeopardize national security. Thankfully Special Counsel Durham caught the FBI in their attempted cover-up, and Danchenko was later indicted.

Long story short, Fiona Hill was buddy buddy from the start with key actors in the Russia Gate conspiracy before she helped conjure up the Ukraine hoax that launched an illegitimate presidential impeachment effort. When the impeachment trial started, Fiona Hill was brought to the Capitol. Under oath and before the whole world, she was forced to admit that she had never even met me before, and she didn't actually know when the supposed back-channel meetings between me and Trump happened. The line of questioning was damning:[36]

"Did you ever figure out what Mr. Patel was doing with respect to Ukraine kind of behind the scenes?"

"I did not…" Hill answered.

"And did you ever learn what [Deputy NSC Director Kupperman] learned after he looked into [Patel's alleged involvement in Ukraine]?"

"I did not…" Hill replied.

"Did you ever see the materials [Patel allegedly brought to the president]?"

"I did not," Hill said.

"Okay. Did you ever learn what materials Mr. Patel was providing?"

"I did not," Hill answered.

"Do you know whether Kash Patel attended that meeting [on Ukraine with the president]?"

"I do not. I had never heard any information to suggest that he was there," Hill replied.

"Okay. Did Mr. Patel have anything to do with Ukraine after that meeting, to your knowledge?"

"I'm not aware that he did…" she said.

In every single reply, Fiona Hill revealed that she didn't actually know a single hard fact. So how could she claim I spoke with Trump about Ukraine when she literally never met me, never spoke to me, and can't even say the date or time of my alleged meetings? Fiona Hill was caught publicly in a massive lie, and how was she repaid? She got a prestigious job back at the Brookings Institute and high-paying media contracts. Another example of mammoth-sized swamp demons politicizing national security and getting rewarded for it.

Vindman was just as embarrassing. During his testimony on Capitol Hill during the impeachment inquiry he was forced to admit that he knew nothing about me either:[37]

"And did Kash Patel have anything to do with the Ukraine portfolio?" the inquirer asked.

"He did not," Vindman responded.

"Did you learn anything else about what [Patel's] involvement was in the Ukraine portfolio?"

"I did not," Vindman said. "I didn't really inquire. I just went about my business."

"Did you ever come across Kash Patel again related to Ukraine matters?"

"I know who he is," Vindman replied. "I know he's on staff. I've, frankly, not had any interactions with him…"

These scenes aren't some Adam Schiff-style fake recreations. These are actual quotes from the sworn testimony of two White House staffers who only faced up to their lies when they were forced to under oath and the threat of perjury.

This is one of the biggest problems at the NSC. People like Fiona Hill, Eric Ciaramella, Alexander Vindman, and all of these other swamp monsters in the politicized permanent bureaucracy work for a president whom they hate and undermine in the most extreme ways. When the Deep State's tentacles spread all the way into the highest reaches of the White House, it severely inhibits the president from serving the people and inhibited me from executing the mission I had signed up for: protecting America.

FIRING BACK

Trump survived the impeachment charade, even though it consumed more valuable months of his term. While folks like Fiona Hill and Alexander Vindman were lauded in the press, they at least got rooted out of the NSC after their baseless attacks. Bolton was forced to resign as well while all this scandal was brewing. Officials across the government were shown the exit for undermining or ignoring our no-fail mission to keep America safe.

I decided that while these firings were good, they weren't enough. The media needed to undergo a major course correction for publishing unfounded, unverified, and false gossip about me, tarnishing my reputation and diminishing my ability to do my job. So I decided to sue for defamation the worst offenders: the *New York Times*, CNN, and Politico. And I filed lawsuits not just for what they did to me during the Ukraine impeachment hoax but for all the manifold lies they told about me while I worked at the White House.

In each of my lawsuits, I listed at length the demonstrable falsehoods the media published, including their claims that I was undermining the Russian investigation, that I was sending information to President Trump from Ukraine, that I was spreading conspiracy theories about Joe Biden, that I was undermining the Biden transition, that I was misrepresenting myself to the president as a Ukraine expert, that I was circumventing NSC process…. The list goes on and on and on.

While these lawsuits are ongoing, I am firmly convinced that the only way to hold the media—the Deep State's mouthpiece—accountable is to make them face real consequences when they publish hearsay and lies. The only thing they understand is something that waters down their bottom line. Nothing else will change their repugnant conduct. Until they do, they have every incentive to keep publishing whatever government leakers tell them to, or at least government leakers who want to undermine Republicans. In that, they are just as responsible for these failed, false takedowns of Trump as the corrupt bureaucrats themselves. One cannot exist without the other.

Outside of these massive distractions, I still had an extremely important job: to coordinate the entire federal government's counterterrorism activities in line with the president's agenda. Right off the bat, we were doing some amazing work, but even there I saw how the Deep State uses much less public and more insidious tactics than impeachment in their dogged attempts to get their way.

CHAPTER 10
The Good...

C learly my time at the NSC wasn't all sunshine and rainbows. I can't say I enjoyed being the target of Deep State intrigue yet again— first during Russia Gate and then during impeachment. But while I worked at the White House, I also saw professional national security and intel staffers do their duty to protect America and serve our interests without regard to politics. However bad it may get (and it's pretty bad in the swamp), it's worth it to remember that there are still good people in government.

Many of these dedicated public servants worked with me to return American hostages, one of the primary duties President Trump tasked me with coordinating. I worked with National Security Advisor Robert O'Brien to secure the release of more than fifty Americans held captive abroad, a record number. In one particularly notable case, in an effort to bring back American journalist Austin Tice and others, I became the first US government official in ten years to travel to Syria and meet in person with representatives of the Assad regime to negotiate for hostages. The trip took years of planning and stealthy regional maneuvering. Most warned me against going, fearful that Assad would kidnap me. But I accepted that as the risk. My job was to bring Americans home, and I was willing to do what was necessary to accomplish that mission. Plus, I figured that if Assad did take me, he'd enrage President Trump. That was my ace in the hole in that Syrian dust bowl.

Each and every one of these hostage returns demanded untold hours of effort, haggling, inside knowledge of who we were dealing with, and fervent devotion to the ultimate objective. The vast majority of people straight down the line who worked to get our hostages home knew that they wouldn't get glowing media profiles written about them or high-paid speaking gigs afterward. They weren't in it for their egos like the political activists at the upper ranks of so many agencies in Washington.

Yet if anything proved how the United States government could use its vast power for good, it was an event that became one of the most pivotal moments in the Trump presidency: a daring raid to take out the head of ISIS, Abu Bakr al-Baghdadi.

TRACKING BAGHDADI

President Trump was elected with a mandate to put an end to ISIS, and I know firsthand that nothing mattered more to him than keeping his promises. The president supported our partners on the ground, expanded the rules of engagement so our military could finally fight without their hands tied behind their backs, and told America's senior military leadership to crush the sons of bitches who thought they could kill and maim without consequences. Soon enough, ISIS was being pushed back on all fronts. Within two years, the ISIS caliphate that was intended to unite all Muslims and subjugate the world was reduced to fleeing gangs of barbarous bandits.

The campaign to totally crush ISIS was already well underway by the time I was commissioned as senior director for counterterrorism in 2019. When I came in, there was a feeling of victory in the air. But the job was not yet finished.

I ran a team that ranged from eleven to eighteen people at any given time with a full portfolio of duties. Not only were we charged with coordinating agencies across the administration to bring American hostages home and take out the leadership of ISIS and al-Qaeda, we also had specific experts combating terrorist financing, countering online terrorist activities, taking on Iran, and stomping out terrorism in every theater of war we were engaged in.

NSC counterterrorism had a suite of offices on the corner of the third floor of the Eisenhower Executive Office Building adjacent to the White House. We had a big space, and we operated kind of like the Animal House of the NSC, with multiple places set up for the team to come together and decompress for a minute or two amid the 24/7 rush of work. Whenever we successfully brought a hostage home, killed a terrorist, or accomplished another one of the president's key objectives, the folks at NSC came to our office to celebrate with a beer or a nice tall glass of bourbon.

As a memento to our office and all of the hostages we successfully brought home, one of the guys on my team ordered an entire custom bourbon barrel that we could use to celebrate at the end of each successful op. Every time our boys got home safely, we'd each pour a glass. Soon, everyone will be able to see our beloved barrel. We all signed it and submitted it to the Trump Presidential Library where it will be on display as a testament to the president's unprecedented concern for American hostages and the work we did.

In the office I also used hockey tape to put up two organization charts on the inside of my door showing the names and faces of all the senior terrorist leaders: one chart for al-Qaeda, one for ISIS. I marked each confirmed kill with a big "X" using one of President Trump's famous sharpies that he gave me personally during my first meeting with him in the Oval Office. Over those initial months, we were making good progress on the lower rungs of the organization charts. But right at the top, untouched, was the secretive leader of ISIS, Abu Bakr al-Baghdadi. ISIS may have been defeated, but we couldn't be satisfied until the mastermind behind it all was brought to justice.

One day that summer, I went into the Oval Office with National Security Advisor Robert O'Brien to present the president with new intel on Baghdadi's whereabouts. Unlike previous false starts, these reports seemed more legitimate—strong enough that the president needed to see it himself. We were getting close, and I was getting animated.

As we showed the president the new intel, I started pacing around the Oval like a silverback gorilla, thrilled at the prospect of finally getting this bloodthirsty killer who enslaved, tortured, and murdered people without remorse. All the while, the president sat there behind the Resolute Desk, cool, calm, and in command like always. When we finished, he said only this: "You know where I stand. I want him dead."

We left the Oval with clear authority to get the job done. Baghdadi was in the crosshairs. Normally, this would be the moment where the politicized bureaucracy would start throwing up roadblocks at every turn. But on this matter, Trump and permanent Washington were on the same page (or those who would slow-walk matters were left in the dark). That meant the Baghdadi raid didn't follow the traditional script. It was an ace operation that broke the bureaucratic mold. In this instance, the DoD and CIA deserve tremendous credit. They ran an impressively tight ship from the earliest days of source cultivation and intelligence gathering on the ground to the final bomb that dropped on the Baghdadi compound.

THE BAGHDADI RAID

By the fall of 2019, those tracking Baghdadi in the CIA and within the military were getting tantalizingly close. We couldn't confirm exactly where Baghdadi was, as he changed locations frequently. But there was a chance we could catch him during a single brief window.

During the final full week of October, the CIA and DoD began making operational decisions to move assets to the Syrian border just in case they were needed at a moment's notice. Every day could be the day we got him—or it could be the day everything fell apart.

On Saturday, October 29, I showed up to the White House to work over the weekend like so many presidential staffers do on a regular basis. I had no meetings scheduled and a pile of office work to do. Pretty much a normal day, except I took the chance to leave the tight collar at home and wear jeans, a T-shirt, and a zip-up hockey hoodie instead. Not long after I arrived on campus, I connected with O'Brien, who informed me of the high-level intel he had just told the president. We were almost certain Baghdadi was in a compound outside of a small city in Syria, close to the Turkish border. The president was being updated regularly, and we needed to prepare the Situation Room in case he authorized a raid.

I quickly threw on the emergency suit I kept on hand in the office. The colors didn't perfectly match, it felt boxy, and I had to rummage around for an old blue tie I hated from my ex-girlfriend. It looked like crap, but I wasn't about to head to the Situation Room with POTUS on campus in jeans. The entire morning my team and I worked with the staff of the White House Situation Room to set up all the feeds and tech we would need to observe the raid live and communicate effectively with the teams on the ground.

No matter where he was, the president was working all day as usual. However, that evening he had a movie night scheduled in the White House to watch *Rambo: Last Blood* with the First Lady, then congressman and future chief of staff Mark Meadows, and actor John Voight. What mattered to us was that President Trump was available and prepared to make the call at any moment.

We always rehearsed at NSC in order to be ready. We called it doing our sets and reps so that nothing would come as a surprise. The only difference was that today was the day we would get the green light. Once we did, we started to move.

The White House and West Wing were still buzzing with activity. Public tours were rolling through the Executive Mansion, allowing visiting tourists to see iconic backdrops like the Grand Foyer, the East Room, and the State Dining Room. Similarly, on Saturdays like this one when the president was not in the Oval Office, he allowed staff to schedule tours of the West Wing. Every time we walked through the hall, there was a wide-eyed tour group looking behind the scenes at where the most powerful man in the world lived and worked.

President Trump loved giving as much access to the public as possible, but considering both the president and the vice president would be present to oversee an intensely secretive operation, we had to close it all up. I spoke with the Secret Service, and by 4:30 p.m. they locked down the entire compound. All tours were cancelled. All access to the West Wing was restricted. West Executive Avenue, the small drive that runs between the West Wing and the Eisenhower Executive Office Building, was teeming with large, armored black Suburbans.

Shortly after, senior members of the administration started showing up. We were running a very tight ship. Outside a select few of us, no staff had been informed of the coming raid. No leaks made it to the media. The Situation Room had only a small number of the most senior officials: President Trump, First Lady Melania Trump, Vice President Pence, Secretary of Defense Mark Esper (who showed up uninvited), Chairman of the Joint Chiefs of Staff General Mark Milley, Robert O'Brien, and my friend and colleague Chris Miller, with whom I was running counterterrorism. Even the White House chief of staff, Mick Mulvaney, was not present.

Actually, I had been in the room as well—as I had every right to be as the president's senior director for counterterrorism. I had spent the entire day setting up the room, along with months beforehand preparing for this moment. But when Esper arrived, he asked what I was doing there. "We're trying to keep things small," Esper said. It was obnoxious. But I wasn't about to get into a pissing match with the secretary of defense right before an op this big. Remember, mission first. I would have my showdown with Esper for his part in slow-rolling the president's agenda later. In the meantime, I posted up in a small room adjacent to the main conference room in the Situation Room suite, where I could quickly jump in to deliver information to the president and his team while keeping track of the feeds.

While Esper had flown in at the last minute uninvited, all the way from Brussels, Director of the CIA Gina Haspel hadn't even bothered to come downtown to the Situation Room from her office at the CIA. She watched from headquarters in Langley, Virginia. I was surprised but figured that she didn't want to be in the room with the president if things went south or the intel turned out to be wrong. That would be typical Gina, a swamp creature if there ever was one.

About 4:00 p.m., POTUS showed up and went around the table. As was his usual practice, he always wanted to be educated on people's opinions, especially when American lives—our soldiers' lives—were on the line. First, he asked for the vice president's opinion. Vice President Pence supported the mission and said that despite the risks, we should do it. The president then consulted every person in the room, including the First Lady, before making his final decision. It was time to get Baghdadi. The boss gave the nod; the raid was a go.

By the time President Trump took office, Russia had a continual presence in the region and soon established a presence in Syrian airspace. This significantly complicated the Baghdadi raid, since we had to go through "their" airspace. A little more than half an hour before our Special Forces broke Syrian airspace, Chairman Milley got on the phone in the Situation Room to contact his Russian counterpart. I vividly remember the call. It was a short but tense conversation. In effect, the chairman told the Russians that America was coming. We weren't targeting Russians. We weren't targeting Syrian government forces or civilians. But we needed them to clear a certain area and get their men out of harm's way. It was the right move to make.

Of course, we didn't tell the Russians we were going after Baghdadi. I doubt it would have mattered. The Russians told the chairman that if we broke Syrian airspace, they were going to shoot us down.

Chairman Milley hung up the phone and reported it to the president. President Trump paused a brief moment and said, "We're going anyway." After all, would the Russians really want to threaten open conflict with the United States over a single mission in Syria, about which they had no details? Rightly so, the president thought not. The chairman then got back on the line and relayed the message. It wasn't a threat. He simply said that whether Russia liked it or not, America was coming in, and they shouldn't shoot because if they did, it would not be a good day for them considering the amount of heat we were bringing.

Within a minute, ████████████████████████████ Russian and Syrian forces fled the area for dear life. The path was open, and the message was sent. Russia may have controlled the skies over Syrian sand, but they weren't going to fight the American military.

SIGNAL JACKPOT

It was a harrowing forty-five-minute-long flight from the moment our helicopters lifted with our Special Forces operators in friendly territory to the time they touched down at the Baghdadi compound. They flew low and fast through sandstorms and high winds that limited visibility. I would trust American aviators (especially these guys) eight days a week, but the conditions were nothing short of awful. Everyone in the Situation Room waited tensely as our soldiers infiltrated.

As the helos approached the objective, ISIS terrorists opened fire. Swift airstrikes made quick work of that threat, and our soldiers touched down.

Chairman Milley had a direct line to the ground force commanders so that any issues or orders could be quickly transmitted from himself or the president. However, nobody back in Washington was there to micromanage. Our Special Forces are highly trained and extremely lethal. Once they were given the objective, they didn't need our help. This is what they do. As I watched them descend, I was reminded of when I conducted global targeting operations with them some years prior. These were good men, and more than anything I wanted every single one of them to make it home safely.

Those in the Situation Room watched everything live from an overhead view. First, they blew a hole in the exterior wall, avoiding any booby traps that may have been rigged at the door. Special Forces operators soon entered the compound where they were confronted by a significant threat from ISIS militants. It was a fierce firefight, but our forces cleared the outer grounds of the compound without a single casualty.

Our teams then evacuated eleven children to safety before continuing the operation. After fully securing the exterior of the compound, the strike team infiltrated the building. Baghdadi was soon chased down a subterranean tunnel and was cornered by a highly trained special operations dog named Conan. Down in the tunnels, Baghdadi hit a dead end. He locked himself in a cell wearing a suicide vest and hid behind his children as a coward.

Up to now, the operation was near flawless, but our soldiers had no idea what tricks might be up Baghdadi's sleeve. The entire hallway could be booby trapped, or ISIS fighters could appear around any corner. They had to proceed with extreme caution.

As a result, while the entire bin Laden raid took less than forty minutes, and most raids leave our soldiers on the ground for less than fifteen minutes, our operators were at the Baghdadi compound for over two hours, an astonishing length of time. Every extra minute our troops spent on the ground brought added risks. Our soldiers could trip a bomb, Baghdadi's guards could be hidden and waiting to attack, or ISIS fighters in the region could descend upon the compound.

As our soldiers closed in, Baghdadi knew death or capture were the only options left. Instead of facing his fate like a man, he detonated his suicide vest. The bomb went off. The building shook. In an instant, Baghdadi killed himself and the three children he was hiding behind. The tyrant who created a regime based on cruelty and oppression died as he lived, driven by evil and murdering innocents. His body was so mutilated by the explosion that we had to confirm his identity using DNA testing on whatever pieces of him could be found. Generally, when a suicide vest clacks off, one's head can go some distance, and sometimes you have to spend time looking for it. Didn't take the boys too long on this day.

Finally, the top terrorist in the world was dead. But we could not rest easy until every single American was out of danger and back on base. That flight back was a long and tense forty-five minutes. The safe return of those soldiers was the only thing on my mind. Thankfully everyone made it back, and I caught my breath for the first time all day.

When our troops finally touched back down, we called Signal Jackpot. Mission accomplished. Baghdadi was dead, and every single American was safe. Conan the dog was the only member of the team injured, and he was welcomed at the White House like a hero later.

The Situation Room cheered and breathed a sigh of relief.

Someone called for another group picture in addition to an iconic photo taken during the raid. Before I knew it, the president looked at me directly and asked for one picture with just the two of us. I was in shock. I was in the Situation Room with the most powerful civilian and military leaders in the world, and the president called me out individually and by name. Two months later, I received a big manila envelope in my office with the picture enclosed. Traced in sharpie in his strong, large, and pointed style, the president wrote, "Great Job Kash," and signed his name at the bottom. That photo reminds me that things can get bad, but that America's national security apparatus is not beyond reform. When we want to, we can use America's massive security and intelligence powers according to their original purpose: not to target our citizens or harass presidents but to rid the world of threats to the American people.

Back in the Situation Room, the president asked for the phone numbers of the Kassig, Sotloff, Mueller, and Foley families. These were the parents of four innocent Americans who were captured by ISIS in Syria and brutally murdered. President Trump never forgot their names, and they were the first people on his mind when the mission was done. He wanted to tell them personally before anyone else broke the news that the animal responsible for the death of their loved ones was finally blown off the face of the earth. President Trump also requested the names and numbers of every commander on the ground. He didn't just want to recognize the senior leaders. Like always, he wanted to personally thank the heroic Americans who put their lives on the line and to tell them that they didn't just do it for America, they did it for every single person who suffered and lost someone they loved because of ISIS.

Then, he looked back at the screens in the Situation Room. We could still see the compound. We had extracted some vital intelligence during the raid, but we didn't have time for a full sweep. Who knows what intelligence could have been left there on the ground. Perhaps worse, we didn't want the building to become a pilgrimage spot and rallying point for the ISIS faithful. The president looked back at the compound on the screen and said three words: "Level that thing." He then left the room with the First Lady, trusting his advisors to finish the job.

Chairman Milley picked up the phone and simply said, "Rubble it. I want to see rubble." He hung up. A minute later, we looked at the screen and saw quick bursts of bright flashes and a large cloud of dust. The compound was completely incinerated. American hellfire rained down and blew the entire place to pieces.

As the missiles hit their target, those of us in the room started cheering and high-fiving each other. I couldn't help myself and shouted, "Fuck yeah!" Chairman Milley then turned to Vice President Pence, who was in between the two of us, and said in a booming voice, "Mr. Vice President, that's what American justice looks like." The vice president, true to his solemn and serious form, slowly responded, "This *is* what American justice looks like."

I don't know what the proper etiquette is for being in the Situation Room with the president's cabinet after killing the world's most wanted terrorist, but dropping the "F" bomb next to the VP can't be on the list. I think on this evening, he gave me a pass.

TELLING THE WORLD

Though the mission was complete, our job was far from done. My team at the NSC gathered phone numbers for the Kassigs, Sotloffs, Muellers, and Foleys and wrote their information down on a separate card. I then worked with my staff to quickly collect pictures and brief bios of every single person on those cards so that the president would have all the background he needed when he made the calls.

I knew that immediately after the raid, the president had headed out to start his movie night with the First Lady and John Voight. It took a bit of time to gather all the necessary information. Regardless, I decided to head straight over to the movie theater in the White House and be available for the president the moment he needed me.

In a short while, the movie ended, and the president walked out with the First Lady right behind him. He saw me there waiting, and I told him, "Mr. President, I have some information for you." He immediately called me over and said, "Kash, let's go. Melania, let's go," and he started walking back the way I came toward the Mansion to the Diplomatic Reception Room. The president and the First Lady sat down. I told him, "Mr. President, I have what you wanted. Thank you for asking for these names. It will mean a lot to them." I then handed him the two cards and the thin folder of information we had gathered over the past couple of hours.

As I prepared to leave, the president stopped me and said, "Kash, how are we going to tell the world we did this? Where should we make the announcement?" This was something I wasn't expecting. History had been made, but now it was the president, the First Lady, and me deciding how to write it.

I brought up a few ideas before the First Lady stood up and said she thought we should do it right there in the Diplomatic Reception Room. She immediately started planning the whole event, moving the military flags in the room around and deciding on the camera angle. It was perfect staging. After that, the president asked me to be back the next day at 7:00 a.m. to prepare for the event and ensure it went just as the First Lady laid out.

Early the next morning with Melania's staging all in place, the president spoke definitively. "Baghdadi was vicious and violent," he said. "And he died in a vicious and violent way, as a coward, running and crying."

The message for every other terrorist around the globe was crystal clear: "Baghdadi's demise demonstrates America's relentless pursuit of terrorist leaders, and our commitment to the enduring and total defeat of ISIS and other terrorist organizations. Our reach is very long."

Within a few short months, the president took a chance to tell the story again, revisit the raid, praise the heroes, and celebrate the end of ISIS during his State of the Union Address. The day of the speech is always stressful at the White House as we verified all the facts in the speech, coordinated with the VIPs, and managed incoming news from the media.

The First Lady had invited as her guests Carl and Marsha Mueller, the parents of Kayla Mueller and two of the people the president personally called shortly after American forces killed Baghdadi. Kayla had served as a humanitarian aid worker in Syria, trying in some way to relieve the deep suffering of the Syrian people during their civil war. In 2013, Kayla was captured by ISIS where she became the personal slave of Baghdadi himself. She was repeatedly raped and tortured during an imprisonment that lasted over five hundred days. Nobody deserved to have Baghdadi brought to justice more than the Mueller family, along with the Sotloffs, Foleys, and Kassigs.

During the speech, just as expected, President Trump spoke about the daring missions of our Special Forces to take out Baghdadi. What viewers didn't know was that President Trump was going to share Kayla's heartbreaking story. As he did, he told the world something that had previously been classified. In each mission, Special Forces teams get to name the operation whatever they want. The heroes of the Baghdadi raid knew Kayla's story, and they wanted to take out Baghdadi for her. So they named the mission Task Force 8-14, a reference to August 14— Kayla's birthday. The president turned to Kayla's parents, saying, "Carl and Marsha, America's warriors never forgot Kayla, and neither will we."

As the chamber roared in applause, Marsha Mueller held back tears while her husband, Carl, held up a picture of Kayla for the world to see. In my heart I knew what I would have told them right then and there: "We would have done it all, and done it all again, even if it was just for you."

Baghdadi was one of the most evil men on the planet, whose cruelty and lust for blood knew no boundaries. Nobody should mourn his death. That bastard is now rotting in hell, and I'm proud that it was America that sent him there.

Of course, the Special Forces who took Baghdadi out deserve the lion's share of the credit. But to plan and execute such an operation takes the coordinated effort of thousands of people all operating to achieve the same mission. That's worth remembering. The Deep State isn't synonymous with agencies and departments like the CIA or NSC or DoD. Instead, Deep State actors have infiltrated those agencies and abuse their power for their own benefit. But when those agencies operate within their lawful authority and as intended, well, that's how you take out terrorists like Baghdadi.

CHAPTER 11
The Bad...

S adly, the flawless execution of the Baghdadi manhunt and raid was more of an outlier than a rule. The norm when I was at the NSC was government bureaucrats slow-walking or hindering the president's agenda, thinking they knew better than the man the American people elected to represent them. Half the time I was at the NSC, I was really just pushing people to do what they had already been ordered to do. Often, half the battle was just figuring out which people tasked with a mission weren't getting the job done, removing said roadblock, and executing.

QUIET OBSTRUCTION

In my sphere of the foreign policy world, President Trump was very direct. He had a few top priorities for the mission: end the forever wars, bring home hostages, kill terrorists, and safeguard America. We had explicit marching orders, but that's not always enough to succeed. When I first realized that, I was very concerned. There is one chain of command, especially when it comes to the national command authority: POTUS to the secretary of defense. Period. When it comes to following the orders of the president, the bureaucracy should move with all haste and urgency. But that would not be the case for a Trump presidency.

Under President Trump, Deep State intentional inaction, paper delays, and obstruction bordered on the seditious.

Never would they openly contradict a direct command from the president. That's not how swamp creatures operate; they are too smart and too evil. Instead, they would slow-walk their actions, selectively hide vital intelligence, leak classified information and private conversations, offer derogatory and anonymous quotes to the press, and present political leadership with a severely limited set of policy responses that only fit the narrative they created. Let's just say with a bureaucracy that sent 95 percent of its presidential election donations in 2016 to Hillary Clinton, it's a miracle that President Trump was able to get anything done.

Aside from reforming the entire federal bureaucracy, which is one of the most deeply entrenched left-wing groups in the entire country, conservatives can only accomplish their objectives while in power through smart and relentless political leadership. For example, in my role at the NSC, I ran something called the Counterterrorism Security Group (CSG), which gathered high-level personnel across the administration who worked directly for the top deputies of the entire alphabet soup of the national security apparatus, including the CIA, the DoD, the NSA, the Defense Intelligence Agency (DIA), and the Office of the Director of National Intelligence (ODNI). The CSG was how we translated the president's policy into concrete actions across the federal agencies regarding counterterrorism.

As the White House policy lead on counterterrorism, my job was to execute the president's national security priorities. Nonetheless, when I pushed these government officials on why particular terrorists we were targeting still ran free, and particular Americans were still hostages, I faced immediate resistance. In one instance, the president wanted to take out a specific senior leader of al-Qaeda, but nothing was getting done. So I asked my counterparts at the DoD and CIA what the holdup was. I was given a standard stonewall response that the NSC ran policy, not operations, so it was not my place to tell them how to get their job done.

They were right. It was not my job to tell them how to do a raid. But as we saw time and again in the Trump administration, if you don't bring the pressure, nothing will ever be accomplished. And it was absolutely my job to enforce the policy of the president, which many did not like hearing. In these circumstances, my direct line to the president was my best leverage.

After pushing on a top official at the CIA, he told me that Director of the CIA Gina Haspel would talk to the president directly about this al-Qaeda terrorist. I responded quickly, "Great, then I will inform the president that Gina will talk personally to him about why your team isn't getting the job done." One way or another, the president would know that the bureaucrats below him were avoiding action.

Soon enough my boss, Robert O'Brien, started getting calls directly from Director Haspel complaining that I was interfering with her people. She wasn't the only one. In other circumstances, Secretary Esper called to make similar complaints and to request I be fired. O'Brien politely reminded them that they were Senate-confirmed presidential appointees serving in the Cabinet and asked why they felt threatened by a mere White House staffer several rungs down the food chain at NSC. Esper and Haspel backed down for the time being, but I learned that nothing makes you enemies faster in Washington than being effective. That's because to be effective, you have to put the mission first and ego last, something these career swamp animals were never willing to do.

INTELLIGENCE SHAKEUP

Outside of counterterrorism ops and hostage matters, the president also asked me to focus on selected declassification efforts. Based on my background leading the Russia Gate probe, he knew I was the best guy for the job. He wanted all the Russia Gate documents as well as everything pertaining to the Hillary Clinton email scandal to be declassified so the public could see the full truth, not just the disinformation fueled by Deep State press leaks. For example, at that time all of the depositions I conducted in the HPSCI where I asked over sixty government and civilian witnesses the Three Cs—if they had any evidence that Trump conspired, colluded, or coordinated with Russia—were still under lock and key for literally no reason. That means only a select few people in Washington knew the truth that those people at the top of the Russia hoax were well aware from the start that the entire thing was bogus.

Such declassification usually happens under the Office of the Director of National Intelligence, but I had experience successfully navigating bureaucratic gymnastics, so to speak. That's why the president asked me to work with ODNI to get the job done.

I barely got started before our effort was stonewalled. At first Dan Coats was the director of national intelligence (DNI). He wasn't malicious, but he was totally asleep. His underlings were running the White House intel operations, and they didn't like Trump. I tried working with Devin Nunes, who was still chairman of the HPSCI at the time, to see if he could put some outside pressure on Coats to release the docs, but it didn't work. Every way I worked it, the answer was always no. At the end of the day, I reminded people that I, and everyone else in the executive branch, worked for the commander in chief, but too many conveniently forgot this law.

I had nothing against Coats personally, but it was clear that as long as he was at the helm of ODNI, nothing was going to get done. I gave my honest opinion to President Trump, and eventually Trump decided to fire Coats. In his place, he named Joe Maguire as acting director. A former Navy SEAL and vice admiral of the Navy, Maguire had a sterling resume. But he had a similar problem as Coats. He couldn't get the job done. I don't think he was necessarily anti-Trump or anti-America first. Maybe he was just too risk averse. Maybe it was the fact that he had the same staff as Coats and was unwilling to contradict them. Regardless, he had a responsibility to follow the president's orders. If that required changing his staff or ignoring their partisan recommendations, so be it. Maguire failed to do it, so soon enough he was on the chopping block as well.

Events surrounding declassification came to a head during President Trump's February 2020 state visit to India. I was honored to go on the trip because I was one of the few senior administration officials of Indian heritage. I speak Gujarati, the dialect used in the region of India where the country's prime minister, Narendra Modi, is from (as is my own family). Trump was slated to fly first to Gujarat and deliver an address to a cricket stadium filled with more than one hundred thousand Indians near my hometown. It was going to be a big moment, both for Trump and Modi, as well as for the US-India relationship. I had arranged for my parents to be there and had worked closely with the president's speechwriters to ensure the remarks were full of cultural references that would resonate with the Indian people.

Around midnight, somewhere over the Atlantic Ocean on Air Force One, the president wanted to talk to me about a number of matters. The plane was entirely blacked out with staffers sleeping, all except for me and President Trump. The president invited me into his office in the nose of the 747 and asked me who I thought should be the director of national intelligence. I gave him exactly the same name I had given him before: John Ratcliffe. The congressman from Texas and former federal prosecutor had been rock solid on the House Intel, Judiciary, and Homeland Security committees. Despite the media blowback, he called the Russian witch hunt and Mueller charade what they were. He was tough, and he knew that the job of the director of national intelligence wasn't just to compile intel for the president but to help reform the broken intelligence community.

The president told me to go and make the call. "Ask him if he'll do it," Trump told me. So I headed downstairs to the belly of Air Force One and hopped on a secure line. Somewhere back in the US, Ratcliffe got a call from a hidden number, the Air Force One operator. The line connected and I spoke. "John, it's Kash. The president wants to know if you'll take the DNI job." Ratcliffe just laughed. We both knew the answer. So I ran back upstairs and told the president, "We are good to go, Boss."

Hours later we landed in Gujarat, where Trump received a king's welcome. I was ecstatic. It was my birthday, I was in my native hometown, and my parents ended up in the front row while President Trump and Prime Minister Modi delivered remarks to over one hundred thousand people. My parents were delayed, and they almost didn't make it.

We had been trying to make arrangements prior to departing from the US, but the logistics were so complicated that the staff assigned to ensure my parents got all the right credentials, invitations, security clearances, directions, and everything else weren't able to get all the ducks in a row in time. Ivanka found out that my parents were not going to be able to make it because folks had dropped the ball, so she made a call from the plane. To this day I don't know what she said. But I do know that when we arrived at the stadium, my parents weren't there. Then, partway through the speech, they walked down the aisle and took the seats we set aside for them right in the front row. You couldn't see it on camera, but right in the middle of the speech, I ran over and gave them a huge hug. One of my most treasured photos was taken that day with me, my mom, and my dad all together smiling in front of the stage with President Trump and Prime Minister Modi speaking near our hometown in Gujarat.

After that incredible moment, I had no idea that the trip was about to get even better, as if that were even possible. The next day in New Delhi, I was part of the large delegation that accompanied the president to his meetings with Prime Minister Modi. At the start of one diplomatic meeting, the group followed Trump and Modi into a very long room, with the two leaders seated up front and staff seated "back benching" along the side. I was surprised I was even allowed in the room, with the national security advisor, the secretary of commerce, the ambassador, and others all present and outranking me. Yet as I walked in, the president turned to me and shouted, "Kash, have you met my friend Narendra?" He urged me to come over, and soon I was speaking to "India's Trump" in our native dialect, with the prime minister asking all about my family and background (of which he already knew, having clearly been briefed on me before our arrival). The leaders introduced the various members of their delegations to each other—when President Trump got to me, he turned to Prime Minister Modi and said, "You don't want to know what he does. He's my intel guy." The whole room started laughing. That statement proved more true than I was aware.

As we awaited Ratcliffe's confirmation for the DNI job, President Trump had agreed to a parallel plan. With the election looming and only a few months left in his first term, he wanted to replace McGuire with another acting DNI. For that job, he chose Ambassador to Germany Ric Grenell, whom I recommended. The idea was that Grenell could do the job and begin declassification while the Senate worked on Ratcliffe's confirmation, which could take months. Grenell had agreed to do it, but without telling me, he told the president he had one condition. "Kash has to be my number two," he said. Ric and I had worked very closely together on hostage operations, and he did an incredible job in Germany leveraging Europe's support to bring American citizens trapped abroad back home. We had a great relationship and a lot of respect for each other. So before I knew it, I was indeed Trump's "intel guy," the principal deputy to the acting DNI. Originally, I turned the job down. But President Trump is a very persuasive guy. I lost that argument, and off to ODNI I went. Not that we would ever get credit from the media for it, but it was the first time in the history of the United States a minority was appointed to this position and, with Ric's appointment, the first time America had an openly gay cabinet secretary.

As we flew back to the States, I was processing my new role. I had a lot of experience with the intel world. I was the national security advisor for the HPSCI and did highly sensitive global targeting with Special Forces while at SOCOM in the DoJ. Not to mention, I'd been rubbing against the intelligence community for months ever since President Trump asked me to work on declassification. I was familiar with the intelligence community and the classification system in general, but I also knew that ODNI had a lot more problems than just refusing to declassify what the president had requested. Not to mention the staff there didn't have a lot of love for me, seeing as I already rocked the boat and made it clear that I wouldn't sit quietly and accept their actions to stonewall direct orders from the president. Ric and I were in for a hell of a ride.

CHAPTER 12
And the Ugly

R ic Grenell and I hit the ground running at ODNI while waiting for Representative Ratcliffe to get through the Senate confirmation process and to formally become the director. One of our first tasks was to declassify the documents President Trump had asked for months and months before, particularly those on Russia Gate. The intelligence community needed a lot of other reforms, such as reprioritization of intelligence collections efforts from our intelligence agencies to advance President Trump's priorities. But we would get to those soon enough.

When ODNI was created after 9/11, one of its primary jobs was to streamline the classification system and to lead declassification efforts. As the head of the intelligence community, ODNI can declassify material from any agency. Incredibly, despite publishing the Nunes Memo in February of 2018, vital parts of our findings were still redacted and classified for no good reason well into 2020. The FBI and DoJ did this on purpose.

Of course, agencies frequently classify documents that actually are state secrets and need to be kept secret for the sake of legitimate investigations or national security purposes. But too frequently agencies classify documents to hide their own corruption. Not only that, but when documents are classified, the American people can't interpret events for themselves. Instead, they become wholly dependent on the government's interpretation of the events through their public statements—or worse, through the media's interpretation driven by selective leaks. That's not even to mention the exorbitant costs to the taxpayer related to managing the unwieldy, complicated classification systems.

Abuses in our classification system are exactly how Adam Schiff could go out there day after day during the Russia Gate investigation and spread utter lies about what we discovered during Objective Medusa. Because we were unable to release the source documents and give the people the full truth, Adam Schiff and his media cronies were able to spread lies with reckless abandon.

After leaving the White House, I started a nonprofit legal offense group, FightWithKash.com with important projects such as DurhamWatch.com to help fix this problem. It started out by simply covering the Durham probe into the origins of the Russia collusion conspiracy. But over time, FightWithKash.com became a centralized hub where all sorts of government documents were published covering Russia Gate, January 6th, and really any other matter of public importance where those in leadership failed to inform the American public. We did so by releasing Inspector General (IG) reports, case filings, declassified notes, emails, department memoranda, and a lot more. It is my firm belief that the people don't need James Comey or the *New York Times* to interpret events for them. They need the hard facts that they can read themselves to make their own decisions. After the massive success of FightWithKash.com, I expanded operations to include a 501(c)3 called the K$H Foundation, which goes beyond public education to provide programs like tuition assistance, educational services, and other programming for veterans and active duty service members.

After starting this government transparency effort, Jan Jekielek, a senior editor and host at the news outlet *Epoch Times*, approached me with a tantalizing offer in the same vein: Would I like to start a show on their channel to discuss Russia Gate, the Durham probe, foreign policy, national security, defense, intelligence, and the Deep State on a regular basis? At first I laughed at the idea and thought he was crazy. Of course I think people should have the ability to find information and know the facts about their government. But part of me still wondered if enough people would be interested in all of this to actually support a show. After all, if you're not engaged in these battles day after day, it's difficult to keep track of all the details. But I decided to take the opportunity to inform people of the facts and walk them through all the major developments happening within government and on the world stage. With that, the show *Kash's Corner* was born—and two years in, it has consistently been one of the top shows on *Epoch Times*. Even more than that, sharing all my findings and insights on video and through podcasts with *Epoch Times* is ultimately what inspired me to write this book.

Back at ODNI, I knew that one of the first things the president wanted declassified was the over sixty depositions I took where senior government officials admitted under oath that they had absolutely zero evidence that Trump colluded, conspired, or coordinated with the Russians. The Nunes Memo had already proven that the Russia probe was based on the Steele Dossier, which itself was paid for by the Hillary Clinton campaign and the DNC. But until we declassified those Three Cs, the American public didn't know the full truth: that every single government official driving the train on the Trump spying operation knew from the very beginning that it was all a load of bull.

Along with those interviews, Ric and I also declassified even more text messages between FBI agent Peter Strzok and his lover Lisa Page. Much of their text conversations had been released before, but the American people never knew the full picture of just how much those charged with investigating Donald Trump hated him and were driven by absolute malice.

As we worked through our declassifications, we gave the agencies involved—in this circumstance, the FBI—the opportunity to weigh in on what we were doing. Just like what happened at the height of Russia Gate, they objected strenuously, slinging false claims that transparency with the American people would do irreparable harm to our national security. So we told them, "Alright, if that's true then just show us what's behind all of the redactions so that we can see what would be so damaging to our national security." With the redactions removed, we saw they were lying through their teeth. The only thing they were hiding from the American people was their own corrupt and unlawful actions.

What we were able to release to the public over massive internal opposition cleared the air on a controversy that was, incredibly, still being discussed in Washington. But we weren't focused on Russia Gate alone. Some of our most influential declassifications centered around Michael Flynn—and ended up exonerating a man who had been set up and persecuted by the Deep State for years.

TARGETING A PATRIOT

A couple of weeks before President Trump took office in January 2017, Senate Minority Leader Chuck Schumer, a Democrat from New York, appeared on MSNBC and issued a threat. Donald Trump had spoken out against the politicization of the intelligence community. As I mentioned earlier, Chuck Schumer then warned that Trump was "being really dumb to do this." "You take on the intelligence community?" he added. "They have six ways from Sunday of getting back at you."

The Democrats and the media smiled at Schumer's threat. They were happy to know they had strong allies in the intelligence community to help them in their total war against President-elect Trump. But the American people heard Schumer's words and shuddered. Schumer was broadcasting what the people had feared: we may vote and choose a president to represent us, but some of our leaders want to turn the electoral process into nothing more than a show to make us feel like the people are the sovereign. In Schumer's world, the Deep State is the real power. If they don't like our choice, unelected, politicized members of the intelligence community will subvert the president and try to take him down from the inside.

Schumer's threat came to fruition in a matter of days. One of the Deep State's favorite mouthpieces and a man who commonly attacks me, *Washington Post* columnist David Ignatius, wrote a story based on a phone call between General Flynn—Trump's incoming national security advisor—and Russian ambassador Sergey Kislyak. In an unlawful breach of diplomatic protocol, the Deep State had leaked the classified call to Ignatius after Obama administration officials illegally leaked Flynn's unmasked identity,[1] overruling protections designed to ensure anonymity for American citizens caught up in surveillance conducted on foreign nationals. (Of course, Comey and the FBI never lifted a finger to investigate who leaked the call, which damaged America's relationship with Russia and undermined the foreign policy of the incoming president.)

Ignatius dutifully reported on behalf of his Deep State master the accusation that Flynn must have said some very bad things and may have even violated a long-forgotten law called the Logan Act, a never-enforced nineteenth-century law that bans private citizens from negotiating with foreign governments. The fact that Flynn was not only doing his job but also doing what every incoming national security advisor does by calling his foreign counterparts didn't matter. The Deep State used Ignatius to cut Flynn. Now there was chum in the water, and the Deep State sharks' feeding frenzy began.

Flynn was a major target for the Deep State. As a former lieutenant general in the Army and the director of the Defense Intelligence Agency under President Obama, Flynn had violated a cardinal rule in Washington by telling the truth. In a public hearing, he reported that ISIS was surging, contradicting the Obama administration's claims that they had ISIS on the run. For that, the national security apparatus, firmly devoted to Obama's foreign policy vision, never forgave Flynn, and neither did the intelligence community.

On top of that, Flynn had been very vocal about the need to reform the intelligence community. As a lieutenant general, he knew that the best intelligence was operational intelligence—information that actually helped people on the ground accomplish their mission. Intelligence reports that took months to rise out of the bureaucratic quagmire in

---

[1]   Traditionally when US spying operations intercept communications between a foreign national and an American citizen, the identity of the American citizen is kept anonymous unless it is absolutely necessary to reveal his or her identity. This is a way to protect the rights and privacy of American citizens. Unmasking is the process by which the identity of the American citizen in these communications is revealed.

Langley or elsewhere in Washington were almost entirely useless. Not only was the intel dated by the time it went through an unnecessary circuit from the sources on the ground back to Washington and then back to those operating on the ground, such intel was often filled with inaccuracies and bad analysis. The fact is that a desk jockey in DC probably knows a hell of a lot less about what's going on in Afghanistan or Syria or Libya than people who actually spend time in Afghanistan or Syria or Libya. As such, Flynn was an advocate for trimming the intelligence community down and refocusing energy to collect usable, actionable intelligence.

As a public defender, federal prosecutor, and someone who worked with our ██████ Special Forces teams at SOCOM, I knew well that intel and evidence from the field were invaluable, which is why I spent so much time travelling to less-than-glamorous sites in the world to track down the truth. Showing up has always been a mantra of mine. You have to go downrange and meet the people putting foot to ass for us. There is a lot more to learn on the ground than whatever is available online or through satellite feeds. But to the intelligence community, what Flynn said was dangerous—at least to them. And what is dangerous to them they automatically assumed was dangerous to the country. Not only would Flynn's elevation to being the president's national security advisor mean that he could implement his plans to cut some of their jobs, those who kept their jobs might be forced to leave their comfortable air-conditioned offices in Washington and actually spend quality time in the places they claimed to be experts on.

For all these reasons, Flynn was a threat to permanent Washington, and he was the initial Trump staffer with a giant target painted on his back. The Kislyak call was just the first step of the trap. Following that, within days after President Trump assumed office, two FBI agents showed up unannounced at the White House to interview Flynn. Then FBI director James Comey would later brag about how he personally sent the agents, subverting the traditional process by bypassing White House lawyers in order to entrap Flynn. The crowd in Comey's interview laughed. Apparently, America's law enforcement agency setting up an innocent man is just a joke to some people. To others it's a repeated violation of the Constitution that Comey-ites used to target their political enemies.

One of those agents Comey sent was none other than Peter Strzok, the man who had formally started the Crossfire Hurricane operation that unlawfully spied on the Trump campaign. The FBI agents were armed with the text of the Kislyak call but didn't tell Flynn. Flynn, trying to do his duty and serve the American people, was happy to help the FBI. He didn't know that the FBI wasn't there to seek his help but to try and trap him. Using the transcript, they attempted to get him to make false statements about what he said to Kislyak. Then, they could prosecute Flynn for lying to the FBI.[38] Of course, how was Flynn supposed to remember every detail of one of the probably hundreds of calls he was making during an insanely busy presidential transition process? And who's to say the FBI's version of what Flynn said would be accurate?

Soon, the manufactured public controversy surrounding Flynn reached a fever pitch, Vice President Pence—concerned about the negative press and worried Flynn privately misled him about the Kislyak call—turned on him. Flynn was out. The Deep State had achieved their first objective. Next, to ensure he never could get close to power again, the Mueller probe prosecuted Flynn for, of course, "lying" to the FBI. Flynn didn't budge—that is until the DoJ threatened to prosecute his son and even reportedly intimated that they would throw him into solitary confinement. Flynn's son at the time had a four-month-old baby. The FBI and DoJ played dirty and changed the calculus. By all appearances Flynn regretted his guilty plea, as he would later try to withdraw it.

FREEDOM FOR FLYNN

When Ric and I got to ODNI, Flynn and the DoJ had been continually pushing back the sentencing hearing as Flynn tried to withdraw his guilty plea. In the intervening years, Flynn had had his reputation irreparably damaged, he faced millions of dollars in legal bills, and he had to sell his house to cover the cost. Even without a prison sentence, the Deep State had destroyed the life of an innocent man who had served our country with distinction. Ric and I did our part to finally stop the injustice by following the law.

The documents we found and declassified were utterly damning and never before revealed to the public. In one of our first drops, we released documents showing that the FBI had planned to set up Flynn all along. Top FBI officials debated before the Flynn White House interview whether the goal was "to get him to lie, so we can prosecute him or get him fired." Despite the FBI's intentions, the agents who interviewed Flynn reported afterward that they believed Flynn was NOT lying and believed he was telling the truth. No matter. In further documents we declassified, we showed how Lisa Page was doctoring the FBI's Flynn meeting notes—or 302s, as we call them—up to seventeen days after the meeting. And she was doing it all while serving directly under Deputy Director Andrew McCabe as his legal counsel. To top it all off, Page should have never been allowed to touch the 302s in the first place. FBI policy dictates only those who were at an interview can write a report on the interview—and even then, only agents and analysts, NOT FBI lawyers. The doctored version of the 302 of the interview was key to the DoJ prosecution of Flynn for allegedly lying to the FBI.

While these declassified docs were making massive waves in the press, we released the full list of people in the Obama administration who unmasked Flynn, setting the stage for the media to publish false reporting on his call with Kislyak and for the whole unjust persecution to get started in the first place. The list was a who's who of the Obama administration—people who had no business spying on the national security advisor of the incoming president, including Obama's national security advisor, Susan Rice; his chief of staff, Denis McDonough; James Comey; CIA Director John Brennan; Director of National Intelligence James Clapper; Ambassador to the United Nations Samantha Power; and even Vice President Joe Biden.[39] Altogether, Flynn was unmasked by at least thirty-nine Obama officials a minimum of fifty-three times, an unjustified abuse of power at the highest reaches of government.

For extra measure, Ric and I foot stomped the whole declassification effort by releasing the Flynn-Kislyak transcript that kicked off the controversy in the first place, allowing the American public to read it for themselves and not just take David Ignatius's word for it. The transcript was normal to the point of being boring. The actual text of the call showed that absolutely nothing improper was said, and in fact Flynn was doing his best to represent the interests of the United States in preparation for his upcoming role in the White House. All the breathless reporting on the call was malicious slander.

Over the course of only a few weeks, Ric and I had dropped truth bombs all over the Deep State. For years corrupt government officials had gone around spouting lies about Russia Gate and Flynn and everything else without any consequences. We used their own documents to show the people that the whole time these officials were liars and crooks. And our efforts had immediate impact. In an embarrassing retreat, the DoJ, which had dogged and prosecuted Michael Flynn for years, was forced to cower in defeat. They didn't just let Flynn withdraw his guilty plea. They dropped their yearslong prosecution effort altogether. Flynn was completely exonerated.

Yet again the Deep State had manufactured a hit job against an innocent man, and yet again we thwarted them. What compounded the Flynn scandal was how the government sat on evidence showing that Flynn was being wrongfully prosecuted. It wasn't just top leaders at agencies but normal bureaucrats at ODNI who were obstructing the truth and preventing true justice from being served—all while contradicting the direct orders of the president who demanded declassification.

The national security apparatus and intelligence community abused the unmasking process and classification system to provoke a baseless political investigation and run cover for the FBI. They politicized the national security apparatus of this country once again. To defeat the Deep State, we have to fix the intelligence community.

CHAPTER 13
Putting Intel in Its Place

B y its nature, the intelligence community frequently operates in the shadows. But that doesn't mean we should be at a loss for how to reform it. In the Baghdadi raid we saw how the intelligence community can work for good—and in the impeachment farce and the takedown of General Flynn we understand how the Deep State has abused the US intelligence apparatus to undermine the people and the president they elected. Left unchecked, our democratic system of government is at risk.

Our task then is to focus on the abuses and to make specific changes that will push the intelligence community back toward its original purpose: providing clear and accurate information to our leaders so that they can make the best decisions possible for the people. Ric and I began instituting some of these changes while at ODNI. The next administration must pick up where we left off and move even further to bring the intelligence community to heel.

TRIMMING THE FAT

Outside of declassification, Ric and I began instituting some long-needed structural reforms at the Office of the Director of National Intelligence. Across the entire federal government, the intelligence community is bloated, politicized, siloed, and riddled with obstructions and obstructionists. General Flynn was completely right in his desire to reform the intelligence community. So we got started. Our first action was to cut down the official ODNI workforce by 10 percent. Part of that came from removing clear waste. When we arrived, there were a large number of unfilled seats, or billets, in the ODNI workforce that Congress was paying for on a yearly basis and that no human being had filled. The last thing ODNI needed was more empty seats, so we cut these unfilled billets entirely and sent the money back to the taxpayers.

That wasn't the only bloat in the office. Over the years, ODNI had grown and grown, much like every other department and agency in the federal government. After all, when agencies have a problem, their response is not to improve; it's just to get larger. But bigger is not better. As a result, ODNI effectively became a massive, partisan public relations firm for the intelligence community. Like the National Security Council, many ODNI staff were detailed over from their home agencies, like the CIA or the NSA—and it showed. The staff at ODNI was much more loyal to their home agencies than to the mission of the Trump administration. Instead of serving the president, these staffers were attempting to implement the priorities of the intelligence community (or at least slow-walk any White House policy that contradicted the intelligence community leadership).

So along with removing the unfilled seats at ODNI, we also sent hundreds of people back to their home agencies or out of government altogether—a change that should be enshrined by Congress in future appropriations legislation that dictates government spending levels. Ric and I began a good work. Future administrations and Congress should codify it and remove at least 10 percent of the positions from ODNI. Sending these employees back served a dual purpose as well. Instead of putting a bunch of people in front of computers at ODNI to create more useless stacks of paper, case officers sent back to their home agencies could actually be sent overseas to collect intelligence, like they are supposed to do.

Because of our cuts, the intelligence community started to target us with leaks at every turn. Shocking I know. One of their favorite attacks was that Ric and I were undermining our intelligence apparatus. Just like the disinformation operations they ran during our declassification work, this argument would be destroyed with truth. In fact, just by removing staff we were making the intelligence apparatus operate more effectively. That's because ODNI bloat actually put up obstacles to intelligence gathering and sharing.

The core purpose of ODNI is to coordinate among the intelligence agencies to both implement the president's agenda and to deliver to the president and other senior members of government hard-hitting, accurate, curated intelligence briefings. This is no easy task. With a multiplicity of intelligence agencies with hundreds of thousands of experts, analysts, spies, informants, and more covering wide varieties of issue areas, ensuring only the most important and accurate information reached its way to the top free from noise was a big job. At times, I personally delivered the Presidential Daily Briefing (PDB) to the boss in the Oval Office. I remember vividly that President Trump made it a priority to focus on national security matters like terrorism, Iran, China, and wars abroad. Meanwhile, the Biden administration has shifted its national security focus to climate change. That means instead of our intelligence experts looking for information on terrorists, they're looking for intel on the setting sun. It's sheer idiocy. But I digress.

Adding more staff at ODNI doesn't exactly make the job of intelligence curating any easier. Instead, additional staffers at ODNI often found themselves trying to justify their existence by trying to do the jobs of the intelligence agencies themselves. They would take intelligence reports written by other agencies and rewrite them just to show that they did something. This is insane. They aren't spies. They don't work in signals intelligence, conduct on-the-ground intelligence collection, or run assets. They were just sitting there collecting a paycheck while adding unnecessary delays and confusion, so we removed them.

This sort of interagency competition causes another problem called stovepiping. Stovepiping is when intelligence that is gathered within an agency is funneled straight up—or stovepiped—to the leadership of the agency without ever being shared with anyone else. Because agencies are jealous of their work, staff in each agency try to hide information from staff in other agencies. That gives them the ability to take credit for particular intelligence findings and successes, inflating their egos and potentially leading to higher positions of authority. This dispositional preference to keep things hidden and secret is endemic in government. The problem is that when it occurs in the intelligence community, it can actually cost lives.

Investigations into 9/11 found that a lack of information sharing prevented the intelligence community as a whole from being able to predict and prevent 9/11. ODNI was created shortly after 9/11 to stop this exact problem by being the central repository where information could be gathered and compiled, breaking down the walls between the different intel agencies. It was the most Washington solution to a Washington problem: if bureaucrats aren't doing their jobs, create more bureaucrats. In the end, unnecessary staff blubber at ODNI ended up creating yet another source of rivalry instead of overcoming the rivalries that already existed. To fully reform the intelligence community, we must not only further cut staff at ODNI but also crack down on the practice of stovepiping and proactively implement intelligence sharing. The director in charge of a reformed, leaner staff at ODNI must keep those staffers hyperfocused on information sharing. That means no ODNI staffer should be doing independent intelligence gathering. Instead, those staffers must be compiling and disseminating information from across the intelligence community to create the most holistic picture possible for decision makers.

ODNI is far from the only intelligence agency with staffing bloat. In order to effectively streamline distribution and sharing of intelligence, the massive size of the existing seventeen intelligence agencies must also be reduced. Just as ODNI had many positions that were carbon copies of the agencies beneath them, many agencies have sub-offices that are really just the same exact thing as offices in other agencies. Instead of coordinating together to get a full picture, each agency keeps erecting new offices and crafting new initiatives in order to try and become a holistic intelligence gathering agency in and of itself. That, and whenever a department creates a new sub-agency, it creates a new bureaucratic black hole that can be walled off, allowing only a select few to access the information inside. Instead of intelligence being something that is collected and shared for the greater good of protecting America, it becomes a status symbol with staffers and agencies and sub-offices all erecting new barriers so they can have new ways to show off who is cool enough to have access and who is not. It's ridiculous, it's childish, and it must stop.

Of course, agencies should stop propping up new offices, especially when another agency already has that base covered. But that is not enough. Congress must also step in. The intelligence community needs a full audit to find duplicity, waste, fraud, and abuse. Congress should conduct a thorough review and revise appropriations to remove duplicative offices and needless paper pushing. And that's not the only action Congress should take. Defenders of transparency and of the people in the House and Senate should immediately form a committee to thoroughly investigate abuses within the intelligence community modeled after the 1975 Church Committee. The Church Committee in the House and the Pike Committee in the Senate reviewed abuses at the CIA, FBI, NSA, and other agencies, uncovering scandal after scandal committed by the Deep State. This included revealing the existence of MKULTRA, a CIA program used to drug Americans with LSD without their consent,[40] as well as uncovering a government counterintelligence program directed against civil rights leaders.[41] Only an open airing of the intelligence community's dirty laundry will restore trust in our national security apparatus.

YOU'RE FIRED

Ric and I didn't have the time to implement these large-scale reforms in the brief period Ric served as the acting director of intelligence. It didn't help that we also faced resistance at every turn. At one point, we heard reports that an ODNI staffer said in a meeting we weren't present at, "We're just going to wait Ric and Kash out." This is exactly how the permanent bureaucracy operates. When anyone bucks the status quo, the bureaucracy knows that their jobs will be there long after the political appointees are gone. The only way the intelligence community will come under democratic control is if officials can be more easily moved, demoted, or even fired for failing to execute the national security no-fail mission of protecting America.

It is a tragedy that people like Alexander Vindman, Fiona Hill, Eric Ciaramella, or the cabal of ODNI staffers who refused to declassify the documents that exonerated General Flynn were ever allowed in the White House. Certainly, some of that can be blamed on Trump's deputies, like Bolton and Coats, who surrounded themselves with the worst of the swamp creatures. The president of the United States can't personally manage the hiring and firing decisions of the thousands of people who work in the White House, much less the millions of people who work in the federal government overall.

But even if the president did have the time to manage those decisions, civil service law prevents him from being able to choose the vast number of government employees whom he relies on to implement the platform he was elected on. While the president can name certain chiefs and heads of departments and agencies, the people who work under those political appointees are almost entirely career bureaucrats he can't fire and who clearly have a political will of their own.

The system was designed over a century ago in an attempt to prevent politicking within the federal government and the buying and selling of government offices. However noble that goal was, the end result was to create a fourth branch of government effectively independent from elected leaders, a branch that can choose to follow or obstruct a president's orders with minimal to no fear of repercussions. In effect, they have zero accountability, which leads directly to the type of gross politicization of the national security apparatus that we have seen time and again.

Democrats and RINOs don't care about this problem, because they are all part of the Washington establishment. George W. Bush and

Barack Obama may have had different policies on some matters, but neither of them ever threatened the politicized federal bureaucracy, so the bureaucracy never seriously attempted to stop them from implementing their agenda. Trump, on the other hand, did threaten the permanent bureaucracy, so it stood against him at every turn. The end result was unaccountable bodies like the intelligence community having veto power over the presidency.

Near the end of his term, President Trump began unrolling reforms to impose accountability on the federal bureaucracy by signing an executive order to create something called Schedule F. In effect, President Trump created a new classification for federal employees that made it easier to fire them if they subverted the president's agenda—no matter who the president was. Sadly, that reform wasn't able to be implemented before the 2020 election. The next president should not only reintroduce that reform immediately but expand upon it to the greatest degree possible. Congressional funding for excess billets must also end. After all, if there isn't money for a useless seat, then no one can sit in it. It's simple math.

But this should be just the beginning. Our Founders created a system where the people were supposed to have the ultimate authority. As long as unelected bureaucrats can abuse their power and subvert the president the people elected without consequence, we don't really have a republic. We need even more aggressive civil service reform if the bureaucracy is ever going to be brought back under the control of our elected leaders—and ultimately under the control of the people.

That is why our civil service system must be transformed at the root. The executive branch should be run and operated by people who work for the president—the only person in our Constitution named as the head of the executive branch. That means Congress must change the law to allow federal bureaucrats to be able to be fired by the president. If an individual or group of individuals within the executive branch is undermining the president, they should be removed from their posts and replaced with people who won't undermine the president's agenda. If the people don't like the president's hiring and firing decisions, they can throw the president out of office. But as long as the president is in office, that person should have the ability to actually implement the policies that he or she ran on without private individuals who have never won a vote of confidence from their fellow citizens being able to stop it.

Likewise, Congress should ban the existence of public sector unions, which, by their nature, establish an antagonistic relationship between federal bureaucrats and the administration they are employed to work for. Nobody is forcing bureaucrats to be federal employees. If they don't like the wages, the benefits, or anything else about the job, they are free to quit and join the vast majority of Americans who work in the private sector. Working in government is a privilege and a service. Many need to be reminded of that by being shown the door. Those who do work for the executive branch should know that they serve at the executive branch's discretion. They should not be able to leverage the power of a union to win concessions from their employer, the president of the United States.

CONTINUED DECLASSIFICATION

As we saw in the previous chapter, one of the worst abuses of the politicized intelligence community is the purposeful classification of documents and materials that have no business being classified. One of the ways the Deep State gets away with this is by creating confusing classification and declassification processes that are different across every single agency. Attempts to impose transparency are met with a wall of bureaucratic mumbo jumbo. Thankfully, Ric and I knew what we were looking for and had an understanding of how the classification process worked through our years working in other agencies. That's why we were able to release Russia Gate and Flynn materials so quickly after being moved into ODNI. But who knows how much is out there blocked from public view that we don't know to look for? How many other Americans are being wrongfully prosecuted and targeted using "intelligence" that doesn't pass muster? Are the Biden FBI and DoJ wrongfully accusing other Americans with false evidence, like they have done repeatedly in the past? Have agency directors and their staff labelled evidence that damages the left as "disinformation"—just like they did with the Hunter Biden laptop scandal?

The only way we can know is by doing a top to bottom reform of the classification system in government. Ric and I began that at ODNI when I launched a group to create a universal classification system. By implementing one single classification system with one single set of universal standards, it makes it a lot easier to determine who can have access to what and what can be declassified and released to the public. When agencies have their own, personal classification systems, it becomes much more difficult to tell if something is classified just because the people at that agency are trying to hide something.

Ric and I began to implement this universal system while at ODNI, which included initiating a multi-year systems overhaul to allow the different computer systems set up at different agencies to "talk" with each other. To this day, the intelligence community cannot actually share information easily because their computer systems are unable to communicate with each other, and their classification systems are all compartmentalized. Unfortunately, the Biden administration put an end to these reforms. But the next president should take back up this banner and fix the utterly broken classification system within the intelligence community.

Another way to reform the classification process would be to erect a permanent office within ODNI that continuously reviews classified material that should be declassified, in whole or in part, for the public interest. This office should report directly to the president. This is just about the only time I will bend my rule against erecting new offices within the intelligence community. Trump was the most transparent president in history, yet the intelligence community continually tried to prevent that transparency because it embarrassed them and the rest of their allies within the Deep State. If a president staffs this office with people truly committed to government accountability and transparency, it will be a hard blow to the Deep State, which can only operate effectively when it operates in secret.

Additionally, those who abuse their access to classified information should be swiftly prosecuted. One of the Deep State's most common tactics is to leak classified documents or internal deliberation to the press in order to smear their opponents. They did it to President Trump, Carter Page, George Papadopoulos, Michael Flynn, me, and countless others. To prevent this from happening, all government employees, including intelligence community employees, should be required to sign nondisclosure agreements, or NDAs, subjecting themselves to criminal prosecution for violating the requirement that already exists that all government devices (including cellphones, laptops, and more) can be used for authorized government work only. Then, those devices should be subjected to mandatory monthly scans across the entire federal government to determine who has improperly transferred classified information, including to the press.

Relatedly, I completely agree with President Trump that we need to reform libel laws in America. Right now, media outlets get away daily with slandering their political opponents by publishing outright lies or negative allegations that have their roots in leaked documents or unverifiable hearsay passed on to them by the Deep State. Just as government employees should be held accountable for their illegal leaks of classified information to the press, journalists and news outlets should also be more easily sued when they publish defamatory stories based on gossip.

Finally, there is currently a policy by which former senior-level employees in the government who hold high-level security clearances are able to keep those security clearances even after they've left the government. For the most part, this is a good practice. For example, former cabinet secretaries are frequently called on to offer their advice and expertise based on their years of experience on very sensitive matters. The only way they can do this effectively is if they retain the ability to view classified materials.

That being said, a significant number of former senior government employees have abused this privilege and used the prestige of their security clearance to attack their political opponents and even rig elections. One of the worst abusers in this regard is former Obama CIA director

John Brennan, who touted his credentials and clearance level to spread the disinformation that the Hunter Biden laptop story was a Russian plant. We already saw how Brennan's disinformation campaign swayed the 2020 election in favor of Joe Biden. Yet Brennan has faced no consequences for leveraging the privilege of his post-government security credentials to help his friend Joe Biden.

Brennan was far from the only one. Like Brennan, former Obama DNI James Clapper leveraged his security clearance to make money as a CNN contributor, where he frequently smears anyone that isn't to his left. Comey has leaked to the press, abused his office, and touted his insider knowledge to land primo book deals to spread his lies. Comey's successor, Christopher Wray, continues to lead the most highly politicized FBI in history where lying, falsifying information, and politically motivated attacks are par for the course. Officials who act like this and use their clearances to engage in political interference campaigns should have their clearances immediately revoked.

***

The intelligence community does some incredible work. It was thanks to them that we found Baghdadi and decimated ISIS leadership. And it's thanks to committed and apolitical staff in the national security apparatus that Americans held hostage far from home have been able to return to their native land safely. Every day committed intelligence and national security staffers do hard, anonymous work in service to our country. Yet their work is tarnished when political actors within the bureaucracy abuse their authority to attack innocent Americans and undermine the president elected by the people. From the NSC to ODNI, I fought back against the national security Deep State and won. They aren't invincible. It just takes warriors willing to fight them smart and hit them head on. When we do that, we put them back in their place and help restore the power of the people over our government.

PART IV

THE DEPARTMENT OF DEFENSE

CHAPTER 14

The Defense Industrial Complex

From the Russia Gate investigation to my time on the National Security Council and in the Office of the Director of National Intelligence, I had fully gained President Trump's trust by fighting for the truth. Tens of millions of Americans saw exactly what I saw—that the Deep State was undermining the Trump presidency and constitutes a perilous threat to self-government. Yet that was a minority opinion in Washington, even within the Trump White House. Incredibly, despite the Russia collusion hoax, the Mueller witch hunt, an impeachment farce, unprecedented leaks, and massive obstruction from the bureaucracy, many people, including many presidential advisors, didn't take the Deep State seriously. That I did, and that I had a track record of taking them on and winning, meant that the president put a lot of faith in me. I soon discovered just how much faith that was.

When it came to confronting members of the Deep State who ran the largest and most powerful bureaucracy in the world, President Trump called on me again. It was a surprise, but before long the president sent me to the Department of Defense.

THE PLAYERS

The Deep State within the DoD operates somewhat differently than its branches in other departments and agencies. Thank God, the military wasn't used as a tool by the Democrats in their attempt to win the 2016 election like how they abused the powers of the DoJ, the FBI, and the intelligence community. But the mandarins at the top of the military establishment do have their own massive egos and interests—and a hearty dose of corruption. All of these failings mean their goals and actions frequently conflict with the national security needs of the United States and the policy priorities of their commander in chief. In the end, their egos and desire for wealth and power weaken American safety and undermine self-government.

This is a problem that preceded the Trump presidency. President Obama, as we all remember, ran on a platform of ending foreign wars. But by the end of his two terms, the wars were still going, and American troops and military assets were engaged abroad in even more foreign quagmires than before. There are many reasons for this, but the most decisive was the influence of the Washington foreign policy blob and the Defense Industrial Complex.

In Washington, effectively every foreign policy "expert" is a wild-eyed hawk. Think tanks, fellowships, foreign policy institutions, and more in Washington almost exclusively train up people whose first reaction to any foreign problem is to call for heavy-handed American involvement. The media rewards the most bellicose writers and talking heads, and people in the foreign policy world walk around attempting to swing a big stick—which to them generally means sending someone else's son or daughter to die in a Middle Eastern desert to advance their theoretical papers.

Congress is particularly bad on this front. Outside of a few brave exceptions, most congressmen and senators want to appear tough on camera and to their constituents. So they continually beef up defense spending (frequently on massively wasteful programs) and call for the president to project power abroad liberally, whether doing so serves American interest or not. Altogether, that means that almost every foreign entanglement has a giant squad of cheerleaders in Washington pushing the president to get more and more deeply involved.

Even more nefarious than these actors is the Defense Industrial Complex. They have different incentives than the foreign policy blob in Washington but the same goal—more foreign conflicts. The Defense Industrial Complex is all centered around the incestuous relationship between senior military leadership within the DoD and the key officers in charge of multibillion-dollar procurement programs on the one hand and the behemoth defense contractors on the other. The agreement they have is unspoken in public but simple: Generals and other senior officers know they will cycle out of service and parachute into the Defense Industrial Complex. Thus while they are "serving," they are actually in bed with the defense contractors. This translates to senior leadership in the DoD putting the American taxpayer on the hook for unnecessary arms purchases, procurement projects, and training missions at soaring costs, all lining the pockets of the defense contractors.

To put it simply, we pay billions for products we don't need for wars we don't need to be in. Then, when the generals and officers who pushed for and elongated those wars get out of the military, they are rewarded with a big fat paycheck by the very companies making all those high-priced goods for the DoD. In effect, they are paid off for keeping the contracts open. This revolving door relationship—and the corrupt hiring and promotion system for military brass that helps keep it running—is at the heart of the Deep State within the DoD. This is not to say that the Defense Industrial Complex doesn't play a pivotal role in many areas. Our soldiers need the best training and equipment, and someone needs to make it. But the bloat must be scalped.

KEEPING THE WARS GOING

With all the chicken hawks in Washington and the incestuous relationship between defense contractors and military brass in mind, we can see how the DoD Deep State implements their plans. Every single time a president—it could be Barack Obama or Donald Trump—tried to end a foreign war or recalibrate America's strategic posture, a massive pressure campaign was immediately implemented to stop him. Foreign policy "experts" scream that America will be less safe if we withdraw from some miserable corner of the earth. Media talking heads who have never served and probably couldn't even take a punch without falling into a puddle of tears then tear into the president as some sort of weakling or coward who will lose his standing abroad if he doesn't get involved. Worst of all, military leaders—eyeballing their plum, post-Pentagon job—bombard the president with descriptions of every way his decision can go horribly wrong (they rarely discuss how engaging in foreign wars has *actually* gone horribly wrong, since doing so would cut against their future bottom line). Then, those same military leaders present the president with a very limited set of options that inevitably keep America engaged—and the wars keep going, and the money keeps flowing. Unless a president is willing to reject the false experts, stand up to the media, and overcome Pentagon obstruction, there's no hope that anything will change.

President Obama faced this. It was about the only time he and the Deep State disagreed. He had eight years in Washington and in both campaigns ran on getting us out of Afghanistan. As I would soon know from firsthand experience, disentangling us from that theater of war was no easy task. But as the years went on, Obama didn't keep his promises. He dug America in further. The military brass would push Obama for more troops, always claim a victory (what that was they could never define) was right around the corner, and warn him that if he pulled out, the whole world would go to hell. Eventually, the DoD Deep State won. They had waited Obama out, and we were still in Afghanistan—not to mention we had expanded other theaters of war in places like Syria and Yemen. To the Defense Industrial Complex, the Obama administration was a major win. America was still being bled dry, and they were getting a big cut of the action.

With the prospect of a Hillary Clinton presidency, the DoD Deep State was salivating. Hillary Clinton was their ideal kind of president. To take one example, Clinton had been a main proponent of taking out Libyan dictator Muammar Gaddafi. However evil he was, his removal led to even more chaos in North Africa and the Middle East, which, to the Pentagon and Defense Industrial Complex, meant more American engagement—and more money. If Clinton were elected, their cash cow would produce more milk than ever before. It doesn't take a Hindu to know such a cow is sacred.

When she lost, the brass at the Pentagon and the executives in places like Raytheon and Lockheed Martin were afraid. They weren't afraid that President Trump vowed to end foreign wars. Obama did the same thing, and words are cheap in Washington. They were afraid that President Trump actually had the stones to keep his promises to the American people and was immune to the sway of permanent Washington. They were right to be afraid.

When President Trump entered office, he faced down the forever war party in and out of government. During his term he successfully navigated relationships with some of the world's worst actors, like Kim Jong-Un of North Korea, reducing the temperature in the international arena and mitigating the risk of a conflagration. He was the first president in decades to not start a new war. And he was enacting very hard fought, careful plans to end foreign wars and draw down our troop presence abroad. The problem was, by 2020, he was running out of time to execute those plans. Nearly four years in, the DoD Deep State had gone through every possible ploy to keep the wars going—including massively slow-walking direct orders from the president. Just like in other areas of government, President Trump recognized that it's not enough to order something. The president may be the head of the executive branch according to the Constitution, but the federal bureaucracy thought it was the true leader. That's why he needed cabinet secretaries, deputies, and aides who have the will, the ability, and frankly the intestinal fortitude to get it done, especially in the face of obstruction.

FIRING ESPER

Up to that point, President Trump didn't have such a deputy at the DoD. Perhaps the biggest roadblock in President Trump's foreign policy agenda was his own secretary of defense, Mark Esper. Esper was a poster child of the Defense Industrial Complex. Before being confirmed as the secretary of defense, he was a major lobbyist for Raytheon, one of the world's largest and wealthiest defense contractors. When he left Raytheon, Esper reportedly was still set to receive a compensation payout from Raytheon in 2022, a payout that one could only assume would impact Esper's decisions as secretary of defense.[42] Outside of the Raytheon connection, Esper seemed to have a good resume. He had been an officer in the 101st Airborne, worked as the chief of staff at the conservative Heritage Foundation think tank, and held staff positions on both the Senate Foreign Relations Committee and the House Armed Services Committee. It was all very impressive but also very Washington. During his tenure at the DoD, we learned that he was a swamp creature, just like so many others.

At every single turn, he always seemed to be subverting the president's agenda. Sometimes he was refusing to draw down our forces in Afghanistan to achieve one of the president's main foreign policy goals. In other instances, he was putting up obstacles to counterterrorism raids in Africa and the Middle East. Days before the election, on Halloween, he had opposed a hostage rescue operation that the president ordered. That act was one of the last straws. Just like with the Baghdadi raid, President Trump had been briefed on the proposed operation, given the risks and rewards, and made his decision. As the head of counterterrorism at the time, I set up the Situation Room with senior officials to observe the raid on our secure systems. Everything was a green light, our Special Forces were on the ramp of the infill aircraft about to jump, and then Esper swooped in and sent word through his channels that the operation was a no-go.

In the Situation Room, I was told what Esper did, so I sent the message back that the commander in chief personally greenlit the mission, so unless there was a threat to our forces, the boys were jumping. A few minutes later, with our rotary wing aircraft on its last pump of fuel, the boys jumped. They executed one of the most flawless rescue operations in Special Forces history. Time on target: less than one minute.

Back in Washington where politics—not our national security or our mission—were being put first, Esper was throwing a fit. He sent a message to the White House the day after our incredibly successful operation that he wanted me fired. All he wanted to do was avenge himself in some personal vendetta. For me, it was never personal. The president gave the order, and even the secretary of defense had to follow those orders or step aside if he refused. Instead, he was politicizing the national security apparatus by recklessly meddling in Special Forces operations. Esper ultimately got the reward he wanted though. He falsely attacked me and President Trump in his book, and the media went from hating him to adoring him. It was a cliché ending to a Washington love story.

Amid all this, the president agreed that Esper had to go. The week after election day 2020, things came to a head. I was in the Oval Office when the president made the call. He had had enough. Esper was out. At the Resolute Desk, the president started to dictate a tweet announcing Esper was fired, which was ultimately sent from an aide's computer. He didn't want to technically fire Esper by tweet, so the president had the aide hold off from sending it in order to give his chief of staff, Mark Meadows, the opportunity to give Esper the heads up. President Trump gave Meadows a two-minute grace period to make the call. Meadows made the call, and the countdown started. After two minutes, the president turned to his aide saying, "Okay, now you can go." Esper had disgraced his office by undermining the president he was nominated and confirmed to serve under. It was good he was out.

My former colleague from the NSC, Chris Miller, was then named acting secretary of defense at my suggestion. I had worked with Chris when I first joined the NSC, and he was the head of counterterrorism at the White House—my future job. From day one I could tell he wasn't some Washington lackey. He was a lifelong Green Beret who was so frustrated with failures within the military that he was about to retire. Then 9/11 happened, and he couldn't hang up his hat. He stayed in, and he ended up being in one of the first Special Ops Forces to land in Afghanistan. In November 2001—less than two months after the Twin Towers fell, the Pentagon was hit, and United 93 crashed in

Pennsylvania—Chris had his boots on the ground. His Special Forces unit helped liberate Mazar-i-Sharif from Taliban and al-Qaeda control, one of the first victories of the war in Afghanistan.

As acting secretary, Chris was beloved by the troops. They knew he wasn't some paper pusher. He was the real deal. He was a soldier secretary, and they knew he wouldn't make decisions to please a political constituency but that he would do what was best for our soldiers—and for America. In that, Chris is just about the definition of America First. He was in Afghanistan before almost any American, so nobody can doubt that he will take the fight to the enemy when necessary. But he also saw our failed leaders squander our initial victories against the terrorists by undergoing a nation-building campaign destined to fail. He knew what needed to be done—and he knew how to do it. You knew this was true because the Deep State raged immediately after he was appointed. But Chris refused to bend the knee to their political attacks. Why? Because he put the mission of America's national security first. He exemplifies service to our nation without politics. To this day I have no idea what news Chris watches, which paper he reads, or even who he votes for. That is the way it's supposed to be. He is the type of American we want every young person who is thinking of enlisting to model themselves after: a person who cares about the safety and security of our nation and its citizens above all else.

Based on his experience and expertise, no one was better for the secretary of defense job in the last days of the Trump administration.

Later that same day when Esper was fired, I got a call too. The president wanted me to head to the Pentagon with Chris to serve as the chief of staff for the Department of Defense. Chris had the vision and capability to accomplish what the president asked, just as the law dictates and how the national command authority should operate. But with such a massive bureaucracy to manage, even Chris needed a deputy to help him execute the mission. Just like with the ODNI job, it was originally a position I was inclined to turn down. But when the president asks you do something, you accept. In retrospect, I went 0–2 against the president. I guess that's why he's the commander in chief!

I was, of course, honored to take the job. So Chris and I packed up and headed across the Potomac to the Pentagon. I didn't receive any glowing media profiles for this one either, but it was the first time in history a minority had ever been named the DoD chief of staff.

Thus began the final seventy-two days of the Trump administration. Beyond the president's directive to end foreign wars in places like Afghanistan, Iraq, Syria, and Somalia, we were also charged with wiping out al-Qaeda senior leadership, killing the emirs of ISIS, bringing back American hostages, increasing aid to veterans, and successfully running vaccine distribution for Operation Warp Speed, all during the height of the Covid pandemic. I had years of experience in almost every one of these arenas. But it was a massive undertaking for anyone. It was time to buckle up and execute the no-fail mission from one of the highest perches of government—the Office of the Secretary of Defense in the Pentagon.

CHAPTER 15

The Largest Organization in the World

Nothing can fully prepare you to run the Department of Defense, the largest organization in the history of the world with three million employees and an annual budget of $740 billion—especially when the senior leadership in that organization is hostile to one of your primary goals and to the commander in chief. Besides the actual Trump card I had with a direct line to the president, I had another quality integral to our success: I don't give a dime about media headlines or their continuous, baseless attacks on me. If you pay attention to the noise, you lose sight of your goals. Not to mention my background experience with national security and the federal bureaucracy between my time at ODNI, NSC, and DoJ folded in nicely in my new role.

It's good we knew what we were doing, because Chris Miller and I had to come in hot. Between my time working with Special Forces at SOCOM within the DoJ and then becoming the chief of staff within the Department of Defense, I put my feet on the ground in every theater of war America is engaged in, travelling to over fifty intelligence and military installations around the world. We didn't do it to get frequent flier status. We did it because I have always believed that nothing can get done unless you show up. Don't mail it in. Forget about writing a fancy letter or setting up some video conference from your air-conditioned DC office. You need to show your troops your face, that you're there, and that you care—that you aren't just some reckless DC rube in it for the hype and for your career. At the end of the day, I always believed that the best way to serve the nation in my role at the DoD was to serve those who put their lives on the line for the mission and to let them see me face to face.

At the DoD alone, Chris and I racked up sixty-five thousand miles visiting our soldiers in war zones. It was an unconscionably large amount of air time, but it was worth it. Every trip had multiple purposes—and one of those purposes was to hear directly from the troops themselves, because their word mattered more than anyone's in Washington.

ENDING FOREIGN WARS

The president had given Chris and me a clear directive to end foreign wars. Our idea was that to do that properly and minimize mistakes, we needed to know the minds of our men and women on the ground. Washington shouldn't be deciding things all on its own. At every single base we went to in every single unit, every single soldier said that we were making the right move. Over the course of those sixty-five thousand miles, there was not a single man or woman on the ground who told us we should stay. With their testimony, we knew without a doubt that we were doing the right thing. What was even more eye-opening was that our soldiers—soldiers who kitted up daily to put foot to ass for America, who lost brothers and sisters in these battles—told us *we* had the hard job. In my sixteen years of government service, that was the most humbling thing I was ever told. Their testimony really put things in perspective. It validated President Trump's foreign policy decisions to buck the swamp and end the wars, and it meant we had to get it right.

After all, the stakes couldn't be higher. Real people pay for the bad decisions made in Washington. The absolute hardest thing I've ever had to do was attend a dignified service transfer of fallen soldiers. I stood there on the tarmac at Dover Air Force Base watching the flag-draped coffins of our fallen carried off. I watched the families, barely hanging on, collapse into tears as the coffin of their loved one was carried to them, waiting to be taken to its final resting place. There's nothing you can say or do to alleviate the agony of those waiting to say their final goodbye.

I met with the families personally before the plane arrived. I saw the pain in their eyes. I heard their broken, tear-stained words that could never fully express their broken hearts. Halfway through meeting them, I ran to the bathroom and wept. I quickly cleared my head and realized that I had to show up for the families, the husbands, the wives, the parents, and the children of the fallen. I had to be there to provide our gratitude and admiration for their sacrifice. So I composed myself and went back out, standing on the flight line to honor the fallen being carried out of the C-17.

These meetings taught me a grave lesson. Deep State thugs were playing a blood sport. To them, their reckless and selfish foreign policy decisions were all about their egos, their paychecks, and their golden parachutes. To these families, it was about their husbands. It was about their fathers. It was about the terrifying prospect of facing life alone when you always thought you would have that person right there in that casket standing at your side. One funeral is too many. One dignified transfer is too many. This was the attitude President Trump carried—and it emboldened me to do everything I could to make sure no other families had to go through that again at Dover Air Force Base.

The most important conflict Chris and I needed to draw down was also America's longest war—Afghanistan. We were tasked with executing a conditions-based withdrawal. That meant the Taliban and Afghan government had to meet conditions along the way to receive benefits from America and secure the peaceful withdrawal of our forces from Afghanistan. We determined whether these conditions were met not through promises or rhetoric but as a result of actual ground-level intelligence. We had a mission. But we needed to get the mission done right because intelligence showed that an immediate withdrawal from Afghanistan would lead to the collapse of the Afghan government in a matter of days and total victory for the Taliban—exactly what happened under Biden.

The conditions President Trump had negotiated were very clear. The Taliban had to fully and completely repudiate al-Qaeda. Second, the Taliban and the Afghan government would have to come together to run Afghanistan since they were the two parties in control of Afghanistan for the last three decades. Third, we told them we would continue to assist with counterterrorism operations in-country with our Special Forces operators. We knew that terrorism wasn't going to be eliminated over-night and needed to keep some footprint, even if it was a much, much smaller presence. Strategically, we were never going to abandon Bagram Airfield, a billion-dollar compound we had built with geostrategic importance not just because it housed thousands of suspected terrorists and was a launchpad for our Special Forces operation but also because of its proximity to Chinese ██████████. Fourth and perhaps most impor-tantly, the Afghan government and the Taliban knew that if an American interest was harmed or an American was killed, we would release the full fury of the American military in Afghanistan. When Trump said that, everyone knew he meant it.

It was a sound plan, and we were progressing steadily toward our ultimate goal. But incredibly, permanent Washington was working qui-etly to undermine it. One of our biggest antagonists was congressional leadership. They were hardly all in. Many yelled at us, but we politely told them that this was the job we were charged to do.

One of the things I'm most proud of from my tenure at the DoD is that during our conditions-based withdrawal, we had zero American casualties. By the time we left office, the strategy was still progressing strongly, and we were able to hand over to the Biden administration a detailed, functional plan to accomplish a goal that the American people had desired for at least the last twelve years.

But the Biden administration threw it out. They didn't even call Chris or me, who had been implementing the plan months prior to their arrival. As dutiful servants of the no-fail mission to keep America safe, we attempted to contact those who took our positions in the Biden administration—putting all politics aside to talk about what was best for America. They refused to engage. Instead, they jeopardized national security with politics.

But Biden's team wasn't just hardheaded. They were petty as well. They went so far as to fire every single one of my employees who were currently out on maternity or paternity leave when Biden took office. I pleaded with the senior leadership at the DoD over email (because they refused to take my calls) to let the staff stay for at least three months, which is the custom. It's not like these people were making decisions that undermined the Biden administration's objectives (like how the bureaucrats operated throughout the Trump administration). They weren't even in the office. They were at home taking care of their newborn children. To the Biden administration, that didn't matter. For all their talk about caring about families, they made new parents unemployed for no other reason than that they happened to be serving American national security while in the Trump administration.

You'd think with Biden's housecleaning that his administration would have a bold and constructive foreign policy. In reality, Biden's foreign policy is actually quite simple: whatever Trump did, do the opposite. I wish I was joking about that. But Biden doesn't have any plans or strategies. The driving force of all of his foreign policy decisions is to do exactly the opposite of Trump so that he can get good press. So with the media cheerleaders behind him, Biden threw out the conditions-based withdrawal plan, leaving no order or structure to achieve our goal to get out of Afghanistan.

But crafting foreign policy to fit a press release doesn't work. Afghanistan descended into utter chaos all because Biden wanted a good headline.

Biden's unilateral evacuation was a massive tragedy, stranding thousands of Americans behind enemy lines and leaving billions upon billions of dollars of military equipment for the Taliban to commandeer. Trump's conditions-based withdrawal specifically kept control of Bagram Airfield in order to methodically remove all Americans and American assets out of the country over the course of months. Instead, Biden let it all collapse in a matter of days. America and the world was left witnessing the embarrassing retreat of American personnel. We watched dismayed as Afghans desperate to get out clung to American aircraft and hurtled to their deaths as the planes took off. Nobody can forget the horrifying scene of people clutching the landing gear on our C-17 only to plummet to their deaths from thousands of feet up.

Worst of all, thirteen American soldiers were murdered in a suicide bombing by a terrorist who was let out of Bagram as a result of Biden's incompetence. Thirteen Americans died because of Biden's politicization of our national security apparatus. Altogether, it was America's worst and most tragic military failure since the fall of Saigon.

As you remember all of this chaos, ask yourself: What if Trump had been the president? Would any of this have happened? No. We know it would have never happened.

In an attempt to save face after this national embarrassment, Chairman Mark Milley and Centcom Commander Kenneth Mackenzie—the worst Centcom commander in uniform at the time—thumped their chests saying that we took out the terrorists that killed our soldiers with a drone strike. It was all a political show. In reality, they hid the harsh facts from the world: they used a drone to execute seven children and thirteen innocent Afghan civilians. That's not America. We don't murder innocent children to cover our political asses. It's not who we are. But it *is* exactly how shameful our leaders are. To them, politics is above all—even above the lives of innocent people. And all this came courtesy of Biden's disastrous foreign policy.

In the end, the failed Afghanistan withdrawal didn't just demonstrate the ineptitude of the Biden administration. It also revealed the utter failures of the military brass. The fact that after twenty years Afghanistan could fall in a matter of days proved definitively that the Pentagon's repeated claims, that victory was around the corner and we just needed another year and another year and another year, were all lies. They were milking the system with no plan for victory. When the structure fell down, the American people ended up footing the bill. Most Americans are paying for the sins of the DoD's corrupt leadership through our nation's massive debt load. Many others, like those thirteen soldiers at Bagram, paid with their lives.

PROCUREMENT AND PAPERWORK

Another heavy lift Chris and I had to work on was negotiating the passage of the National Defense Authorization Act (NDAA), the bill that sets out exactly how much money the Department of Defense gets and for which programs and sub-agencies. On top of that, we also were in a position to reroute budget procurement efforts. Analyzing and reforming these processes are vitally important, since ultimately this is how the money gets funneled into the Defense Industrial Complex.

The DoD is an insanely large bureaucracy with branches in every region of the world that manages not only a civilian workforce with hundreds of thousands of people but over a million uniformed service members as well. It takes a lot of money to run the United States military, and a lot of that money is actually worth it. Soldiers deserve their pay. We should arm them with the absolute best weaponry, armor, vehicles, ships, planes, tanks, training, and more. They deserve medical care, housing allowances, and benefits for their service to our nation. But as a nation—and especially as Republicans—we must get rid of this false idea that the Department of Defense always needs more money and that that money is always spent well. Having worked as the chief of staff for the DoD, I have seen firsthand multibillion-dollar projects shuttered for failing to perform. These are programs that never should have been started and never should have received funding in the first place. These projects didn't help America. The only ones who benefited were in the Defense Industrial Complex, who were still paid fat fees despite completely failing at their objective.

With Chris as the acting secretary and me as his chief, we were able to reroute budget procurement efforts to places we thought needed it instead of burning money on boondoggles. We set new priorities and established much higher standards for the receipt of funding, so the DoD knew what direction we were heading. But they also knew they could wait us out. Chris and I were appointed by the president and had the constitutional authority to make decisions. But that's just the case on paper. At the DoD there are other power centers outside of presidential authority. They were there before us, and they would be there making decisions long after we were gone. And they were already working to subvert our mission.

This would happen in large and relatively small ways. In one instance, the president wanted to give a Presidential Unit Citation to the elite Special Forces unit that helped to take out the most evil and lethal terrorist in the last one hundred years, Iran's Quds Force leader Qasam Soleimani. He was single-handedly responsible for more American service member casualties than any other terrorist. The operation to take him out was one of the most successful and well-executed missions in history, right up there with the Baghdadi and Osama bin Laden raids.

The Presidential Unit Citation is essentially the Medal of Honor for a group of people, and there is absolutely no doubt that these Special Forces operators deserved it. Yet even in this seemingly uncontroversial action, the bureaucracy did what it does best and told Chris and me that it just couldn't be done. They made all sorts of excuses about how we just didn't have enough time to file all the paperwork even though we had weeks left in the administration.

By this time I had long learned how the Deep State works. When they want something done or hidden, they operate quickly and without delay. When they don't want something done, the paperwork inevitably takes forever to appear, and all of a sudden dozens upon dozens of people need to review it, offer their comments, and give their approval. For good or bad, government operates through paper pushing, and if you want to get something done, you have to know how to move paper. For the Presidential Unit Citation, we really just needed the president's formal, personal sign-off. So one day in the Oval Office at a meeting with the president along with officials from the DoD, I asked about the status of the citation. Someone chimed in that the paperwork just wasn't ready yet. I told them that wasn't a problem at all. I had just so happened to have worked directly with the acting secretary of defense to get the paperwork processed. Then I pulled out the Presidential Unit Citation and slapped it on the Resolute Desk. All it needed to be complete was the president's signature, and the boss was more than happy to sign it. The unit was rightly honored, and no pencil neck at the DoD was able to obstruct it.

UNCONSTITUTIONAL SUBVERSION OF THE CHAIN OF COMMAND

Yet obstruction and malfeasance in the DoD happens in matters even more gravely consequential than the Presidential Unit Citation. An entire parallel power structure separate from the president has been erected within the DoD to keep the wars going and the money flowing to the Defense Industrial Complex. It all centers around a good ole boys' club of senior leadership made up of generals and other flag officers who occupy the most senior ranks in the different branches of the military. This is the power center that most directly subverts the president's constitutional authority as commander in chief. The Joint Chiefs of Staff operates as the central node of this boys' club, with the top generals in each branch all represented. Just like in the FBI where field agents must go to DC to suck up to senior leadership in order to get a promotion, in the DoD everyone knows that the only way to get a star (or more stars) on your shoulder is through the Joint Chiefs, particularly through the chairman of the Joint Chiefs of Staff.

If you've read the Constitution, you know this shouldn't be the case. The president is the sole commander in chief of the armed forces. He can call upon the opinion of his cabinet on military matters. He can call on the opinion of uniformed military officers as well. He can even delegate responsibility to the secretary of defense to execute objectives. But the president and only the president is at the head of the military. Our Founders did this for a very good reason. They wanted to ensure that the military was always and forever under civilian control, led by a person ultimately accountable to the people. As we've seen throughout history, republics fail when the military becomes an independent political actor competing with civilian leadership.

This vital principle of civilian leadership of the military is not only under assault in America, it's already being proactively subverted. During the end of President Trump's term, Chairman of the Joint Chiefs of Staff Mark Milley undermined the chain of command multiple times, establishing himself as the ultimate operational authority, not the president. It was the exact type of move our Founders feared and that should make every American shudder.

In one terrifying instance near the end of President Trump's term, Chairman Milley called the Chinese to tell them that if we were going to attack them, he would warn them first. This was insanity. Trump was not planning on attacking the Chinese nor did Milley have any reason to believe Trump wanted to attack the Chinese. But with this admission, Milley was broadcasting that in such an outlandish circumstance, he would subvert the chain of command and undermine the authority of the commander in chief to the benefit of our main global opponent. As proof of just how much of a political animal Milley is, he told this to reporter Bob Woodward knowing that the press would throw all standards to the wind and praise him. Instead of spending his time worrying about how to protect our boys downrange, the highest-ranking uniformed officer in America found time to leak sensitive information to the media for a favorable headline. Milley has never been an apolitical military leader. He is the Kraken of the swamp.

For betraying his oath of office and undermining the Constitution, Milley should be fired. But because he acted against Trump, the media lauded him as a hero. On top of all of that, around the same time Milley reportedly said that he feared the military could not control the president.[43] This was a terrifying insight into his mind. No American should *ever* want the military to control the president of the United States. That he believes the military should means that Milley should be kept as far away from power as possible.

Milley's damaging political subversion of the chain of command and presidential authority was not only unprecedented. It's flagrantly illegal. Congress removed executive command authority from the chairman of the Joint Chiefs in the 1950s. National command authority runs from the president of the United States to the secretary of defense—period. Then the secretary of defense can delegate to the ground force commanders running operations. What no one can ever do is delegate operational decision-making to anyone in the office of the Joint Chiefs of Staff, and certainly not to the chairman. That is expressly prohibited by statute.

The chairman of the Joint Chiefs of Staff is purely an advisor to the president who can inform him his opinion on what the risks and benefits are of operations and help him understand our military capabilities and deployments. Contrary to popular belief, he is not the head of the military. He does not have the authority to disrupt orders or use his high-level knowledge to undermine directives from the commander in chief. When Milley subverted the operational command structure, it was one of the most explicit threats to civilian control of the military in American history.

Chairman Milley undermined civilian control of the military in more systemic ways as well by illegally inserting himself into the process by which military leadership is chosen. The Constitution makes it clear that the president, with the consultation of the secretary of defense, runs the military, which means they should choose its leaders. The reality is that the chairman of the Joint Chiefs of Staff exercised that authority. I intervened while this process was happening when I worked at the DoD. Chairman Milley presented me with a binder of fifteen people to be promoted to higher officer positions within the military, telling me that these were the folks we were going to go with. I told him that's not how this works. We would review his *recommendations*, and then Acting Secretary Miller and the president would make that decision. Usually, civilians at the head of the DoD never actually review what the chairman of the Joint Chiefs gives them, meaning for all intents and purposes, the chairman chooses who runs the military.

As I looked over Milley's list, I quickly found that half of them had major problems, so I sent them back. These people weren't just unqualified. They were clearly political hacks loyal to Milley who didn't merit the position. Milley was trying to install yes-men instead of choosing the best leaders for the job. I called him on it, and he was forced to agree.

This entire officer selection process is undeniably corrupt and unconstitutional. It also leads to very bad outcomes for America. For the military to operate most effectively, it must be a meritocracy. Leaders should be chosen based on their proven abilities. At the highest level, this demands uncanny logistical talent, strategic vision, and unwavering loyalty to the Constitution. The current promotion structure does not reward ability. It rewards those who are the best at demonstrating their loyalty to the Joint Chiefs of Staff and their increasingly political whims. The fact that the Joint Chiefs operated like corrupt leadership in other agencies and in Congress should frighten Americans.

This is why America doesn't win wars anymore. A large number of our generals and flag officers aren't actually capable of winning wars. That's not why they were promoted. They were just the best at politicking and sucking up to the top brass. So we continue to make strategic blunder after strategic blunder because those at the top politicize the national command authority.

It's also why the money keeps flowing to the Defense Industrial Complex. Those at the most senior levels of the military who occupy key positions in the procurement system generally get the biggest payout from defense contractors when they leave the military. Why in the world would they ever promote someone who would threaten their bottom line? Those who are principled enough to stand up for the best interests of the American people and call for reforms in Pentagon procurement (especially in R&D) are quickly passed over, left to wallow in middle management at best. Many of them, knowing they will never reach the top unless they are willing to play the sleazy Washington game, end up leaving the military altogether. The whole thing leaves our enlisted men and women on the ground extremely demoralized. They know that the best almost never reach the top, and they're led almost entirely by political hacks instead of men and women of honor. Of course, there are a large number of incredible officers in the military who deserve our respect and thanks. But only a few good apples are able to rise through the barrel and make it up to the top of the ranks. When they do, they are ostracized and undermined if they don't get in line.

Perhaps most insidiously, this corrupt network of politicized officers has begun to disintegrate our proud American military through increasingly aggressive attempts at radical left-wing social engineering. This is one of the primary reasons why the military brass is turning woke. The rot here starts at the top. Chairman Milley is one of the most political animals in all of Washington. I am not exaggerating when I say he is more political than Nancy Pelosi. For all the reasons described, he also has the military leadership under his thumb. So when he says that the military has to study critical race theory and when the Pentagon proclaims that it is going to root out what it calls domestic extremism—a term the establishment uses for anyone who supports Donald Trump—the whole military structure follows suit. Officers know where their bread and butter comes from. Speak up, and you'll be punished. But if you purge the military of conservatives and force woke training on our military personnel? Well, that might just get you a promotion.

That's how you get a military brimming with left-wing propaganda where the chairman of the Joint Chiefs of Staff proudly declares that our soldiers need to understand "white rage." But Milley doesn't need radical left-wing literature to understand white rage. He just needs to look in the mirror.

Of course, under the Biden administration civilian leadership is just as bad. Under President Biden, Secretary of Defense Lloyd Austin issued a majorly revised campaign plan, or camplan, that the DoD uses to run the entire military. There are different camplans for each combatant command throughout the military, and they are designed to direct our massive military structure to a unified goal. Austin's first ever camplan for the United States military focused on climate change. That's right. Not terrorism. Not China. Under President Biden, the military's primary mission is to fight the weather.

Adding insult to injury, Secretary Austin and the Biden administration made it undeniably clear that American security is not even close to the military's top priority when they imposed a vaccine mandate on our service members. These are the fittest members of American society in an age cohort at effectively no risk of Covid. Yet they had their due process and religious liberty rights grossly violated by being fired for refusing to take the vaccine. This was unjust to them personally and negatively impacted military readiness. What President Trump did with Operation Warp Speed was miraculous. I am proud that we made vaccines available to any American who wanted one. But nobody should ever be forced to take it—especially not our service members. Congress must put in law that every service member fired because of this gross politicization of our armed forces must be rehired with an apology and full back pay.

The result of all of this unprecedented politicization of the military is that good soldiers know that loyalty to America and demonstrated capabilities aren't rewarded and that having normal conservative opinions is punished. As a result, morale has plummeted. Meanwhile, patriotic Americans just aren't joining the military as much anymore. Every single branch failed to reach its 2022 recruitment numbers. Young Americans want to serve their country. But increasingly people wonder if the military under its current leadership actually serves America or if it just serves the Democrat Party and the radical left-wing activists who run their show.

Altogether, the deficiencies of our leadership, the waste and fraud in our procurement process, the politicization of the armed forces, and the resulting decline in enlistment undermines the single, overarching goal of the military: to keep America safe. The DoD Deep State is a threat to American security.

PEACEFUL TRANSITION OF POWER

Amid all this politicking and our work to reform the DoD, Chris Miller and I also had another vital task. We had to lead a transition of power. As the chief of staff for the Department of Defense, I was, by regulation, the head of the presidential transition. But the DoD is the largest agency in government, and it took a significant amount of effort to ensure incoming staffers for the Biden administration were brought up to speed so they could govern effectively and defend our nation. The reality was that I supervised the transition, but it was career staff at the department who implemented it. Regardless, it was a heavy lift for everyone involved.

While we were doing legwork to get the Biden team informed, the media and the Deep State were spinning a different narrative. As has happened so many times now, the press spread utter lies, attacking me personally. Like always, they wanted me to be the story, and not the great work we did. So they reported based on anonymous leaks from career bureaucrats, this time claiming that I was putting up obstacles to the transfer of power. By the time these stories came out, the Washington cabal was addicted to the idea that Trump was some sort of dictator who was going to stage a violent coup. As one of Trump's top lieutenants, they came after me again to support their new fantasy.

But the documented facts of the transition put this lie to rest. President Trump ordered us to lead the transition in November (nobody has ever been able to answer how someone could be inciting an insurrection while he has ordered a transfer of power), and we moved full steam ahead. Under our leadership, the DoD completed over 260 requests for information and sent the Biden team forty-three initial transition books adding up to over 7,200 pages. We held well over two hundred interviews with Biden team members upon their request, far exceeding what other administrations have done. We spent thousands of man hours with large groups of individuals conducting these interviews, setting up meetings, providing access to the Pentagon for the Biden team, giving them clearances, and producing millions upon millions of documents for them to review. All said and done, it was a master class in how presidential transitions go—even in the face of the egregious lies in the press. We treated transitioning the largest no-fail mission on God's green Earth just as carefully as running that mission. I am proud we accomplished both objectives without fail.

In all of my positions in government, I spent the shortest time as chief of staff at the DoD. Yet that time was during one of the most consequential periods in American history. What I saw at the DoD terrified me and convinced me that American democracy is under threat. Though, of course, the media was wrong about the cause. It wasn't Donald Trump who threatened our democracy. It was the Deep State, which had extended its reach into the military and was using our armed forces to destroy rule by the people.

CHAPTER 16

Mission First

W e cannot allow the DoD to remain in its current state. We must reform our military not just for ourselves but for the sake of every honest American in uniform. That's because we are proud of our military and of the men and women who serve. We honor those in uniform. We respect their willingness to sacrifice. When our family, friends, and neighbors volunteer to serve, we cheer them on with admiration and pride. This is what makes corruption in the Department of Defense so disheartening. It's not just that crooked officers and generals are burning taxpayer money and lining their pockets. It's that when people put on that uniform, they intend to serve something above politics and Washington intrigue. They don't want to be used for some woke project or put into harm's way to boost the Defense Industrial Complex's bottom line. They want to defend America—their home and the greatest country on Earth. And they want to remain guardians for self-government and warriors against all tyrants who would seek to control the fate of the American people from above.

Perhaps more than any other government organization infiltrated at the top by the Deep State, the United States military is filled with loyal, patriotic, honorable Americans who signed up to give something back to the country that gave them everything. They, more than anyone else, are betrayed by the corrupt leaders at the top. The vast majority of military members are loyal to our country, yet the DoD Deep State is still subverting our Constitution. This reveals an age-old truth: a fish rots from the head down. That fact shouldn't depress us, because it means the way forward is clear. To fix the Department of Defense, we must cut off the head.

SWEEPING CLEAN THE JOINT CHIEFS OF STAFF

The entire body of the Joint Chiefs of Staff must be completely revamped. Too much power has been seized by the chairman, especially over hiring and operational decision-making. Considering he is prohibited by law from having such power, the chairman must be reined in. As I saw so clearly while at the DoD, every officer who wants the next star on his shoulder cowers in front of the chairman of the Joint Chiefs because he has monopolized the nomination processes, subverting the chain of command and undermining the ability of the president to execute his constitutional authority. All flag officers (generals and admirals) must be selected solely by the secretary of defense and the president based on merit. In fact, that's the law. The president and secretary of defense are the constitutionally delegated leaders of the armed forces, and the officer class must look to them above everyone else for their career advancement. That will ensure civilian control of the military exists in reality, not just on parchment. The chairman of the Joint Chiefs of Staff can still offer his advice—if requested to do so by the president and the secretary of defense. That's all he is legally permitted to do.

This reform will demand a secretary of defense who understands the constitutional structure of our armed forces and is willing to go to bat to defend civilian control of the military. This incestuous system of the chairman of the Joint Chiefs choosing the military's top officers loyal to him arose out of negligence on the part of civilian leaders, and it cannot be allowed to continue. Under Esper's leadership, the Joint Chiefs ran wild over civilian leadership of the DoD, and it did untold damage to America's national security mission.

But choosing officers shouldn't be a completely top-down process no matter who does it. Most uniformed armed service members are enlisted Americans. They are the ones who show up at a recruiting office and sign a contract to join the greatest fighting force in the free world. In fact, 85 percent of our military is enlisted. The remaining minority are the officer class who graduate from increasingly woke service academies or went through officer candidate school at some point. In the current system, almost every single—if not all—of the flag officers are chosen from the very small 15 percent of uniformed officers in the military based almost entirely on the officers above them. There needs to be a process where enlisted personnel have an opportunity to formally weigh in on officer candidacy. They spend time with people in the foxhole, as it were. They actually know people's leadership capabilities on the ground in intense, life-or-death situations. I know from personal experience that many of the people following orders from officers would have never recommended those same officers for commanding positions. They didn't see a resume. They didn't care if the officer above them was really good at kissing ass. All they knew was who was a good leader worth following and who was bad. Having the support of the enlisted men and women shouldn't be the only qualification for being an officer and rising up the ranks, but it's a hell of a lot better than the current system, which rewards with extended careers those who are best at maneuvering the Joint Chiefs of Staff's political gauntlet.

As we saw, many of those generals and flag officers loyal to the chairman of the Joint Chiefs above all are also highly political and ineffective. These second-rate commanders lead to strategic and battlefield failures and manipulate the military to serve the chairman's woke political ends. To push back against woke radical left-wing engineering in the military and to ensure we have generals who have the will and ability to win—instead of just a will to continue military quagmires for the benefit of the Defense Industrial Complex—the next president and secretary of defense must be willing to fire bad officers.

The media, the Democrats, and other functionaries of the Deep State will undoubtedly attack this move as undermining the military.

They will make it seem like this attempt to stop the politicization of the military is actually part of a plan to politicize the military. We must be resistant to these attacks. We don't want a politicized military. We want a military led and filled with soldiers loyal to the Constitution. That can only happen if we remove those who are loyal to the left-wing agenda and to the Defense Industrial Complex.

Relatedly, the president and secretary of defense must retake control of operational decision-making. Too often general officers and flag officers find themselves taking tasks and orders directly from the chairman's office, which is illegal. The chairman is not in the chain of command by law and for very good reason. The operations of the Office of the Secretary of Defense must be run by the only person under law authorized to do so: the secretary of defense. Any chairman of the Joint Chiefs who refuses or has refused to follow this chain of command, like Mark Milley, must be immediately removed from office.

In line with these priorities, the office of the Joint Chiefs of Staff must be reduced in size. There are too many staff working for the chairman trying to justify their existence with needless paperwork. The bureaucratic bloat is worse than unnecessary. It is used as a tool to illegally insert the Joint Chiefs into civilian decisions. When I served in government, all the time people would refuse to act or would slow-walk presidential decisions because they were waiting for the chairman or someone else's signature on some "package" of proposals. They would refuse to budge until someone who had no right to be in the process had their staff review it and give an official green light. All the different offices and power players would then send these "packages" around to each other, using them as pieces of leverage to barter with one another for more authority or more control over processes and decisions they had no right to be involved in. All this system does is allow politics to influence the national command authority and corrupt the no-fail mission of the national security apparatus.

Cutting the staff at the Joint Chiefs will massively curtail this illegitimate, wasteful, and dangerous meddling. Practically speaking, the chairman can only dip his hands into pots he shouldn't be in because he has staff doing the legwork. For example, in the nomination process he has staff who cull candidates and put together the binders that the chairman would give to the secretary of defense announcing his choices. Without staff to do that, he can't influence the nomination process nearly as much. The chairman should have some staff. But he should not have so many that he can get involved in jobs far outside the scope of the Joint Chiefs.

FIXING PROCUREMENT

Perhaps the largest and most needed DoD reform of all is a complete overhaul of its research and development arm. This is the beating heart of the Defense Industrial Complex because it is where Congress funnels billions upon billions of dollars every year on countless wasteful, ineffective, and failed programs. Too often the Defense Industrial Complex bleeds the DoD even when they deliver products that don't work or aren't useful. Case in point is USS *Gerald R. Ford*, a monster aircraft carrier that cost north of $10 billion that serves limited warfighting purposes in today's battle space. Not only that, the point of the ship is to launch planes, but its aircraft catapult system was dangerously faulty and cost three times the originally quoted price. The *Gerald Ford* doesn't work, and we don't need it. We still have plenty of nuclear-powered aircraft carriers to fill gaps in our mission. Our fixed and rotary aircraft can launch from many different platforms around the world. Not to mention, one shot is all that's needed to take out thousands of our soldiers and sink a $10 billion ship. We don't need to put all our eggs in that one basket, and doing so is actually dangerous.

Even when procurement projects do "work," the Defense Industrial Complex creates inferior equipment and matériel on a monumentally delayed timeline. Meanwhile, nobody with power does anything because those with the most direct authority over these boondoggle programs are eying their post-DoD paychecks from the very defense contractors they are supposed to be watching over and holding to account. We must remove waste, fraud, and abuse not only to save taxpayers untold amounts of money but also to restore the integrity of our military. This will require revamping the entire research and development department.

In terms of how contracts are made and money is spent, the next president and secretary of defense must install the appropriate leaders for the DoD's massive R&D programs. These programs are led by a tandem of undersecretaries of defense, one for research and engineering and the other for acquisition and sustainment. Together, the two undersecretaries combine forces to run the whole program—from cyber to engineering, from contracts to ship building, and from prototype tech to nuclear defense. The next president must install undersecretaries who run these programs without looking to the overlords in the Defense Industrial Complex. These undersecretaries must be given clear authority to shut down wasteful programs and to refuse to sign contracts for projects that don't have a reasonable chance of success and of actually improving our military capabilities. And most importantly, they must only sign off on programs that are in total alignment with the commander in chief's priorities.

In the current processes, the secretary of defense must sign off on large contracts personally. Too often the secretary has been a rubber stamp. This must end. The secretary must review closely these contracts as well and act as a backstop to ensure no more wasteful programs are authorized. And I really mean none. Our standard must be to permit ZERO waste and fraud. When government is comfortable with screwing up just a little bit, it opens the floodgates to massive abuse.

Longer-term, the next administration must work proactively with Congress to change DoD budgeting. Far too often Congress's knee-jerk reaction is just to throw more money at the problem. The problem is not that the DoD has too little money. It's that it is spending the massive sums of money it gets poorly. Congressmen need to be informed that just because someone with stars on their shoulders or an impressive title from the Defense Industrial Complex says something is good doesn't make it so—and just because an idea for a new military program sounds exciting and advanced doesn't mean it can actually happen in the real world.

To that end, the Department of Defense must undergo another audit—and face penalties if they fail. Thus far the Pentagon has failed three straight audits with officials unable to say where money has gone, how much was spent, or what return the taxpayer has gotten. The department still can't detail its assets and liabilities—something that should be expected of any organization. There is a bipartisan effort in Congress to punish those components of the DoD that fail an audit by removing some of their taxpayer funding. These efforts should be supported—and this should be a frontline priority in conjunction with the other reforms discussed. The DoD's continued failed compliance is unacceptable. They are receiving taxpayer money, and the taxpayer has a right to know how that money is being spent.

Limiting the funding to what is necessary and what works will help control the power of the Defense Industrial Complex and weaken the Deep State within the DoD. To truly crush the elements within the DoD who are not loyal to the Constitution and who don't follow the lawful authority of the president, we must also shatter the revolving door between the Pentagon and the Defense Industrial Complex. Strict rules must be implemented to outright ban those from the Defense Industrial Complex from joining the DoD and from senior members within the DoD moving over to the Defense Industrial Complex. If you want to serve, fantastic—go and serve. If you want to make money, awesome—go make money. But we must prevent this rotating cycle of corruption that destroys the integrity of our national command authority and bends the knee of the American taxpayer to the overlords of the war machine. Stopping the revolving door will prevent swamp from subverting the authority of the president for personal gain and the enrichment of the arms manufacturer they came from or are heading to.

A full-scale anti-lobbying effort will dramatically reduce waste and curtail the incentives that exist for the brass to push for and elongate endless foreign wars. Our nation's top generals can start concerning themselves with the security of the United States of America and the well-being of the soldiers under their command—not the golden parachute they are stitching together for their retirement from uniformed service.

ELIMINATE THE OFFICE OF NET ASSESSMENT

In many ways the Deep State within the DoD appears to operate independently of other Deep State actors. However, the DoD is much more intertwined with nefarious domestic political interference campaigns than it initially seems. At the DoD, this interference comes frequently through something called the Office of Net Assessment (ONA). ONA has a rather bland-sounding job of assessing future risks, trends, and needs for the military. Their speculative work is supposed to prepare America for future threats and warfare. Theoretically. In reality, ONA has been captured and is frequently used as a federal cutout to create sources that feed the rest of the Deep State, like the FBI, in order to carry out domestic disinformation campaigns against political opponents in willing violation of the law.

Case in point, ONA paid over a million dollars to a contractor for "research" by the name of Stefan Halper. This is the same Stefan Halper who was sent by the FBI to spy on Carter Page and George Papadopoulos during the 2016 campaign as part of the Russia Gate scandal. That means the DoD was paying the salary of an FBI spy in order to dig up "research" one can only presume was used to attack Donald Trump, while that same person was double dipping and also getting paid by the FBI. The inspector general found that Halper's work with the DoD was really just a shell. Halper was charged with doing research for the DoD, including on Russia. Yet though Halper said he talked to Russian intelligence officers, he couldn't submit any proof that he did so, and the sources Halper allegedly contacted said they never worked with him. Meanwhile, ONA couldn't provide all of their contract documents with Halper when asked and couldn't demonstrate if Halper had actually complied with the law while doing his work.[44] There are no coincidences in government. The DoD didn't just accidentally pay one of the key figures in Russia Gate over $1 million for shoddy work *on Russia*. Through ONA, the DoD was a party to the Russia Gate scandal.

To top it all off, the Office of Net Assessment has not actually produced a net assessment in fifteen years. Instead of analyzing future trends and preparing our military as best as possible, ONA is operating as a multimillion-dollar cash cow that funds "research"—research that can be used to damage their political opponent. All this means that the military was directly involved in an unprecedented criminal conspiracy spearheaded by the government gangsters at the FBI and DoJ.

While at the DoD, Chris and I removed those who were responsible for hiring Halper at ONA. The inspector general had proven without a doubt that Halper should have never been there—and should have never received seven figures for his so-called work. The entire office is another tool of the politicized bureaucracy using public funds to destroy the America First agenda. It should be eliminated in its entirely.

At the same time, the Inspector General office proved in the ONA case, and in many others, that it retains the ability to operate effectively, professionally, and, perhaps most importantly, apolitically. Acknowledging this, the inspector general must be protected and preserved from capture by left-wing activists. Right now, the institution is working. But conservatives must keep a watchful eye and nip in the bud any attempts at politicizing this important office. The inspector general has stymied the Deep State time and again by steadfastly reporting the truth. As a result, the Deep State undoubtedly has the inspector general in its sights. We must remain vigilant.

***

The soldiers, sailors, Marines, airmen, and guardians of the United States military deserve leaders who will only send them into battles that America must fight to secure our no-fail mission and that we know we can win. The rot at the top of the DoD is a scandal beyond measure, a threat to our country, and endangers the very best and bravest young people our nation has to offer. The next president can fix this problem by reforming the senior levels of the military, removing politics from the DoD, installing accountability, and doing one thing above all else: putting the mission first. Then and only then will the military be restored as the guardian of—not the rival to—self-government.

PART V

JANUARY 6TH

CHAPTER 17

The Insurrection That Never Was

O n January 6th, 2021, I was at the Pentagon in the Office of the Secretary of Defense, as I was almost every day since being named the DoD chief of staff. I knew the president was holding a big rally on the mall, but there was no possible way I could attend. We had so much to do with the transition, Afghanistan withdrawal, and planning for the inauguration, among all the other normal operations of the DoD to keep America safe—that's the no-fail mission, and it does not take a knee and rest, even for a moment. The countdown clock to the end of the administration was ticking, and Chris and I were continually rushing around the office. But as the day went on, I started to notice something strange on TV. The Office of the Secretary of Defense is a SCIF, a secure room, so we didn't have any cell phones. We did have several TVs with cable news on, and they were all showing the same thing. There was a very large crowd gathering at the Capitol, and it seemed all the regular tactics of crowd control were either not implemented or ineffective. Chris and I began to monitor what was going on at the Capitol more closely, but at that point, like most every American, there was little we could do as we started seeing barriers overrun and people streaming through the doors.

It was getting increasingly obvious that whatever the hell was going on, the security forces on the ground were not up to the task. That's when we finally got the call we were waiting for—the call the law required and the one we needed.

OVAL OFFICE AUTHORIZATION

Shortly after the US Capitol Police ordered the evacuation of the Capitol Complex around 1:30 p.m., the secretary of the Army was on the phone with Washington, DC, Mayor Muriel Bowser.[2] The National Guard reports to the secretary of the Army who reports to the secretary of defense, and Mayor Bowers was on the line calling for the National Guard to be deployed, and deployed immediately. Of course, we did exactly that. That's one of the jobs of the National Guard: they provide assistance to law enforcement upon request; they never supplant local authority. But what really pissed me off was that this completely uncertain situation and reactive response should have never happened in the first place. That's because the president had, days before January 6th, explicitly authorized the National Guard to be deployed if needed.

Under our federal system of government, local police forces are the first and primary force used to quell domestic disturbances. The law is crystal clear about the deployment of the military within the United States. It is *never* allowed unless two very specific conditions are met. First, the president has to authorize the use of the National Guard. Second, state and local authorities (meaning governors or, in the case of DC, the mayor) or federal law enforcement (in this case, the Capitol Police) must make the request for National Guard assistance. This two-part system makes complete sense. Nobody wants the president to have unilateral authority to deploy military troops within America as he pleases. That's a recipe for tyranny. Likewise, we can't just have the National Guard deployed whenever a mayor or governor requests it, or else the National Guard just becomes the local police force subject to the whims of local

---

2   The Department of Defense released the gold-standard, official timeline of the event, which can be found in Appendix C.

politicians. The law follows the principles laid down by our Founding Fathers to ensure the military is never able to run this country.

As I've pointed out, President Trump already did everything within his legal authority before January 6th. He actually brought up the idea of authorizing the National Guard himself. I had been in the Oval Office having a meeting with the president on a completely separate, sensitive national security matter days before anyone breached the Capitol. As the meeting wrapped up, he turned to the group of us in the room, including me, Acting Secretary Miller, Chairman Milley, and Chief of Staff Mark Meadows and brought up January 6th—the day the votes for the presidential election would be certified in Congress and the day that he planned to hold a big rally on the Ellipse adjacent to the National Mall. President Trump always drew in a very large crowd, and he expected there to be another large crowd that day. So, in order to be very cautious, he told us that he authorized the DoD to deploy anywhere from ten thousand to twenty thousand National Guard troops anywhere that was needed in the nation to keep the peace. Boom, step one complete.

At the DoD, we do reps and sets—we *always* prepare. The last thing we ever wanted was to be caught with our pants down, so we started gearing up the guardsmen immediately. Bags were packed, and busses were at the ready. We prepared everything we could up to the limit of the law. But here's the kick: we couldn't employ and deploy troops unless the appropriate authorities made the request for backup. That's not a preference. That's the law.

Up until the afternoon of January 6th, we had only one of the two necessary conditions to deploy the guard. Without the request from Mayor Bowser, our hands were tied. And that's not to say we didn't proactively reach out to Mayor Bowser and others before January 6th to ensure the district had ample security. Like I said, the president was well aware that we should expect a historically large crowd to come to his rally that day. When he authorized the National Guard to be used if requested, we quickly reached out to offer our assistance not only to Mayor Bowser, but to the sergeants at arms in the House and Senate who manage the US Capitol Police and are charged with security of the Capitol Complex itself. Mayor Bowser had requested some support at metro stations and for traffic control. But she made it explicit in a written and signed letter delivered to the administration on January 5th that she was requesting no additional support from the National Guard. Likewise, the day before that on January 4th, the US Capitol Police also confirmed that they had no request for support from the DoD. In fact, their own internal documents say that we, the DoD, approached them four separate times before January 4th to ask if they needed National Guard assistance, and each time the sergeant at arms of the Senate, who reported to Chuck Schumer, and the sergeant at arms of the House, who reported to Nancy Pelosi, said no. Don't take my word for it. Their records prove it. Bowser's letter and the Capitol Police documents are all publicly available.[3]

President Trump and his administration followed the law down to the last period. We did everything possible to prepare. But there was no way—absolutely no way—that the president was *ever* going to unilaterally deploy troops in Washington, DC, or anywhere in America. This narrative that President Trump was going to hijack the military and execute a "coup" is a total farce. The commander in chief is the only person who can order a presidential transition, and President Trump had already sent the order to transition the government months before. How could he be performing a coup while already having ordered us to prepare to hand the reins of power to the Biden administration? Yet again the hard facts get in the way of the fake news mafia disinformation campaign.

In the afternoon of January 6th, I was fit to be tied. No good American wants what we saw that day to ever happen at the US Capitol. Yet immediately, the Trump administration was being blamed. The same politicians who castigated Trump for simply showing strength by walking across Lafayette Square while American cities were burning were now condemning Trump for not sending troops in, gun blazing, even though they had refused to make the legally necessary request to prevent what happened on January 6th. And if we got that request beforehand, we

---

[3]   All of these documents can be viewed in Appendix C.

know for a fact that events would have been different as evidenced by exactly what happened once we got the green light.

With Mayor Bowser's request finally received in the afternoon, we were all systems go. Having been around government for a while, and knowing we are ultimately accountable to the people of America, I ordered that the DoD create a simultaneous timeline of events to keep a clear record of exactly how we operated during these tense moments. True to form, our men and women delivered, and that timeline is the quintessential document that has withstood all scrutiny, including multiple congressional investigations, because it was signed off on by the secretary of defense, the secretary of the Army, the chairman of the Joint Chiefs of Staff, myself, and others. That timeline reveals a miracle. American National Guardsmen and women arrived at the Capitol in the early evening, roughly four hours after we got the request from Mayor Bowser. They quickly began securing a perimeter, and within roughly two hours, the Capitol building was secure. From National Guard authorization to establishing a secure perimeter to completing the mission and returning order so that Congress could do their job took less than six hours.

You have to remember, the National Guard isn't filled with full-time military personnel. They are doctors, teachers, parents, and other everyday citizens who volunteer a portion of their time for the national defense. You can't just call them up and deploy them within a few minutes. It takes hours, if not days. But our preparation showed what's possible. On January 6th we were able to conduct the fastest cold start deployment of the National Guard since World War II. It was an operational miracle, frankly. It's what we do.

In the coming days, thousands of troops surged into Washington, DC, the largest troop mobilization within the district since the Civil War. As Chris Miller, the soldier's secretary, was wont to do, we walked the perimeter in the middle of the night to thank our men and women, continuing throughout the next day and stopping by every checkpoint we could to shake a hand and say thanks. We also questioned why in the world none of the local or federal authorities like the Capitol Police or the Department of Homeland Security or FBI were putting up a no-climb fence around the perimeter of the Capitol. I called them, and all they were concerned about was who was going to pay for it (another sign that they really weren't *that* concerned about a "coup"). At that time, the details around January 6th were still extremely murky, and we had no idea what would or would not happen in the coming days. We had to be prepared for anything. So I made the call, ordered the fence, and had it installed overnight by our National Guard forces. It's amazing how quickly and effectively we can operate when you don't politicize the national security of this country.

At the DoD, one of our primary goals was to ensure Washington remained at peace, and the inauguration went off without a hitch. That's exactly what we did. The following days were quiet. The haphazard riot at the Capitol was a one-time event, and President Biden was inaugurated on January 20th with little fanfare and zero violence.

THE NARRATIVE DEFEATS JUSTICE

With order restored you'd think that our goal would be to do a thorough security review, what we call an after-action report, to ensure a breach of the Capitol never happened again. You'd think the government would try to separate out the wrongdoers from people who happened to be in the wrong place at the wrong time to prosecute the genuine law breakers. You'd think that our leaders in Congress would start a gold-standard, bipartisan commission to figure out exactly what happened and who was responsible. Sadly, that's not what our government did. From the very beginning, it was clear the Democrats intended to use January 6th as a political weapon to demonize their opponents and solidify their power. Justice and the truth were pushed to the side, and the political narrative became more important than anything else.

I could sense this was happening from the very beginning. During the middle of the riot, as the DoD was still doing everything it could to deploy the guard to safeguard the Capitol Complex and our election procedures, Speaker Pelosi called to ask us when the congressional food service was going to be reopened. It didn't really seem like a question from someone terrified for her safety or concerned for the greater good. Yet even as her primary concern was getting the staff back to work to make her a sandwich, Pelosi and Senate Democrat Leader Chuck Schumer were asking us where the tanks, armored personnel carriers, and Humvees were. They explicitly asked for an Abrams M1 tank to come in. We had to politely ask them what the purpose was. Were we just going to start mowing down American citizens with .50-caliber belt-fed machine guns in downtown DC as if it were downtown Qandahar?

By everything we could see, the crowd at the Capitol was unarmed or armed only with non-lethal objects like bottles, flag poles, or bike racks. This wasn't some trained military force marching into the legislature with M16s and grenades. You don't send a tank into a riot. It doesn't make sense. That is, it doesn't make sense if your purpose is to restore order while reducing the risk of injury and loss of life. Obviously, that was far from what the likes of Schumer, Pelosi, and Bowser cared about. They cared about optics, and they wanted to be able to yell and scream that a tank was needed to stop what they would soon absurdly be calling an "insurrection"—the next iteration of their disinformation campaign to get Trump.

This narrative that January 6th was an insurrection is gaslighting at is finest. The media took it up quickly, and soon every organ of power promoted the same line that this was an insurrection, and that Trump was trying to overthrow the government. Russia Gate and my recurring battles with the Deep State had taught me to never underestimate the length the ruling class will go to—or the lies they will tell—to defeat Trump and delegitimize the MAGA movement. Even so, this was a whole new level. They were trying to convince the people that Trump was a dictator and that his supporters, the most outwardly patriotic group in America, were actually trying to destroy our Constitution and end our republican form of government.

Even at the very beginning, the details never added up to support these insidious claims. How could Trump both be staging an insurrection while he also authorized National Guard troops to defend the Capitol and deployed them at lightning speed once the legal request came in? Trump couldn't be both defending the Capitol and attempting to overthrow the Capitol at the same time. It makes no sense.

That wasn't the only discrepancy. In his speech on the mall that day, President Trump told his supporters to march to the Capitol "to peacefully and patriotically make your voices heard." He explicitly called for peace—and in fact the rabble-rousers who sparred with authorities and overran police lines were already agitating at the Capitol before President Trump even finished his remarks. Meanwhile, we learned later that the FBI had information before January 6th about a possible riot, but they never shared that information with the DoD or anyone else. Why not? They have provided no explanation.

Video later released showed Capitol Police standing to the side next to wide open doors in certain sections, allowing protestors to walk in unobstructed. Other videos showed protestors who did enter walking on the designated paths within the Capitol building that are sectioned off by velvet ropes—hardly the actions of a force bent on the coordinated and violent destruction of our democracy. There were clearly very bad actors in the crowd, including those who were smashing windows, attacking police officers, destroying property, and treating a building owned by the American people with disrespect. But these weren't commandos. It wasn't a hostile military unit advancing through the building. In fact, the only people who died on January 6th itself amid the chaos were four Trump supporters—two who had heart attacks or strokes, one who was ruled to have died from amphetamines but was seen on video being beaten by a cop while unconscious after being trampled by the crowd, and the last, an unarmed woman who was fatally shot by a Capitol Police officer.

The media never stopped spreading the story that a different Capitol Police officer was bludgeoned to death by the mob using a fire extinguisher. But this was a total lie. That police officer died on January 7th from two strokes. The medical examiner found his death was natural, and there were no external or internal injuries to be reported.[45] The so-called insurrectionists didn't actually kill anyone. Again, that's not exactly the sign of a coup. Instead, this narrative is the sign of a disinformation campaign.

POLITICAL PROSECUTIONS

January 6th was a national tragedy, and those who broke the law should be prosecuted swiftly for the crimes they committed. As a former public defender and federal prosecutor, I am unwaveringly in favor of upholding the law fairly and equally in all circumstances. But in the aftermath of the riot at the Capitol, the ruling class went far beyond fairness and equality. They bastardized due process. They immediately used January 6th as a tool to demonize half of America, crush dissent, and imprison defendants in perpetuity while they awaited horrendously delayed trials.

It began with the protestors actually there that day. Despite the breathless politicized accusations that the mob was actually a crowd of insurrectionists, dwindling few people are being tried for the crime of insurrection—an actual crime that is deemed as grave as treason and is punishable by death. In fact, those who are being charged are largely being prosecuted for misdemeanors like trespassing, resisting arrest, or not allowing Congress to perform its official duties. There is video evidence that some who are being prosecuted by the Biden DoJ were actually trying to stop violence and urge peacefulness among the crowd.

Despite the fact that the prosecutions themselves are spotty and almost entirely for very low-level offenses, significant numbers of Trump supporters were held in custody in terrible conditions and without bail. All of this is gravely unjust. As a public defender, I argued over one thousand bond hearings. Criminals are generally only held without bond if they are a flight risk and a threat to themselves or the community. Being held without bond is usually reserved for hardened criminals like murderers or narco-traffickers. Yet in America's two-tiered system of justice, conservatives accused of misdemeanors are held without bail while hardened criminals are being released back into the community without even a slap on the wrist.

We see it everywhere as radical left-wing prosecutors open the doors of prisons. An illegal immigrant by the name of Luis Rodrigo Perez was released after posting bail in New Jersey after being held for domestic violence. He went on to murder three people and wound two others.[46] In New York, a criminal named Anthony Ibanez was released after committing robbery. He went on to attempt to rape a fifteen-year-old girl and was only stopped when a stranger stepped in to fend off the attacker.[47] A man named Frankie Harris was also released after being charged with sixteen offenses, including third-degree assault and endangering the welfare of a child. After left-wing prosecutors let him go free, he was caught on surveillance footage strangling and raping a sixty-four-year-old woman who was left unconscious to die.[48]

This dereliction of justice is happening in blue cities across America. But in the case of January 6th, we are witnessing political persecution. People with no previous criminal record who are accused of committing crimes way less violent and sickening than the rapists and psychopaths mentioned above are being locked up with no hope of release as they wait months or even years for their trial. The only way this happens is if a prosecutor makes the request for detention and a federal judge agrees. Both the prosecutors and the judges are equally at fault in the unlawful deprivation of liberty of so many when it comes to January 6th.

Meanwhile, authorities have commonly resorted to throwing January 6th protestors in solitary confinement. This is the most extreme way to detain a prisoner and is only allowed to be used if the prisoner is at risk of doing harm to the general prison population or of being harmed by the general prison population. In solitary confinement, prisoners are deprived of the basic human need for socialization and left in horrible conditions we can only imagine. Try this on for size: find the smallest bathroom you have access to, stay in it for twenty-three hours a day, and the other hour you get to walk around in a larger cage. Where is the American Civil Liberties Union calling for the rights of the accused here?

As a public defender, I represented people held in solitary confinement. When I would meet with them, generally I would be sat across a protective glass barrier. The guards would let me in then leave the room as I was there with my client. After our meeting the client would be taken away, then I would ring the bell for the guard to come and get me. One time when I did this, nobody came. I ended up being stuck in solitary confinement myself for just three hours (I'm convinced this type of thing happens to a lot of defense attorneys), and, let me tell you, it was not fun. I've always said prosecutors need to spend a night in jail before they start their duties so they know what it's like to cage a human being. Then they might have a small idea that to put somebody in solitary confinement for twenty-three hours a day should only be undertaken in the most grave circumstances.

Meanwhile, Stephen Colbert's crew got a complete hall pass from the Department of Justice even after breaking the same laws that January 6th protestors have been charged with violating. Colbert's production team showed up to the Capitol and started wandering through the halls when they didn't have a right to be there. Colbert's crew was told they could not be there, and it was unlawful to be there. They were given warnings. They did not leave. In fact, they caused such a commotion that a Democrat staffer actually had to call the Capitol Police, who came and rightfully arrested them. Yet the DoJ refused to prosecute Colbert's staff. What's the difference between them and the Trump supporters on January 6th? Just their political ideology. It's yet another example of the two-tier system of justice destroying Americans' faith in our justice system.

All the while, federal prosecutors have used a common Deep State trick. They didn't prosecute people who should, by all public accounts, be prosecuted, and those they did prosecute they publicly smeared. Federal investigators continue to release very scary sounding indictments against January 6th protestors to make it sound like they committed way worse crimes than anyone is actually being convicted of.

Even more shady, there are all sorts of strange agitators who were at the Capitol on January 6th and stirred up the crowd to breach the Capitol beforehand but who have faced no consequences. The most famous of these is a man named Ray Epps. Epps and others like him were caught on video pushing people to do illegal activities and to storm the Capitol building. Yet they have not been detained or prosecuted by the DoJ. Federal law enforcement has used cell phone data, video evidence, bank records, and more to track down just about everyone who was at the Capitol that day. Yet we're supposed to believe they can't find these guys? It's not that they can't. It's that they don't want to. Epps literally went from being on the FBI's most wanted list to being removed from it overnight.

When some of the last remaining honest journalists ask questions about these instigators being ignored by the FBI, the feds don't say a word. Even when Senator Ted Cruz asked a top FBI official, Jill Sanborn, in a congressional hearing whether or not there were federal agents embedded in the crowd, Sanborn dodged every question.[49]

"Did any FBI agents or confidential informants actively participate in the events of January 6th? Yes or no?" Senator Cruz asked.

"Sir, I can't—I can't answer that," Sanborn said.

"Did any FBI agents or FBI informants actively encourage and incite crimes of violence on January 6th?" Cruz asked.

"Sir, I can't answer that," Sanborn replied.

"Ms. Sanborn was Ray Epps a fed?" Cruz followed up.

"Sir I cannot answer that question," Sanborn said again.

The answers weren't, "No, they are not," or, "No, Ray Epps is not a fed." If the answer was no, she would have said so. Sanborn's answers were corrupt FBI government speak for, "We don't have to answer you with the truth, because if we did we would yet again reveal our own corruption." All the signs of a cover-up are on full display—as is the two-tiered justice system we have become so familiar with. What's most terrifying is that the persecution of the establishment's political opponents didn't stop with the protestors who were at the Capitol that fateful day. Soon, they expanded their reach to target any American who has ever dared to wear a MAGA cap.

CHAPTER 18

Made-Up Domestic Terrorism

The false narrative that January 6th was an insurrection staged by Trump supporters and urged on by President Trump himself quickly became the most powerful weapon the ruling class had against Trump—and against the over seventy million Americans who voted for him in the 2020 election. The Deep State's machinations to take out Trump and silence his supporters had been going on for years. They leaked, they lied, they covered up, they obstructed, they subverted, they broke the law, and their wings in the media, the Democratic Party, corporate America, Big Tech, and the cultural institutions of our country joined them in concert, promoting their disinformation across the board.

The incredible thing was that despite all this, the Deep State never actually succeeded in taking out President Trump. In fact, he was still massively successful. The Deep State was failing. Worst of all for them, during the Trump administration millions upon millions of Americans were awakened to the existence of the Deep State, learned the truth, and stopped listening to them and their lies.

You must remember that the Deep State isn't actually that many people. It doesn't even represent close to the majority of our country. They control the levers of power in and out of government, but as long as the people retain any form of control in the ballot box or in public opinion, then the influence of the Deep State is limited. It depends on a lot of people either having no idea what's going on or being led to believe that what the Deep State is doing is actually good. When those people stop listening, the Deep State starts to lose control. That's how we begin the process to defeat it, but it's also when the Deep State becomes even more erratic and dangerous.

FACE OFF

After all we've been through, the mask is off, and we can see the Deep State not as they posture themselves or pose for the camera but face-to-face as they really are. Over four years of President Trump, the Deep State delegitimized itself and showed the American people that they are the opposite of public servants. Now, vast swaths of our country recognize that the Deep State is nothing more than a cabal of government gangsters and their allies, who politicize the power of the federal bureaucracy, the media, and more to illegally persecute their enemies, inflate their egos, enrich themselves, and entrench their power.

We learned this long before January 6th—and that made the Deep State and the ruling class desperate. Like a caged raptor backed against a wall, their desperation made them more dangerous too. They began to think that if people like us could no longer be led like sheep with their cover-ups, fake media narratives, selective leaks, show trials, FBI entrapment, and all of the other unlawful operational methods at their disposal, then we must be forced out of the political process altogether. Because people like us continue to act and think freely, we are a threat to their power. In their mind, that means we must be removed so we can never threaten their power again.

January 6th gave the Deep State and the entire ruling regime afraid of the America First movement the perfect vehicle to label normal, patriotic, God-fearing Americans as not just racists or white supremacists (something they had been falsely charging for years) but as insurrectionists or even domestic terrorists. In the past, they charged us with having bad opinions. They said our policies would hurt the country or even that we were bad, mean people. Now, they have gone a giant step further to make the ridiculous claim that we want to overthrow the government. This escalation in rhetoric is intended to try and legitimize their efforts to move the political battlefield from the court of public opinion much closer to the court of law, where they can prosecute MAGA Republicans by politically weaponizing federal law enforcement. Really it moves us one step closer to a world where dissent isn't just deemed objectionable, but it's ruled illegal. That isn't America—it's Venezuela, Russia, Iran, China, the Democratic Republic of Congo, or all the other hell holes of the world that we are happy we don't live in.

The Deep State's moves to outlaw dissent aren't a conspiracy theory. It's the damn near explicit message of the person who is currently the most powerful man in the world and who is one of the greatest allies the Deep State has ever known: President Joe Biden. President Biden desecrated perhaps the most sacred place of American national memory—Independence Hall in Philadelphia, Pennsylvania, where the Declaration of Independence was signed and where the Constitution was drafted—to declare in a September 2022 speech that "equality and democracy are under assault." [50] Who, in his mind, was the aggressor? Was it the Chinese? Was it the Russians or Islamic terrorists? Was it those who spent years subverting the duly elected president of the United States in order to effectively reverse the will of the people? No, to President Biden and his allies, Enemy Number One is Donald Trump and MAGA Republicans whom he says "represent an extremism that threatens the very foundations of our republic."

As he, the Deep State, the media, and the Democrats have done for years now, Biden highlighted January 6th in his speech, calling the protestors and rabble-rousers there that day "insurrectionists who placed a dagger to the throat of our democracy." Just to make sure he covered all the normal radical left-wing talking points, he called MAGA Republicans like us all white supremacists too, an accusation that never ceases to amuse a person named Kash Patel.

It was not only laughable but frankly sadistic that immediately after demonizing in the most extreme terms every single American who voted against him in the 2020 election, Biden then said that America can't "let anyone or anything tear us apart." It was classic misdirection as we've seen in so many other places in this book. He was accusing us of doing exactly what he was doing in his speech, and he knew he could get away with it (at least with a lot of Americans) because the fake news mafia was at the ready to deploy their disinformation tactics on his behalf yet again.

What Biden said in Philadelphia was remarkable because it came from the mouth of the president of the United States. Frankly it was the most divisive and dangerous thing a president has ever uttered about his fellow Americans. But Biden was only repeating what all his allies in the ruling class have been screaming for years on end now. Their rhetoric is growing more extreme and more overt because they want the general public to believe that when the DoJ presses charges against you, when the FBI breaks down your door, or when the Deep State spies on your communications, that you deserved it because *you're* the enemy, after all.

Whistleblowers have revealed in multiple ways how the Deep State is continuing to weaponize the power of the state against internal dissidents. To pump up public support for their attacks on conservative Americans, the FBI leadership has been reportedly pushing agents to artificially inflate data about domestic terrorism to make the problem seem much worse than it is.[51] Meanwhile, a whistleblower came forward to reveal that FBI agents are being moved off child trafficking cases in order to conduct politically targeted cases on MAGA Republicans.[52] That shows you explicitly their priorities: they think that conservatives are more evil than child traffickers. By labelling us as insurrectionists, that is exactly the message they are trying to send.

The supreme irony in all of this is that they are the ones who have actually done everything in their power to overthrow our constitutional government, not us. They are the ones who used a Clinton-paid foreign agent to spread propaganda in a desperate ploy to justify spying on a presidential campaign—all culminating in multiple attempts to undermine a sitting president after they didn't accept the results of the election. They are the ones who erected a special counsel to harass the Trump administration for years. They are the ones who attempted to impeach the duly elected president over absolutely nothing. They are the ones who covered up their own crimes and leaked classified information in order to destroy the president and discourage and silence the people who voted for him. They are the ones who subverted the chain of command and the constitutional authority of the commander in chief. *They* are the criminals; *we* are the ones who are persecuted. All the while the real threats facing America are utterly ignored. They put the mission last.

TRUTH SOCIAL

Biden's Independence Hall speech laid out the battle lines clearly. But the hammer started coming down on the America First movement long before Biden declared that those who don't support him are enemies of democracy. One of the most immediate actions the ruling class took after January 6th was to attempt to ban all dissent online. Social media companies had already been shadow banning and silencing conservatives online for years. They had demonstrably rigged the 2020 election by throttling the Hunter Biden laptop scandal. And their meddling continues into the Biden administration, as we learned in 2022 that at least forty-five officials from the White House and various federal agencies, including the FBI, directly communicated with Twitter, Facebook, and YouTube to restrict free speech on political issues.[53] But it was shortly after January 6th that the social media giants made their most direct assault on free speech. Within days of the breach of the Capitol, Donald Trump, the president of the United States, was banned from Twitter and Facebook, while other companies like Instagram, YouTube, TikTok, and Pinterest, among others, silenced those who voiced concerns about the integrity of the 2020 election.[54]

Millions of Americans were rightly terrified that social media companies could blacklist the sitting president and ban conversations on certain subjects they don't want people to discuss. That's why Parler, a social media app devoted to free speech, quickly became the most downloaded app in America. Everyone wanted to be in a place where the regime didn't censor their speech. But the tech companies wouldn't allow that either. In an unprecedented display of power, giants like Amazon, Apple, and Google effectively banned Parler from the internet, removing it from their app stores and hosting services so that people couldn't download or use it anymore.[55]

These hostile actions against the American people convinced President Trump that the only option was to create an alternative platform free from the control of the Big Tech giants who are so tightly aligned with the Democrat Party. That's why shortly after leaving office, he founded Truth Social, a truly independent social media platform that never violates free speech. Devin Nunes, my old boss in the House, left Congress and became the CEO of Truth Social, and the company got off to a great start.

Soon after, both Devin and President Trump asked me to sit on the board of Truth Social. They needed reliable people who shared their vision. I had my former boss and my former-former boss both asking me for help, so I said, "Of course." Now, I am proud to be providing not just Americans but the world (Truth Social has already premiered in the UK, with plans to expand further) an alternative to the Big Tech thought police on offer today—all on a platform that isn't riddled with bots like Twitter.

THE SHAM JANUARY 6TH COMMITTEE

As the Democrats took full control of Washington in January 2020, it didn't take long for them to start up yet another witch hunt against President Trump and his supporters. This one they called the House Select Committee on January 6th, and it was to become one of the primary vehicles used by permanent Washington to build up and spread the false narrative that the riot at the Capitol was actually an insurrection to overthrow our democracy.

The select committee was highly politicized from the start. Under normal, non-politicized circumstances, the leaders of each party are able to choose which members of their party will be on which committee. Yet when Republican House Leader Kevin McCarthy selected strong members like Jim Jordan and Jim Banks to represent our party on the select committee, Nancy Pelosi acted completely against tradition and blocked them from being seated. In order to spread the disinformation that the January 6th committee was really bipartisan, Pelosi then found the two biggest Trump-hating Republicans in the House, Liz Cheney and Adam Kinzinger, and put them on the committee instead.

If the House really cared about finding the truth, they would let all sides be able to put up their best representatives to call witnesses and ask questions equally. But the Democrats didn't care about the truth. They only wanted to spread the narrative they had pre-chosen from the very beginning. Every Republican except for the RINOs Cheney and Kinzinger ended up boycotting the panel because it was clearly being propped up as a show trial. Thankfully, Wyoming voters delivered Liz Cheney her due reward and retired her in her 2022 primary, and Kinzinger didn't even bother to run again for his seat, choosing instead to retire in disgrace.

With a deeply partisan cast of characters running the show, it's no surprise that the committee has been a national embarrassment to Congress and an abject failure to the American people they serve. The "unselects," as President Trump calls them, have held much of their hearings and gathered significant amounts of testimony behind closed doors. They don't want the public to see the unvarnished testimony even of their own handpicked witnesses. Instead, just like the Deep State within the executive branch, they leaked and hid information selectively to support the narrative.

For example, Liz Cheney released an edited video of Chairman Milley claiming that Vice President Pence—not President Trump—ordered the National Guard to be deployed in Washington. This is utterly ridiculous. Mark Milley, as we know, proactively violated the chain of command. Yet he still knows what the chain of command is—and so should Liz Cheney, whose father is former vice president and former secretary of defense Dick Cheney. Cheney and Chairman Milley know that the vice president has no authority to order or authorize troop deployments. Only the president can do that, which he executes through the secretary of defense—that's the only national command authority under the law, period.

The simple truth is that President Trump authorized the National Guard. The January 6th committee released General Milley's disinformation to purposefully make it look like President Trump was not proactively involved in restoring order. The fact that the troops Trump authorized were the ones who restored order that day totally undermines the insurrection narrative—as does the fact that it was the political angling of people like Bowser and Pelosi who prevented the deployment in the first place. All of this was another example of how the radical left creates a fictional narrative when the facts are against them, then shoves the lie down our throats via the fake news mafia.

The committee was also happy to leak the fact that Milley compared Trump to Hitler and Trump supporters to Nazis. It was all part of the show meant to frame Trump supporters as enemies of the nation. Chairman Milley should have been doing his job instead of engaging in politics to curry favor with the Biden administration. If he were a man of honor, he would have told the truth and helped restore America's faith in the DoD.

The committee would pull stunts like this regularly. Whenever something bad was said about Trump or his supporters, it was made public. Yet the opposite was also the case. Whenever any facts arose that defended the conduct of the Trump administration, the committee hid them. I watched them do it personally.

At the very beginning of the House's big political show, I was the first person subpoenaed by the January 6th unselects. Yet again my name was paraded through the press, and I received death threats and attacks. The committee was happy to let me be smeared publicly. Yet they weren't happy to publicly release my testimony. That's because they spent the vast majority of time asking me not about January 6th but about everything from Afghanistan to Somalia to Russia Gate and more—they were on a fishing expedition to find damaging information about Trump on any subject possible. When they did finally ask me about January 6th, I told them the total and complete truth that the president had authorized the National Guard to be deployed days before, that local authorities rejected our offer, and that once we did receive the legally required request, we mobilized with unprecedented skill and efficiency. That contradicted the narrative, so the committee never released my testimony, despite my repeated calls for them to do so.

Furthermore, I entered into the record the DoD timeline and numerous other exhibits that the public should have access to regarding January 6th. Months later, my lawyer and I reviewed my transcript and discovered that the January 6th committee had unlawfully omitted each of my exhibits. When we put them on blast for it, they said it was a clerical error, a laughable excuse.

One such exhibit they left out was the Biden DoD Inspector General report on January 6th. The Biden administration IG demonstrated commendable fairness and devotion to the truth, serving as an example for how investigators should operate as they review important events to ensure integrity of mission and call out failures, if there are any. Biden's IG concluded that "DoD officials did not delay or obstruct the DoD's response" and, further, that "the DoD's actions...were appropriate, supported by requirements, consistent with the DoD's roles and responsibilities...and compliant with laws, regulations and other applicable guidance."[56] The facts don't lie, so the sham January 6th committee has done everything in its power to ensure the facts don't get out. We executed the mission; they implemented a disinformation campaign.

Ironically, it was liberal media darling Liz Cheney who, in a Fox News interview, ended up providing the clearest proof that Trump was not trying to overthrow the government. In her interview, Cheney declared that according to the Department of Defense and the former acting secretary of defense, President Trump never gave the "order" to deploy the United States military in DC on January 6th. Well, Liz Cheney was right. But she was wrong to think this helped her case. In reality, it blew it up.

Back in my public defender days, if you could use the government's own evidence to exonerate your client, you were walking your client right out of the door of the courthouse as a free and innocent man. This was like one of those moments. That's because a president can't order troops to deploy domestically for law enforcement purposes. In fact, unilaterally ordering troops into the Capitol is the definition of a coup or an insurrection. As we all well know, the president can only *authorize* the use of troops. Liz Cheney is smart enough to know this. She was just doing a sleight of hand. She certainly knows that most people would not know the ins and outs of the law governing National Guard deployment, so she obviously wanted to make it seem like Trump was failing in his duty because he didn't do what he was legally barred from doing. Meanwhile, if he broke the law and did what Liz Cheney was apparently calling on him to do, he would have actually been staging the insurrection that Cheney and her ilk have been screaming about. Heads I win, tails you lose.

But the American public is more perceptive than Cheney gives them credit for—and we quickly saw through her spin. So I would like to thank Liz for exonerating the very man she has been falsely persecuting with her words on Fox News, some of the few truthful words she has ever spoken. I have since half-joked that if there were ever a trial on this matter, I would do two things to defend Trump: enter into evidence the Biden DoD Inspector General report and call Liz Cheney to the stand. I rest my case, Your Honor.

The facts are the facts are the facts. No matter how the fake news mafia tries to cover it up, or the January 6th committee tries to spin it, or Big Tech tries to manipulate it, January 6th was NOT an insurrection. It was NOT a coup. It was NOT an assault by domestic terrorists on our democracy. It was a completely avoidable tragedy and an embarrassment for our nation where the people who broke the law must be prosecuted. But that was it. The disinformation narrative being jackhammered into our faces is a lie with one purpose: to destroy dissent.

CHAPTER 19

Fight to Win

After a tumultuous end to Trump's first term, the Deep State got what it wanted. The radical left, led by the Biden administration, moved with devastating speed to strip away the hard-won gains of the previous four years and to put up roadblocks of every kind to stop investigations into the truth behind the Deep State's nefarious actions. The Durham probe has been hobbled. Critical Russia Gate documents remain under lock and key. Not to mention the policy failures of the Biden victory alone are enormous, including everything from the disastrous evacuation of Afghanistan to the costly and dangerous proxy war with Russia in Ukraine, to the terrifying economic impacts of inflation, to the Democrats' insane green ideology imposed in a vain attempt to control the weather while demolishing the economic security of the American people. Only the most hardened partisan could rate the Biden administration thus far as anything more than an abject failure. Our nation is weaker, poorer, and more divided than anyone could have ever imagined during the boom days of the Trump presidency. And all the while, the worst actors in the Deep State have scurried right back to their positions of power to manipulate our democracy and abuse their power for the satisfaction of their egos and their own political gain.

Flush with victory, the Deep State in the government, the Democrat Party, the media, Big Tech, and all the major power centers of America are using their power to entrench a two-tiered system of justice, persecuting their political opponents and banning dissent. They are working with astonishing effectiveness to censor conservative thought while the all-powerful national security state, intelligence apparatus, and federal law enforcement structures have been weaponized to track, target, and purge those who don't support the regime. They have erected a system where elites in the media and government collude in an attempt to destroy the careers and reputations of people like me who stand in their way and expose their corruption. And they are so arrogant in their mission and spiteful of the American people that they have publicly labelled half of America as irredeemably evil extremists who are a threat to democracy.

The Deep State's war against self-government and red America has now become official government policy. Biden's secretary of homeland security said domestic extremists are a greater threat to America than radical terrorists.[57] Meanwhile, Biden's secretary of defense announced a military-wide plan to purge the ranks of extremism.[58] We don't have to look far to see what they mean. Biden himself labelled all Trump supporters as extremists and white supremacists, which means the Biden administration has been weaponized to treat conservative Republicans as the enemy. The Biden DoD is also imposing woke so-called anti-racist training and perverse gender ideology on the world's greatest fighting force in a way that pushes patriotic, Constitution-loving Americans from the ranks. While senior leadership in the military bows to the left-wing narrative, our force readiness and preparedness has similarly been gutted. The Biden administration's politicization of the military is destroying the no-fail mission to keep America safe.

Red-blooded American soldiers aren't the only targets. When a memo called moms and dads who opposed critical race theory in schools "domestic terrorists," the Biden Department of Justice used that memo as an excuse to target parents. The Biden administration absurdly went so far as to attempt to create what they called a "Disinformation Governance Board" through the Department of Homeland Security to monitor and squelch messages and information that the administration doesn't support. The board was set to be run by an actual purveyor of disinformation by the name of Nina Jankowicz, who personally helped spread the false Russia Gate conspiracy. The Biden administration was slammed so hard for trying to start a Ministry of Truth that they paused their plans…only to resurrect them once again with a new White House task force on disinformation run by Vice President Kamala Harris.

Yet nothing demonstrates the ruling class's frenzy to persecute political opponents more than the Mar-a-Lago raid, where the same Deep State actors who executed the worst scandal in American history through Russia Gate literally plundered the home of a former president.

All around us a politicized federal bureaucracy has been weaponized. Back in 2016, the Deep State had to operate in the shadows to spy on candidate Trump and, when they were found out, they did everything they could to hide their crimes. Today, anyone who supports candidate Trump is openly deemed a de facto terrorist. Americans like you and me have always been the enemy. But now those who are against us are operating out of the shadows. The Deep State is in the open.

DARKEST BEFORE THE DAWN

Despite all of these trials, I am not without hope. We should not be surprised that our opponents are using every authority in technology, media, and in the state to crush us. To them, nothing is more important than power, and they will destroy everything—even our glorious constitutional republic—in order to keep power. To them, censoring conservatives, labelling regular moms and dads as terrorists, prosecuting innocent Americans, and erecting a two-tiered system of justice is all part of the plan. What is heartening—and what has certainly not been part of their plans—is that tens of millions of Americans are refusing to bend the knee to the Deep State.

What terrifies the Deep State is that despite spending years relentlessly spreading disinformation and despite every illegal thing they have done to abuse and manipulate us, not only do we not believe them anymore—we now see them clearly for who they are. We know the truth, and that is what gives me hope.

For sixteen years, I worked for the government in service of our nation. I never expected to be there that long. Now, I am a private citizen, and I have had the privilege of meeting other patriots everywhere I go when I travel the country. No matter where I am, I see the same thing: dedicated citizens who see the corruption of the Washington regime and who are resolved to defend America. As Trump put it, it's time to "drain the swamp."

By and large, these are people who would rather live quiet lives raising their families, running their businesses, and volunteering at their schools and houses of worship. But they have been forced to rise up and defend our Constitution and our way of life. These brave Americans recognize that the Deep State may be firing everything it has at Trump, but they are only targeting him because he is standing in front of us. With Trump pushed out of office, we have been exposed and are now in the crosshairs more and more.

That is why the people I meet are no longer satisfied just voting every two to four years and then going on with our lives. They know it is not enough. They are getting involved in their school boards to save their kids from propaganda—just as I have been doing my part to help reshape American education through my *Plot Against the King* children's book series that teaches the importance of service, mission, faith, and truth. People are reading up on the facts free from the lens of the mainstream media, and they are telling their family, friends, and neighbors what they have learned. They are taking up space in the streets and at our nation's capital to peacefully protest and petition their government—as is their constitutional right. They are putting daily pressure on our political leaders not just to talk a big game but to play to win with legislation, investigations, and concrete actions.

Now, we must take our fight to the next level. The last thing America needs is more conservative commentators and complainers who post about problems without ever doing the hard work of finding solutions. We need to get much more serious about training and credentialling doers and leaders who can take positions in local government, state government, in Congress, and perhaps most importantly within presidential administrations. At every single level, in every single office, we need people with the guts and intelligence to take on the Deep State and who have the strength to withstand the attacks—fighting for the truth and defeating the disinformation campaigns. We need people who are unafraid to stand for America.

Nobody should ever underestimate what one person with a clear mission, loyalty to the Constitution, and aggressive chops can accomplish. After all, I grew up as an unknown, first-generation Indian American hockey fanatic in Queens and Long Island. I got bad grades in law school. I spent years as an unknown public defender. Yet for some unplanned reason, I ended up being the lead investigator who uncovered the greatest political scandal in American history—and for seven years now, I have been on the front line in every single major battle that the Deep State has waged against the American system of self-government. Not only that, but time and again in these battles I won—despite feeling like the whole world was against me—because I did one singular thing. I fought for the truth.

If that's what one person can do, think of what all of us can do together. Imagine what will happen when we all tell the government gangsters that they can threaten us, defame us, and attack us, but we will not submit to their destruction of America.

We still have spirit in us. We still have hope. So get out there. We have a fight to win. Put the mission first.

APPENDICES

APPENDIX A

Top Reforms to Defeat the Deep State

Throughout this book (particularly in chapters 3, 8, 13, and 16) I have detailed an extensive list of reforms that could be implemented in order to curb governmental abuses, prevent corruption, and end the Deep State threat to self-government. Below is a collection of the top reforms that should be implemented.

OVERALL REFORMS

- **Aggressive Congressional Oversight**: Congress must much more aggressively subpoena documents and witnesses to uncover wrongdoing in every branch of government. This includes the formation of a new Church Commission, modeled after the congressional body that uncovered CIA crimes like MKULTRA and spying operations on the civil rights movement. If the bureaucracy resists, the strategy of fencing should be much more commonly used to withhold appropriated funds until agencies comply with congressional requests.
- **Prosecute Leakers**: The Department of Justice has the forensic capabilities to discover leakers. Every single one of them should

be found and prosecuted for violating federal law. Additionally, government employees should be required to sign NDAs, subjecting themselves to criminal prosecution for violating the requirement that already exists that all government devices (including cellphones, laptops, and more) can be used for authorized government work only. Then, those devices should be subjected to mandatory monthly scans across the entire federal government to determine who has improperly transferred classified information, including to the press.

- **Civil Service Reform**: The next president should reinstitute Schedule F, a Trump administration policy creating a new classification for federal employees that made it easier to fire them if they subverted the president's agenda. Additionally, Congress must change the law to allow federal bureaucrats to be able to be fired by the president. If an individual or group of individuals within the executive branch is undermining the president, they should be removed from their posts and replaced with people who won't undermine the president's agenda.

DEPARTMENT OF JUSTICE REFORMS

- **Curb Policy of Pursuing Trials Within DC**: In 2020, Washington, DC, voted 92 percent for Joe Biden and less than 6 percent for Donald Trump. A future attorney general must change DoJ rules to cease prosecuting trials in a place with such a biased jury pool unless it is absolutely necessary.
- **Ban Jurisdiction Shopping**: Jurisdiction shopping allowed corrupt FBI agents to leverage a highly biased federal judge in order to secure the search warrant to raid Mar-a-Lago. A future attorney general must ban judge shopping and jurisdiction shopping.
- **Reform the FISA Court**: FBI agents must be required to work with DoJ prosecutors in order to submit a FISA warrant application, forcing them to follow all proper legal procedures. FISA Court judges should not serve in one-month rotations but should

be properly trained with long-term appointments so they have familiarity with the cases presented to them and laws at hand. A public defender position should be present at all FISA Court proceedings to advocate for the accused, and a court reporter should transcribe every FISA Court hearing for the record.

FEDERAL BUREAU OF INVESTIGATION REFORMS

- **Move the FBI Headquarters out of Washington**: Whether through Congress or the president, the FBI headquarters should be removed from Washington, DC, to prevent institutional capture and curb FBI leadership from engaging in political gamesmanship. FBI agents should no longer be required to serve stints in Washington in order to be promoted; rather, promotions should be based on field experience.
- **Cut the General Counsel Office**: Instead of operating as a purely investigatory body, the General Counsel office within the FBI has taken on prosecutorial decision-making. In effect, they are centralizing power to both investigate and prosecute crimes, even though it is the job of Department of Justice alone to prosecute crimes. The General Counsel office should be significantly reduced in size.

INTELLIGENCE COMMUNITY REFORMS

- **Create a Permanent Declassification Office**: The next president should erect a permanent office within the Office of the Director of National Intelligence (ODNI) that continuously reviews classified material that should be declassified, in whole or in part, for the public interest. This office should report directly to the president.
- **Cut the Size of the Intel Community**: The number of staff at ODNI and throughout the intelligence community, including the CIA and the NSA, must be drastically reduced to eliminate

duplicative offices and cut down on information silos and the practice of stovepiping—where intelligence officials funnel important information directly up to the agency heads without sharing it with others. Intelligence agencies must be refocused on ground-level intelligence gathering.

DEPARTMENT OF DEFENSE REFORMS

- **Reestablish Civilian Control of the Military**: Politicized, ineffective officers must be immediately fired by the next president. At the same time, the next administration should end the process whereby the chairman of the Joint Chiefs of Staff effectively chooses flag officers. Promotions at the highest levels of the military should be done on merit and solely upon the discretion of the president and the secretary of defense.

- **Fix the Procurement Process**: The current procurement process is not only wasteful, it operates as a blood money scheme where high-level Pentagon employees continue bad programs and pursue foolish engagement abroad to enrich their future employers within the defense industry, or the Defense Industrial Complex. The next president must appoint a secretary of defense and undersecretaries of R&D who refuse to rubber-stamp wasteful projects. Congress must restrict budgeting to cut waste in procurements as well. Lastly, laws and/or regulations must be implemented that ban employees within the Defense Industrial Complex from being hired at the Pentagon and to restrict Pentagon employees from later working within the Defense Industrial Complex.

These reforms are hardly exhaustive—and they don't include the full breadth of recommendations included in this book. However, even if these policies alone were to be implemented, the Deep State would be mortally wounded, and the American people would be able to retake control of their country.

APPENDIX B

Members of the Executive Branch Deep State

This list only includes current and former Executive Branch officials and is not exhaustive. It does not, for example, include other corrupt actors of the first order such as Congressmen Adam Schiff and Eric Swalwell, members of Fusion GPS or Perkins Coie, Christopher Steele, Paul Ryan, the entire fake news mafia press corps, etc. Alphabetical by last name.

- **Atkinson, Michael** – Former Intelligence Community Inspector General
- **Austin, Lloyd** – Secretary of Defense under President Biden
- **Auten, Brian** – Supervisory Intelligence Analyst within the FBI
- **Baker, James** – Former General Counsel for the FBI, currently a member of the Brookings Institute, former Deputy General Counsel at Twitter
- **Barr, Bill** – Former Attorney General under President Trump
- **Bolton, John** – Former National Security Advisor under President Trump
- **Boyd, Stephen** – Former head of Legislative Affairs at DoJ under Deputy Attorney General Rosenstein

- **Biden, Joe** – President of the United States
- **Brennan, John** – Former Director of the CIA under President Obama, currently a Senior National Security and Intelligence Analyst at NBC and MSNBC
- **Carlin, John** – Acting Deputy Attorney General, former head of National Security Division at DoJ during Russia Gate investigation by FBI
- **Ciaramella, Eric** – Former NSC staffer within the Obama and Trump administrations
- **Cipollone, Pat** – Former White House Counsel under President Trump
- **Clapper, James** – Former Director of National Intelligence under President Obama, currently a National Security Analyst at CNN
- **Clinton, Hillary** – Former Democrat Party Nominee for President and Former Secretary of State under President Obama
- **Comey, James** – Former FBI Director
- **Dibble, Elizabeth** – Former Deputy Chief of Mission at the US Embassy in London
- **Esper, Mark** – Former Secretary of Defense under President Trump
- **Farah, Alyssa** – Former Director of Strategic Communications under President Trump
- **Farkas, Evelyn** – Former DoD official under President Obama
- **Flores, Sarah Isgur** – Former Head of Communications at DoJ for AG Sessions
- **Garland, Merrick** – Attorney General under President Biden
- **Grisham, Stephanie** – Former Press Secretary for President Trump and Chief of Staff for Melania Trump
- **Harris, Kamala** – Vice President of the United States
- **Haspel, Gina** – Former Director of the CIA under President Trump and current advisor at King & Spalding law firm
- **Hill, Fiona** – Former NSC staffer who worked with Vindman and Ciaramella
- **Heide, Curtis** – FBI Agent

- **Holder, Eric** – Former Attorney General under President Obama and current Senior Counsel at Covington law firm
- **Hur, Robert** – Special Counsel to investigate Biden and former PADAG under Rosenstein
- **Hutchinson, Cassidy** – Aide to Mark Meadows
- **Jankowicz, Nina** – Former Executive Director of the Disinformation Governance Board in the Biden administration
- **Lerner, Lois** – Former Director of the IRS under President Obama
- **Lynch, Loretta** – Former Attorney General under President Obama
- **Kupperman, Charles** – Former Deputy National Security Advisor under President Trump
- **Mackenzie, Kenneth** – Retired US Marine Corps General and former Commander of the United States Central Command
- **McCabe, Andrew** – Former Deputy Director of the FBI under President Trump
- **McCarthy, Ryan** – Former Secretary of the Army under President Trump
- **McCord, Mary** – Former Acting Assistant Attorney General for National Security at the DoJ and currently the Executive Director for the Georgetown Law Institute for Constitutional Advocacy and Protection
- **McDonough, Denis** – Former Chief of Staff for President Obama and currently Secretary of Veterans Affairs
- **Milley, Mark** – Chairman of the Joint Chiefs of Staff
- **Monaco, Lisa** – Deputy Attorney General of the United States
- **Moyer, Sally** – Former Supervisory Attorney at the FBI and currently Legal Counsel at Cloudflare
- **Mueller, Robert** – Former Director of the FBI and Special Counsel
- **Ohr, Bruce** – Former Associate Deputy Attorney General
- **Ohr, Nellie** – Former CIA Employee and Independent Contract for Fusion GPS
- **Page, Lisa** – Former Legal Counsel for Deputy Director of the FBI Andrew McCabe and currently a National Security and Legal Analyst at NBC and MSNBC

- **Philbin, Pat** – Former Deputy White House Counsel under President Trump
- **Podesta, John** – Former Counselor to President Obama
- **Power, Samantha** – Former Ambassador to the United Nations under President Obama, currently Administrator of the United States Agency for International Development
- **Priestap, Bill** – Former Assistant Director for the FBI Counterintelligence Division
- **Rice, Susan** – Former National Security Advisor under President Obama, currently Director of the Domestic Policy Council under President Biden
- **Rosenstein, Rod** – Former Deputy Attorney General under President Trump and current partner at King & Spalding law firm
- **Strzok, Peter** – Former Deputy Assistant Director of the FBI's Counterintelligence Division
- **Sullivan, Jake** – National Security Advisor under President Biden
- **Sussmann, Michael** – Former legal representative for the Democratic National Committee and former partner at Perkins Coie law firm
- **Taylor, Miles** – Former DHS official under President Trump, aka "Anonymous"
- **Thibault, Timothy** – Former Assistant Special Agent at the FBI's Washington Field Office
- **Weissman, Andrew** – Former Deputy under Special Counsel Mueller
- **Vindman, Alexander** – Former Director for European Affairs on the NSC under President Trump
- **Wray, Christopher** – Director of the FBI under President Trump and President Biden, former partner at King & Spalding
- **Yates, Sally** – Former Deputy Attorney General under President Obama and briefly the Acting Attorney General under President Trump

The Nunes Memo, January 6th Timelines, and Other Documents

THE NUNES MEMO

UNCLASSIFIED ~~TOP SECRET//NOFORN~~

January 18, 2018

Declassified by order of the President
February 2, 2018

To: HPSCI Majority Members

From: HPSCI Majority Staff

Subject: Foreign Intelligence Surveillance Act Abuses at the Department of Justice and the
          Federal Bureau of Investigation

Purpose

This memorandum provides Members an update on significant facts relating to the Committee's ongoing investigation into the Department of Justice (DOJ) and Federal Bureau of Investigation (FBI) and their use of the Foreign Intelligence Surveillance Act (FISA) during the 2016 presidential election cycle. Our findings, which are detailed below, 1) raise concerns with the legitimacy and legality of certain DOJ and FBI interactions with the Foreign Intelligence Surveillance Court (FISC), and 2) represent a troubling breakdown of legal processes established to protect the American people from abuses related to the FISA process.

Investigation Update

On October 21, 2016, DOJ and FBI sought and received a FISA probable cause order (not under Title VII) authorizing electronic surveillance on Carter Page from the FISC. Page is a U.S. citizen who served as a volunteer advisor to the Trump presidential campaign. Consistent with requirements under FISA, the application had to be first certified by the Director or Deputy Director of the FBI. It then required the approval of the Attorney General, Deputy Attorney General (DAG), or the Senate-confirmed Assistant Attorney General for the National Security Division.

The FBI and DOJ obtained one initial FISA warrant targeting Carter Page and three FISA renewals from the FISC. As required by statute (50 U.S.C. §1805(d)(1)), a FISA order on an American citizen must be renewed by the FISC every 90 days and each renewal requires a separate finding of probable cause. Then-Director James Comey signed three FISA applications in question on behalf of the FBI, and Deputy Director Andrew McCabe signed one. Then-DAG Sally Yates, then-Acting DAG Dana Boente, and DAG Rod Rosenstein each signed one or more FISA applications on behalf of DOJ.

Due to the sensitive nature of foreign intelligence activity, FISA submissions (including renewals) before the FISC are classified. As such, the public's confidence in the integrity of the FISA process depends on the court's ability to hold the government to the highest standard—particularly as it relates to surveillance of American citizens. However, the FISC's rigor in protecting the rights of Americans, which is reinforced by 90-day renewals of surveillance orders, is necessarily dependent on the government's production to the court of all material and relevant facts. This should include information potentially favorable to the target of the FISA

~~TOP SECRET//NOFORN~~

PROPERTY OF THE U.S. HOUSE OF REPRESENTATIVES

application that is known by the government. In the case of Carter Page, the government had at least four independent opportunities before the FISC to accurately provide an accounting of the relevant facts. However, our findings indicate that, as described below, material and relevant information was omitted.

1) The "dossier" compiled by Christopher Steele (Steele dossier) on behalf of the Democratic National Committee (DNC) and the Hillary Clinton campaign formed an essential part of the Carter Page FISA application. Steele was a longtime FBI source who was paid over $160,000 by the DNC and Clinton campaign, via the law firm Perkins Coie and research firm Fusion GPS, to obtain derogatory information on Donald Trump's ties to Russia.

   a) Neither the initial application in October 2016, nor any of the renewals, disclose or reference the role of the DNC, Clinton campaign, or any party/campaign in funding Steele's efforts, even though the political origins of the Steele dossier were then known to senior DOJ and FBI officials.

   b) The initial FISA application notes Steele was working for a named U.S. person, but does not name Fusion GPS and principal Glenn Simpson, who was paid by a U.S. law firm (Perkins Coie) representing the DNC (even though it was known by DOJ at the time that political actors were involved with the Steele dossier). The application does not mention Steele was ultimately working on behalf of—and paid by—the DNC and Clinton campaign, or that the FBI had separately authorized payment to Steele for the same information.

2) The Carter Page FISA application also cited extensively a September 23, 2016, *Yahoo News* article by Michael Isikoff, which focuses on Page's July 2016 trip to Moscow. This article does not corroborate the Steele dossier because it is derived from information leaked by Steele himself to *Yahoo News*. The Page FISA application incorrectly assesses that Steele did not directly provide information to *Yahoo News*. Steele has admitted in British court filings that he met with *Yahoo News*—and several other outlets—in September 2016 at the direction of Fusion GPS. Perkins Coie was aware of Steele's initial media contacts because they hosted at least one meeting in Washington D.C. in 2016 with Steele and Fusion GPS where this matter was discussed.

   a) Steele was suspended and then terminated as an FBI source for what the FBI defines as the most serious of violations—an unauthorized disclosure to the media of his relationship with the FBI in an October 30, 2016, *Mother Jones* article by David Corn. Steele should have been terminated for his previous undisclosed contacts with Yahoo and other outlets **in September**—before the Page application was submitted to

UNCLASSIFIED

the FISC in October—but Steele improperly concealed from and lied to the FBI about those contacts.

b) Steele's numerous encounters with the media violated the cardinal rule of source handling—maintaining confidentiality—and demonstrated that Steele had become a less than reliable source for the FBI.

3) Before and after Steele was terminated as a source, he maintained contact with DOJ via then-Associate Deputy Attorney General Bruce Ohr, a senior DOJ official who worked closely with Deputy Attorneys General Yates and later Rosenstein. Shortly after the election, the FBI began interviewing Ohr, documenting his communications with Steele. For example, in September 2016, Steele admitted to Ohr his feelings against then-candidate Trump when Steele said he **"was desperate that Donald Trump not get elected and was passionate about him not being president."** This clear evidence of Steele's bias was recorded by Ohr at the time and subsequently in official FBI files—but not reflected in any of the Page FISA applications.

a) During this same time period, Ohr's wife was employed by Fusion GPS to assist in the cultivation of opposition research on Trump. Ohr later provided the FBI with all of his wife's opposition research, paid for by the DNC and Clinton campaign via Fusion GPS. The Ohrs' relationship with Steele and Fusion GPS was inexplicably concealed from the FISC.

4) According to the head of the FBI's counterintelligence division, Assistant Director Bill Priestap, corroboration of the Steele dossier was in its "infancy" at the time of the initial Page FISA application. After Steele was terminated, a source validation report conducted by an independent unit within FBI assessed Steele's reporting as only minimally corroborated. Yet, in early January 2017, Director Comey briefed President-elect Trump on a summary of the Steele dossier, even though it was—according to his June 2017 testimony—"salacious and unverified." While the FISA application relied on Steele's past record of credible reporting on other unrelated matters, it ignored or concealed his anti-Trump financial and ideological motivations. Furthermore, Deputy Director McCabe testified before the Committee in December 2017 that no surveillance warrant would have been sought from the FISC without the Steele dossier information.

UNCLASSIFIED

TOP SECRET//NOFORN

5) The Page FISA application also mentions information regarding fellow Trump campaign advisor George Papadopoulos, but there is no evidence of any cooperation or conspiracy between Page and Papadopoulos. The Papadopoulos information triggered the opening of an FBI counterintelligence investigation in late July 2016 by FBI agent Pete Strzok. Strzok was reassigned by the Special Counsel's Office to FBI Human Resources for improper text messages with his mistress, FBI Attorney Lisa Page (no known relation to Carter Page), where they both demonstrated a clear bias against Trump and in favor of Clinton, whom Strzok had also investigated. The Strzok/Lisa Page texts also reflect extensive discussions about the investigation, orchestrating leaks to the media, and include a meeting with Deputy Director McCabe to discuss an "insurance" policy against President Trump's election.

UNCLASSIFIED

TOP SECRET//NOFORN

KASH PRAMOD PATEL

OFFICIAL DEPARTMENT OF DEFENSE JANUARY 6TH TIMELINE

CONTROLLED UNCLASSIFIED INFORMATION

MEMORANDUM FOR RECORD

SUBJECT: Record of Events and Activities of the Office of the Secretary of Defense and Acting Secretary Miller Related to the Civil Disturbance and Efforts to Support Local Law Enforcement Response on 06 and 07 January 2021

This memorandum memorializes the discussions and actions leading up to and in response to the violent attacks on 06 January 2021. The below timeline is a compilations of notes and correspondence for the events that occurred.

Unless noted otherwise, internal Department of Defense participants generally included the Acting Secretary of Defense (A/SD), Deputy Secretary of Defense (DSD), Chairman of the Joint Chiefs of Staff (CJCS), A/SD Chief of Staff (COS), A/SD Senior Military Advisor (SMA), Deputy Chief of Staff (DCOS), Principle Military Assistant (PMA), Executive Secretary (ExecSec), Special Assistant to the Secretary of Defense, Acting Assistant Secretary of Defense for Legislative Affairs (LA), Assistant Secretary of Defense for Public Affairs (PA), Office of the General Council (OGC), DSD SMA (DSMA).

31 December 2020

- Mayor Muriel Bowser and Dr. Christopher Rodriguez, DC Director of Homeland Security and Emergency Management Agency, deliver a written request for D.C. National Guard (DCNG) support to DC Metro Police Department (MPD) and Fire and Emergency Service.

02 January 2021

1330   SecArmy briefs the A/SD and CJCS on the mission requirement. Codifies briefing with a letter. No decision made.

03 January 2021

- Carol Corbin/OSD HD&GS confirmed with John Erickson from USCP, who works for Deputy Chief Sean P. Gallagher (Protective Services Bureau Commander) that USCP was not requesting DoD support.

1300   The Acting Secretary of Defense (A/SD) meets with select Cabinet Members (A/AG, SEC/Interior, A/SEC DHS, and APNSA) to discuss DoD support to law enforcement agencies and potential requirements for DoD support.

1645   A/SD and CJCS meet with APNSA prior to meeting with POTUS.

1730   A/SD and the Chairman of the Joint Chiefs of Staff (CJCS) meet with POTUS, POTUS concurs in activation of the DCNG to support law enforcement.

SUBJECT: Record of Events and Activities of the Office of the Secretary of Defense and Acting Secretary Miller Related to the Civil Disturbance and Efforts to Support Local Law Enforcement Response on 06 and 07 January 2021

04 January 2021

- USCP confirms there is no requirement for DoD support with the Secretary of the Army (SECARMY).

0900   DoD Senior leaders Small Group. The A/SD, in consultation with CJCS, SECARMY, and DoD General Counsel (DoD GC), reviews the Department's plan to be prepared to provide support to civil authorities, if asked, and approves activation of 340 members of the DCNG to support Mayor Bowser's request.

  o Support provided in response to Mayor Bowser's request includes support at:
    ▪ Traffic Control Points: 90 personnel (180 total/2 shifts); Metro station support: 24 personnel (48 total/2 shifts); Weapons of Mass Destruction Civil Support Team: 20 personnel; and Internal Command and Control: 52 personnel.
  o A/SD also authorizes SECARMY to deploy a Quick Reaction Force (40 personnel staged at Joint Base Andrews) if additional support is requested by civil authorities.

1700   A/SD and CJCS sync w/Cabinet Members (A/AG, DOI, DHS OPS, APNSA)

1745   A/AG call with SecDef and CJCS

05 January 2021

- Mayor Bowser delivers a letter addressed to the Acting Attorney General (A/AG), A/SD, and SECARMY confirming that there are no additional support requirements from the District of Columbia.
- 255 DCNG arrive in DC and begin to manage traffic control points alongside local law enforcement.

06 January 2021

0800   A/SD Miller requests a rehearsal of ONE following recent FAA reporting. (A/SD, COS, SMA, DCOS, PMA, JMA, EXECSEC)

0830   A/SD Miller convened a conference call with CJCS Milley to discuss the prospect of civil disturbance and the Department's role in support of local law enforcement efforts. (A/SD, CJCS, SMA, MA, PMA, COS, DCOS)

0845   A/SD Miller convened a SVTC with LA, PA, and Budget Affairs (BA). A/SD relayed the following guidance: DoD would support local law enforcement efforts and would not be

2

CONTROLLED UNCLASSIFIED INFORMATION

SUBJECT: Record of Events and Activities of the Office of the Secretary of Defense and Acting Secretary Miller Related to the Civil Disturbance and Efforts to Support Local Law Enforcement Response on 06 and 07 January 2021

the lead federal agency in support of today's efforts; and, A/SD was to be notified should crowd sizes exceed 20k, as this was the number previously highlighted by DC Police as within the capacity of local law enforcement to maintain order. (A/SD, COS, Covelli-Ingwell, Johnston, Kovatch)

1130   A/SD participates in ONE Rehearsal. (Additional attendees: NORTHCOM CDR, DJS, DJ2, DJ3)

1302   Press: VPOTUS releases a letter via Twitter regarding his role in the electoral process.

1315   A/SD informed of demonstrators beginning to march to U.S. Capitol.

1326   USCP orders evacuation of Capitol complex.

1334   SECARMY phone call with Mayor Bowser in which Mayor Bowser communicates request for unspecified number of additional forces.

1340   Press: Reports of potential explosive devices at DNC/RNC headquarters. Cannon Building evacuated.

1349   Commanding General, DCNG (CG-DCNG) Walker phone call with USCP Chief Sund. Chief Sund communicates request for immediate assistance. MG Walker SVTC with Army leadership immediately informing them of the request.

1410   Chief Sund contacted MG Walker again to request immediate assistance and stated 200 Guardsmen were needed and to send more if they are available.

1422   SECARMY phone call with DC Mayor, Deputy Mayor, Dr. Rodriguez, and MPD leadership to discuss the current situation and to request additional DCNG support.

1430   A/SD, CJCS, and SECARMY meet to discuss USCP and Mayor Bowser's requests.

1445   Joint Staff leadership establish open bridge for senior leader discussion and situational awareness updates.

1447   Press: Speaker of the House requests National Guard support to clear the Capitol.

1500   SECARMY directs LTG Piatt to contact DCNG to prepare available Guardsmen to move from the armory to the Capitol complex, while seeking formal approval from A/SD for deployment. LTG Piatt contacts DCNG and informs them to prepare to move 150 personnel to support USCP, pending A/SD's approval.

1500   A/SD determines all available forces of the DCNG are required to reinforce MPD and USCP positions to support efforts to reestablish security of the Capitol complex.

3

CONTROLLED UNCLASSIFIED INFORMATION

SUBJECT: Record of Events and Activities of the Office of the Secretary of Defense and Acting Secretary Miller Related to the Civil Disturbance and Efforts to Support Local Law Enforcement Response on 06 and 07 January 2021

1504   A/SD, with advice from CJCS, DoD GC, the Chief of the National Guard Bureau (CNGB), SECARMY, and the Chief of Staff of the Army (CSA), provides verbal approval of the full activation of DCNG (1100 total) in support of the MPD.

1505   Immediately upon A/SD approval, Secretary McCarthy directs DCNG to initiate movement and full mobilization.

In response, DCNG redeployed all soldiers from positions at Metro stations and all available non-support and non-C2 personnel to support MPD. DCNG begins full mobilization.

1518   A/SD NG Mobilization discussion. DSD recommends DoD support to DoI at Lafayette Square to free law enforcement officials to support Capitol response. A/SD clarifies no military police from out of state authorized to mobilize.

1519   SECARMY phone call with Sen. Schumer and Speaker Pelosi about the nature of Mayor Bowser's request. SECARMY explains A/SD already approved full DCNG mobilization.

1526   SECARMY phone call with Mayor Bowser and MPD police chief. Relays there was no denial of their request, and conveys A/SD approval of the activation of full DCNG.

1528   HASC Chairman Smith call with A/SD to discuss DoD support.

1530   Interagency Sync call. Review of efforts to date: no active duty troops, need to restore Capitol security, conducts review of the process of the use of federal troops and process to be followed for mobilization. (Additional attendees via phone: D/FBI, D/DHS, WH (Cipollone))

1535   A/SD informed of DC Mayor's curfew effective 1800, 6 January until 0600 7 January

1536   Release of CCIR conveying A/SD approval of full activation of DC National Guard.

1537   ExecSec directs PFPA to secure A/SD, Dr. Esper, and DSD residences following public announcement of VANG activation.

1540   Update call with A/AG Rosen. No decisions. Interrupted with request for call from Congressional leadership at 1544.

1544   Congressional Leadership call with A/SD. Rep Hoyer makes request for active duty troops. No commitment offered by A/SD. Schumer: Tell POTUS to tweet everyone should leave. We need help. A/SD explains commitment provided to DC, NG. (A/SD, DSD, CJCS, Pelosi, Schumer, Smith, McConnell, Hoyer)

4

CONTROLLED UNCLASSIFIED INFORMATION

SUBJECT: Record of Events and Activities of the Office of the Secretary of Defense and Acting Secretary Miller Related to the Civil Disturbance and Efforts to Support Local Law Enforcement Response on 06 and 07 January 2021

1546   CNGB phone call with the Adjutant General (TAG) of Virginia to discuss support in Washington DC. TAG said Governor had ordered mobilization of forces at 1532.

1548   SECARMY departs Pentagon for MPD HQ.

1555   CNGB phone call with TAG of Maryland to discuss support in Washington DC. TAG said governor ordered the mobilization of the rapid response force. TAG reports Governor had ordered mobilization of the rapid response force at 1547.

1600   DOD Releases Statement on National Guard mobilization.

1604   DHS Secretary Call with A/SD.

1608   VPOTUS call. VPOTUS at Capitol. Building not secure. What is the timeline? FBI must clear. CJCS briefs VPOTUS on status of FBI HRT, USSS, ATF, and DCNG efforts. VPOTUS relays direction to "clear the capitol." A/SD and CJCS do not say no; underscore DoD is in a supporting role for local law enforcement efforts. VP: why were more troops not provided in advance? CJCS: we fulfilled everything DC Mayor asked for. A/SD asked if more troops needed. VPOTUS replied no. Ends 1609.

1610   SECARMY arrives at MPD HQ.

1610   CNGB Meeting (in-person). Discuss numbers, timeline, seek review of authorities for activation. Estimate of 90 minute timeline from activation to arrival. No decisions. Joined by OGC at 1618 and review authorities for mobilization of NG forces. Agree no active duty, NG dispatched with riot gear only. No arms. CJCS gives advisement to mobilize MD, VA, but not deploy.

1613   WHS provides report on PFPA. Confirms deployment of PSD officers to homes of A/SD, DSD, Dr. Esper. Informs of ask from USCP to send 15-20 officers under mutual aid agreement. PFPA recalled and will be on standby within 30min. No deployment unless/until authorized by A/SD. WHS clarifies these available PFPA staff are line officers, not equipped for civil disturbance as that was not the request. Intent by US Capitol Police is to use PFPA officers for perimeter clearing and security. Not confronting demonstrators. Provides additional details on Pentagon security and notification of the standup of the Pentagon Operations Center.

1617   A/SD informed of press report on POTUS tweets video stating "Go home and go home in peace."

1619   Call with SecArmy. SecArmy IVO Lafayette Park, briefs details of plan, to include maneuver of TCPs, mobilization, kit, shifts. A/SD authorizes. Guard will be in riot gear and have no lethal weapons. PFPA will support Capitol police with 15-20 additional

5

CONTROLLED UNCLASSIFIED INFORMATION

SUBJECT: Record of Events and Activities of the Office of the Secretary of Defense and Acting Secretary Miller Related to the Civil Disturbance and Efforts to Support Local Law Enforcement Response on 06 and 07 January 2021

PFPA officers. A/SD, CJCS, SECARMY, and CNGB discuss availability of NG forces from other States in the region. A/SD gives voice approval for out-of-State NG forces to muster and to be prepared to deploy to DC.

1625   A/SD views and approved DoD Press Statement.

1625   Report received of Georgia and Kansas Capital being overrun.

1626   Regional NG Authorities Discussion with A/SD, CJCS, OGC, CNGB.

1627   CJCS notes that if the report given of the Georgia and Kansas capital being overrun is accurate it is a nationwide insurrection.

1632   SecArmy phone call. SecArmy provides status update and recommends support for clearance and perimeter operations in support of USCP. A/SD and CJCS acknowledge and A/SD approves. A/SD gives permission for SecArmy to provide public notification.

1633   CJCS provides his best military advice that "We must establish order and involuntarily mobilize thousands of National Guard for 30 days to secure the inauguration. This is going to happen again."

1635   SECARMY authorizes DCNG to depart DC Armory to support USCP at the Capitol.

1636   A/SD informed of press report FBI deployment to the Capitol.

1637   A/SD informed of press reporting of explosive device found on Capitol Hill.

1640   A/SD Call with Congressional leadership. Speaker Pelosi and Senator Schumer request assistance securing perimeter and guarding access points. Accuses National Security apparatus of knowing that protestors planned to conduct an assault on the Capitol. A/SD relayed no prior knowledge of the scope of actions seen today. (A/SD, DSD. CJCS, COS, DCoS)

1640   SECARMY phone call with Governor of Maryland. Governor to send MDNG troops to DC.

1647   A/SD informed of Mayor Boswer - SecArmy Press Conference

1648   A/SD formally approves deployment of 20 PFPA officers under mutual aid agreement with DC Council of Governments to support crowd control efforts at the Capitol Building.

6

SUBJECT: Record of Events and Activities of the Office of the Secretary of Defense and Acting Secretary Miller Related to the Civil Disturbance and Efforts to Support Local Law Enforcement Response on 06 and 07 January 2021

1652   DOD Press Statement on full activation of D.C. National Guard: STATEMENT BY ACTING SECRETARY MILLER ON FULL ACTIVATION OF D.C. NATIONAL GUARD

1700   Cabinet-level Discussion. A/SD convenes. DHS updates on efforts to deploy non-scalable fencing at Capitol. WH (Cipollone) informs 350 federal agents at the Capitol building. 1 death confirmed of woman shot at Capitol. CP not requesting additional law enforcement as of 1710. CJCS asked to confirm, citing obvious disconnect with political leadership (Pelosi, Schumer) who just relayed desire for DoD intervention. CJCS relayed VPOTUS guidance to see Capitol building cleared to enable legislature to get back to work immediately. Reiterated DoD mission is in support of law enforcement efforts led by DOJ. WH (Cipollone) directed DHS to "send everything they can at this point" to the Capitol. A/SD relayed no need for federal troops – no objections raised. Agree to reconvene at 1800. Ends at 1715. (NSA O'Brien, A/AG Rosen, A/D/DHS Wolfe, Sec Bernhardt, WH Legal (Eisenberg, Cipollone, Philbin)

1702   Departure of 154 DCNG from DC Armory in support of USCP.

1715   SecArmy Update Call. 150 DC NG QRF staged to support law enforcement effort. Effort to clear Capitol expected to take hours, not days. Will call back at 1800. Ends at 1720.

1720   Agenda Discussion for 1800 call. Agree Bowditch should lead with update; will then turn to each D/A to identify support options needed and will review across D/As; special projects (non-scalable fencing); and conclusion. DoD consensus that Rich Donoghue (D/AG) should be interagency lead for coordination going forward.

1720   D.C. National Guard begin arriving to the U.S. Capitol with 154 Soldiers

1725   A/SD call with WH (Cipollone), DOJ reaffirmed as the lead federal agency for response coordination.

1740   DCNG arrived at U.S. Capitol, swear in with USCP, and begin support operations.

1745   A/SD signs formal authorization for out-of-State NG to muster and gives voice approval for deployment in support of USCP.

1750   WHS Email Update: Threat Working Group held by USNORTHCOM and JTF-NCR at 1700. Confirmed deployment of 20 PFPA officers to support USCP under mutual aid agreement. Approx 400 DCNG currently being deployed. SecArmy authorized full callup of ~1110 guardsman support. At the request of USCP, PFPA officers will be deputized to perform police functions/duties in DC.

7

SUBJECT: Record of Events and Activities of the Office of the Secretary of Defense and Acting Secretary Miller Related to the Civil Disturbance and Efforts to Support Local Law Enforcement Response on 06 and 07 January 2021

1800   Interagency Sync Call. SecArmy commits to clearing House and Senate areas by 2100. First discussion of defense around Capitol. CG DCNG Commits to full mobilization by midnight. A/SD asks DOI if it needs additional support, and he says no. (DHS, DOJ, FBI, DOI)

1814   154 Soldiers from the D.C. National Guard In Position with the Capitol Police and MPD Establish Perimeter on the West Side of the U.S. Capitol

1915   VPOTUS Interagency Call. Donoghue leads. Briefs Capitol building cleared, not secured. Facilitating reentry to chambers, votes to resume at 2000. No significant damage to building. All exposed entrances to be guarded. VPOTUS back in Senate Chamber Office. Speaker Pelosi requests support for food delivery. Confirmed concessions will be available for Congressional members. (VPOTUS, Donoghue, Schumer, Pelosi, McConnell)

1936   SecArmy Update Call. Capitol secured, votes to be conducted at 2000. SecArmy requests and A/SD approved for Sec. 284 EEE funding for the fence around the Capitol. Discuss long term posture for forces and agree mobilization to be extended into next week. Paperwork forthcoming. Will receive next update in 45min. A/SD instructed no press engagement. WH direction that DOJ (D/AG Donoghue) to handle press engagement as rep to lead federal agency. Agree to 2100 update call.

2015   DSD received official request from DHS CFO, Mr. Troy Edgar, for funding support options for emplacement of fencing around the Capitol. DSD relays A/SD VOCO approval for DoD funding of the fence.

2000   USCP declares Capitol is secure.

2100   SecArmy Update Call. SecArmy provides update on available National Guard forces. Expects non-scalable fencing to be installed tomorrow. Receives DSD approval for funding for DHS efforts. DSD to press DHS for expedited delivery and installation. SecArmy provides recommendation for 30-day mobilization of multi-state NG forces. A/SD and CJCS agree 30-days sends a signal to protestors. SecArmy to stay at DC MPD HQ with DC Mayor to facilitate coordination. Gives praise for D/DIR FBI Bowditch efforts to coordinate.

2115   GEN Hokanson raises intent to activate National Guard force on orders through 30 Jan under 502 authority. 502 authority requires request from any federal agency in addition to any request by DC Mayor. OGC not present, will seek to confirm whether Legislative Branch fits the definition of a federal agency. GEN Hokanson states we can have 6200 by

8

SUBJECT: Record of Events and Activities of the Office of the Secretary of Defense and Acting Secretary Miller Related to the Civil Disturbance and Efforts to Support Local Law Enforcement Response on 06 and 07 January 2021

Saturday with riot gear and no weapons. GEN Hokanson updates no further issues in states with other reported disturbances today. Agree to reconvene at 2300. Ends at 2122.

2118   A/USD(C) sends e-mail to Mr. Edgar with approval of Emergency and Extraordinary Expenses (EEE) Funding Support to DHS, in the form of reimbursement of expenses through the Economy Act.

2157   Received final HQDA G3/5/7 Update (#5) email on D.C. Civil Disturbance.

2158   SA meets with DCNG leaders at DC Armory to discuss force flow and 30 day mobilization orders.

2323   E-Mail containing DHS Points of Contact for Capitol Fence effort was sent to Secretary McCarthy to facilitate DIRLAUTH for construction scheduled to commence at 0900, 07 Jan 21

2345   Final SecArmy Update Call with A/SD, MG Walker (CG DCNG), and CSA. SECARMY provided an update of National Guard. The non-scaleable fence is on site and will take about 20 hours to erect. GEN Hokanson clarifies that NG forces will be in riot gear with no batons.

07 January 2021

0015   Final DOD Internal Synch with A/SD, DSD, CJCS, CNGB, CoS, SMA, PMA, DCoS, and EXECSEC

0900   SecArmy update to A/SD & CJCS. SecArmy Provides current disposition of NG. They also discuss posture of NG forces leading into the inauguration. SecArmy plans to have 2500 NG personnel in DC on 08 JAN with 850 on duty at any given time.

0955   A/SD has meeting with PA and LA.

1041   A/SD and Sec Bernhardt conduct phone call. Sec Bernhardt socializes that he may ask for NG support of around 150 personnel to help guard the monuments.

1145   A/SD has phone call with A/SEC DHS Wolf. A/SEC Wolf expresses appreciation for DOD support and DHS has no new request for support from DHS.

9

OFFICIAL U.S. CAPITOL POLICE JANUARY 6TH TIMELINE

DEPARTMENT TIMELINE
UNITED STATES CAPITOL POLICE
TIMELINE OF EVENTS FOR JANUARY 6, 2021 ATTACK

This document memorializes critical events leading up to and during the January 6, 2021 attack at the U.S. Capitol.

The timeline is as follows:

WEDNESDAY, DECEMBER 16, 2020

- The United States Capitol Police (USCP) learns that different groups of protesters are organizing demonstrations on U.S. Capitol grounds related to the January 6, 2021 joint session to certify the electoral vote count.

- Special Event Assessment issued for January 6, 2021 demonstrations.

  - Initial assessment indicates two groups of demonstrators – a group called "Donald, You're Fired," an anti-Trump group, and a group called "Patriots United March," a pro-Trump group.

  - Initial assessment finds "no information regarding specific disruptions or acts of civil disobedience targeting this function."

FRIDAY, DECEMBER 18, 2020

- The USCP begins developing Civil Disturbance Unit (CDU) action plan for January 6, 2021 event.

TUESDAY, DECEMBER 22, 2020

- Metropolitan Police Department ("MPD") hosts first multi-agency teleconference in which agencies share intelligence and initial planning for the January 6, 2021 event. The following agencies are represented:

  o MPD
  o United States Park Police (USPP)
  o Washington Metropolitan Area Transit Authority (WMATA)
  o Federal Bureau Investigation Washington Field Office (FBI WFO)
  o Federal Bureau Investigation Headquarters (FBI HQ)
  o Supreme Court Police
  o United States Secret Service (USSS)
  o DC Fire & Emergency Medical Services (FEMS)

WEDNESDAY, DECEMBER 23, 2020

- Revised Special Event Assessment issues for January 6, 2021 demonstrations.

Review of the Events Surrounding the January 6, 2021, Takeover of the U.S. Capitol   *2021-I-0003-A, February 2021*

DEPARTMENT TIMELINE

- Revised assessment includes that on December 19, 2020, POTUS called for supporters to come to Washington, DC on January 6, 2021, for a big protest called "Be There, Will Be Wild."

- Revised assessment identifies four pro-Trump groups holding protests at the US Capitol: (1) Women for America First; (2) Stop the Steal; (3) Women for a Great America; and (4) The One Nation Under God Foundation.

- Revised assessment identifies three counter-protester groups: (1) They/Them Collective; (2) DC Youth Liberation Front; and (3) Shutdown DC; Refuse Fascism DC

- Revised assessment indicates: "The protests/rallies are expected to be similar to the previous Million MAGA March rallies in November and December 2020, which drew tens of thousands of participants. It is also expected that members of the Proud Boys, Antifa, and other extremist groups will rally on January 6, 2021."

- Revised assessment finds "no information regarding specific disruptions or acts of civil disobedience targeting this function. Due to the tense political environment following the 2020 election, the threat of disruptive actions or violence cannot be ruled out."

- Initial draft of USCP CDU Operational Plan issues to Assistant Chief Chad Thomas, Uniformed Operations, and is approved.

  - Initial CDU Plan proposes perimeter fencing to secure Union Square, along Constitution Avenue between First Street NW and First Street NE, and perimeter fencing along First Street NE between Constitution Avenue and Independence Avenue.

  - Initial CDU Plan proposes deployment of four CDU platoons of officers in riot gear (Hard Platoons).

  - Initial CDU Plan proposes deployment of eight Grenadiers, including two with each Hard Platoon, equipped with chemical munitions.

  - Initial CDU Plan proposes deployment of USCP SWAT Teams to provide tactical response and counter-sniper over-watch.

MONDAY, DECEMBER 28, 2020

- Chief of Police Steven Sund participates in MPD-hosted bi-weekly law enforcement partners meeting in which intelligence and planning for January 6, 2021 event discussed. Law enforcement partners participating in the bi-weekly meeting include:

  - MPD
  - USPP
  - USSS (Uniformed and non-uniformed)
  - Amtrak Police Department
  - WMATA
  - Federal Air Marshalls

Review of the Events Surrounding the January 6, 2021, Takeover of the U.S. Capitol　　　　　*2021-I-0003-A, February 2021*

LAW ENFORCEMENT SENSITIVE

DEPARTMENT TIMELINE

TUESDAY, DECEMBER 29, 2020

- USCP personnel attend multi-agency teleconference hosted by MPD in which agencies briefed on intelligence and planning for the January 6, 2021 event.

- Joint Session Perimeter Plan issues to Assistant Chief Thomas and is approved.

WEDNESDAY, DECEMBER 30, 2020

- Revised Special Event Assessment issues for January 6, 2021 event.

  - Revised assessment indicates that "[a] number of individuals and groups are calling for their supporters to travel to Washington, DC, on or before January 6, 2021, to show support for POTUS and for overturning the election results. The protests/rallies are expected to be similar to the previous Million MAGA March rallies in November and December 2020."

  - Revised assessment indicates that "Stop the Steal has posted a webpage entitled 'wildprotest.com' that includes a map of the Capitol grounds indicating they will be gathering on the Senate Fast Front Grassy Area 9 on January 6, 2021. The webpage states 'We the People must take to the U.S. Capitol lawn and steps . . . [.]' They plan to show support for the Members of Congress who are expected to file objections to the certification of the electoral vote."

  - Revised assessment indicates that a Member of Congress is confirmed as a speaker in the "Stop the Steal" event.

  - Revised assessment indicates that "there have been several social media posts encouraging protesters to be armed."

  - Revised assessment found "no information regarding specific disruptions or acts of civil disobedience targeting this function. Due to the tense political environment following the 2020 election, the threat of disruptive actions or violence cannot be ruled out."

- Deputy Chief Timothy Bowen, Uniformed Services Bureau (USB), directs USB division commanders to bring in ALL available personnel for the joint session and demonstrations on January 6, 2021.

- USCP cancels "Ready Reserve" assignments for January 6, 2021.

THURSDAY, DECEMBER 31, 2020

- USCP Intelligence and Interagency Coordination Division (IICD) holds an internal briefing to review the December 30, 2020 Special Event Assessment with officials at the rank of Captain and above.

DEPARTMENT TIMELINE

SATURDAY, JANUARY 2, 2021

- Carol Corbin (DOD) texts USCP Deputy Chief Sean Gallagher, Protective Service Bureau, to determine whether USCP is considering a request for National Guard soldiers for January 6, 2021 event.

SUNDAY, JANUARY 3, 2021

- USCP Deputy Chief Gallagher replies to DOD via text that a request for National Guard support is not forthcoming at this time after consultation with COP Sund.

- Revised Special Event Assessment for January 6, 2021 event issues to USCP Executive Team and Deputies to both the Senate Sergeant at Arms and House Sergeant at Arms.

    - Revised assessment indicates that approximately six Members expected to speak at demonstration events scheduled on Capitol Grounds.

    - Revised assessment indicates that "some of militia members who are participating in this event and staying in Virginia, plan to march into Washington, DC on January 5th, while armed."

    - Revised assessment indicates "[t]here is also indication that white supremacist groups may be attending the protests."

    - Revised assessment states:

        Due to the tense political environment following the 2020 election, the threat of disruptive actions or violence cannot be ruled out. Supporters of the current president see January 6, 2021, as the last opportunity to overturn the results of the presidential election. This sense of desperation and disappointment may lead to more of an incentive to become violent. Unlike previous post-election protests, the targets of the pro-Trump supporters are not necessarily the counter-protesters as they were previously, but rather Congress itself is the target on the 6th. As outlined above, there has been a worrisome call for protesters to come to these events armed and there is the possibility that protesters may be inclined to become violent. Further, unlike the events on November 14, 2020, and December 12, 2020, there are several more protests scheduled on January 6, 2021, and the majority of them will be on Capitol grounds. The two protests expected to be the largest of the day—the Women for America First protest at the Ellipse and the Stop the Steal protest in Areas 8 and 9—may draw thousands of participants and both have been promoted by President Trump himself. The Stop the Steal protest in particular does not have a permit, but several high profile speakers, including Members of Congress are expected to speak at the event. This combined with Stop the Steal's propensity to attract white supremacists, militia members, and

LAW ENFORCEMENT SENSITIVE

DEPARTMENT TIMELINE

others who actively promote violence, may lead to a significantly dangerous situation for law enforcement and the general public alike.

- USCP increases the size of Dignitary Protection details for Members with four agents to six agents during the week of January 3, 2021.

- USCP extends coverage for Dignitary Protection details to 24/7 coverage.

- USCP posts Dignitary Protection Agents at the residence of certain Congressional Leaders due to open source intelligence.

- USCP mandates that each Dignitary Protection detail include MP7 or M4 assault weapons.

- USCP Investigations Division and IICD extend coverage to 24/7 operations during the week of January 3, 2021.

- USCP embeds an analyst from the National Capitol Region Threat Intelligence Consortium (NTIC) with the IICD analysts during the week of January 3, 2021.

MONDAY, JANUARY 4, 2021

- USCP IICD holds internal briefing to review the January 3, 2021 Special Event Assessment with officials at the rank of Captain and above.

- USCP IICD issues the January 3, 2021 Special Event Assessment to all USCP officials at the rank of Sergeant and above.

- USCP personnel attend multi-agency teleconference hosted by MPD in which agencies brief on intelligence and planning for the January 6, 2021 event.

- COP Sund attends briefing for the January 6, 2021 event with law enforcement partners, including the following agencies:

  o MPD
  o DC National Guard
  o HSAA
  o SSAA
  o Architect of the Capitol
  o USSS (uniformed and non-uniformed)
  o FBI (Washington Field Office and HQ)
  o USPP
  o Metro
  o Amtrak
  o US Army Military District

- COP Sund asks Senate Sergeant at Arms (SSAA) Michael Stenger and House Sergeant at Arms (HSAA) Paul Irving for authority to have National Guard to assist with security for the January

LAW ENFORCEMENT SENSITIVE

DEPARTMENT TIMELINE

6, 2021 event based on briefing with law enforcement partners and revised intelligence assessment.

- COP Sund's request is denied. SSAA and HSAA tells COP Sund to contact General Walker at DC National Guard to discuss the guard's ability to support a request if needed.

- COP Sund notifies General Walker of DC National Guard, indicating that the USCP may need DC National Guard support for the January 6, 2021, but does not have the authority to request at this time.

- General Walker advises COP Sund that in the event of an authorized request, DC National Guard could quickly repurpose 125 troops helping to provide DC with COVID-related assistance. Troops would need to be sworn in as USCP.

- Revised Joint Session Perimeter Plan issues based on request by the SSAA and HSAA to change existing perimeter.

- SSAA notifies USCP that access to the Senate side of the Capitol is to be restricted to Senators and staff with offices in the Capitol.

- USCP issues "USB Operational Posture for the Joint Session of Congress on January 6, 2021," which provides for the following activities beyond routine in-session staffing:

  - Pre-screener officers at each Member/Staff building entrance for House and Senate Office buildings;

  - Increased exterior patrols;

  - West Front is closed for Inaugural preparations;

  - East Front Plaza access is restricted to Members/Staff;

  - Additional Officers posted at the North and South Barricades to facilitate access;

  - Additional Officers posted at the subways to monitor access to the Capitol;

  - House Wing of the building restricted to Members and staff with offices in the Capitol; and

  - 271 officers and officials assigned to CDU platoons.

- USCP personnel investigate threat to fly a plane into the U.S. Capitol to avenge the death of Qasem Soleimani on January 6, 2021.

TUESDAY, JANUARY 5, 2021

- USCP issues new CDU helmets to CDU "Soft" Platoons 1, 3, 4.

LAW ENFORCEMENT SENSITIVE

DEPARTMENT TIMELINE

- USCP IICD begins issuing demonstration updates with information about activity related to the January 6th demonstration that are occurring in the DC Metropolitan area.

- COP Sund holds joint task force briefing to discuss January 6, 2021 event and Inaugural events with police chiefs in the National Capitol Region, the HSAA and SSAA, USSS, FBI, and DC National Guard.

- COP Sund, Assistant Chief Yogananda Pittman, Protective and Intelligence Operations, and Assistant Chief Thomas tour the outer perimeter.

- Final Joint Session Perimeter Plan revised based on feedback from SSAA and HSAA to restrict access to the Capitol Square using bike rack with USCP CDU personnel. HSAA approves the revised plan.

- ACOP Pittman coordinates movement of physical barriers with Security Services Bureau and Architect of the Capitol to conform to new plan.

- COP Sund informs SSAA and HSAA in separate discussions about the DC National Guard ability to provide 125 troops if necessary

- Final CDU Operational Plan for the January 6, 2021 event issues.

    - Final CDU Plan includes seven CDU platoons, including four Hard Platoons, totaling 276 sworn employees.

    - Final CDU Plan includes the use of less lethal munitions by Grenadiers, including the pepper ball launcher systems and FN-303.

    - Final CDU Plan indicates that CDU platoons are scheduled to report at three distinct reporting times; 0800 hours, 1000 hours, and 1200 hours. This ensures CDU coverage from 0800 hours on January 6, 2021, through 0400 hours on January 7, 2021.

    - Final CDU Plan includes deployment of USCP SWAT teams to act as counter-assault ground teams and provide counter-sniper support.

    - Final CDU Plan indicates that counter-sniper teams must monitor for protesters open carrying or concealing firearms.

    - Final CDU Plan indicates that officers will not independently employ force without command authorization unless exigent circumstances justify immediate action.

    - Final CDU Plan indicates that projectiles will not be fired indiscriminately into crowds.

    - Final CDU Plan indicates that "[i]n the event the protest group size exceeds [USCP] capability to obtain compliance, motors and scouts will create a "box" around the mobile protest group and will block approaching traffic to mitigate any vehicle pedestrian collision."

DEPARTMENT TIMELINE

- At approximately 1900 to 2000 hours, USCP task force agent embedded with the FBI emails Intelligence Operations Section a memorandum from the FBI Norfolk office providing additional details regarding the January 6, 2021 event.

- USCP assigns two DPD agents each to the House Floor and the Senate Floor on January 6, 2021. A DPD Sergeant is assigned to manage the agents.

- USCP assigns DPD team of agents and officials to the Ellipse event on January 6, 2021, due to Members attending the event.

WEDNESDAY, JANUARY 6, 2021

WEDNESDAY, JANUARY 6, 2021	
TIME	**EVENT DESCRIPTION**
Approximately 0600 hours	USCP deploys counter surveillance agents to monitor and report back on demonstrators at the Ellipse, at metro stations in the area, and around Capitol and Supreme Court grounds, including numbers, their attire, packages or equipment they are carrying, directions from which they are coming or going, any gathering locations, and any suspicious activity.
	USCP deploys DPD agents to the Ellipse as protection for Members in the event of any threats.
	USCP assigns agents to all emergency evacuation vehicles for Congressional Leadership in the House Garages.
0743 hours	USCP begins releasing demonstration updates related to the January 6, 2021 event..
0823 hours	The Department receives intelligence regarding the radio frequency that some of the demonstrators are using to communicate. The Department intercepts the frequency and assigns an intelligence analyst to monitor the frequency and protester activity.
0845 hours	75 to 100 demonstrators walk up Constitution Avenue near North Barricade.
0926 hours	Approximately 50-60 people on the House Egg.
1000 hours	Metro transit personnel investigates suspicious package at Capitol South Metro. USCP personnel respond to assist.

LAW ENFORCEMENT SENSITIVE

DEPARTMENT TIMELINE

WEDNESDAY, JANUARY 6, 2021	
TIME	**EVENT DESCRIPTION**
1002 hours	Suspicious package at Capitol South Metro is cleared.
1022 hours	USCP demonstration update indicates that unconfirmed count put crowd size at 25-30k at the rally on the Ellipse. Update also indicates that organizers of the Ellipse event planning a march to the Capitol after POTUS speech.
1048 hours	USCP demonstration update indicates that large crowd of protesters gathered on East Front remain peaceful.
1051 hours	One group originally permitted for Senate East Front Grassy Area 9 will no longer be demonstrating.
1058 hours	Demonstration group gathers in the Senate Park on the C Street side of the Russell Senate Office Building. Also steady flow of demonstrators walking along Louisiana and Constitution heading west.
1058 hours	USCP learns that another agency has recovered two firearms from an unattended vehicle in Northwest, DC and reports it over the radio for situational awareness.
1059 hours	Approximately 200 Proud Boys gather near Garfield Circle move toward Senate Egg.
1109 hours	Approximately 400 demonstrators on the East Front stretching from Senate Plaza to House Plaza.
1111 hours	USCP demonstration update indicates that MPD found a vehicle with a rifle and scope in plain view at L'Enfant Plaza.
1114 hours	USCP personnel investigate suspicious package at the Supreme Court of the United States ("SCOTUS"), 100 block of East Capitol Street.
1115 hours	JEMNS alert sent: The USCP is continuing to investigate a Suspicious Package at the Unit Block of Second Street NE. Staff and other personnel are directed to AVOID THIS AREA until further notice.
1124 hours	USCP personnel monitors 3-4 counter demonstrators setting up "props" on 3rd Street and Pennsylvania Southeast.

LAW ENFORCEMENT SENSITIVE

DEPARTMENT TIMELINE

WEDNESDAY, JANUARY 6, 2021	
TIME	**EVENT DESCRIPTION**
1126 hours	USCP investigates a twitter posting indicating that a militia was being formed on Capitol Hill by the Silver Arm Band. Allegedly a man was handed a flyer near the U.S. Capitol that states that a national militia is being organized on Capitol Hill to defend the Constitution and the Republic and that members must wear silver armbands signifying that they are lawful combatants.
1135 hours	Additional demonstrators arrive on the Capitol Square.
1139 hours	JEMNS alert sent: The USCP is continuing to investigate a Suspicious Package at the Unit Block of Second Street NE. Staff and other personnel are directed to AVOID THIS AREA until further notice.
1144 hours	Approximately 100-150 demonstrators walking up Delaware Avenue from Union Station.
1151 hours	USCP demonstration update indicates that MPD is responding to reports of a man with a rifle at 15th & Constitution Avenue NW.
1151 hours	USCP demonstration update indicates that DHS is investigating two handguns found in a vehicle during a security check at 550 12th Street SW.
Approximately 1157 hours	POTUS Trump begins speech at the Ellipse.
1204 hours	USCP clears suspicious package at SCOTUS.
1215 hours	JEMNS alert sent: The USCP has cleared the incident with the Suspicious Package at the Unit Block of Second Street NE.
1229 hours	USCP personnel reports hearing the sound of a Taser at the Senate Egg. USCP personnel advised for situational awareness and officer safety.
1230 hours	Very large group reported as heading to the U.S. Capitol from eastbound on Pennsylvania Avenue at approximately 7th Street.
1233 hours	USCP demonstration update indicates that USPP have detained a person armed with a rifle at 17th Street near the WWII memorial.

LAW ENFORCEMENT SENSITIVE

DEPARTMENT TIMELINE

WEDNESDAY, JANUARY 6, 2021	
TIME	**EVENT DESCRIPTION**
Approximately 1236 hours	USCP personnel and USSS escort VPOTUS Pence into the U.S. Capitol.
1239 hours	JEMNS alert sent: Due to Demonstration Activity, the following road closures are in effect: First Street between Constitution and Louisiana Avenues NW and Constitution Avenue between First and Third Streets NW.
Approximately 1244 hours	USCP personnel investigate explosive device at RNC headquarters.
1245 hours	D.C. police camera captures what looks like a wall of people suddenly arriving about a block west of the Capitol.
1246 hours	USCP personnel shut down Constitution Avenue due to approach of large group of demonstrators.
1248 hours	JEMNS alert sent: The USCP is responding to suspicious package at the 300 Block of First Street SE.
1249 hours	USCP K-9 units sweep Command Post at 1st and D Streets SE and conduct additional sweeps on 1st Street.
1252 hours	USCP deploy additional personnel to begin clearing residences and businesses near RNC Headquarters.
Approximately 1253 hours	Insurrectionists at the front of the large group amassing near the Capitol Reflecting Pool pick up a metal barrier and push it into USCP officers. A crowd begins to press onto the restricted Capitol grounds.
1255 hours	USCP directs all available USCP units to respond to the West Front of the Capitol to assist with breaches along the perimeter. USCP personnel instructed to lock Lower West Terrace door and south side.
1256 hours	USCP directs units to respond to Upper West Terrace area to contain insurrectionists.
1256 hours	USCP personnel evacuate construction workers.
1258 hours	COP Sund asks for and receives assistance from Acting Chief Contee MPD.

LAW ENFORCEMENT SENSITIVE

KASH PRAMOD PATEL

DEPARTMENT TIMELINE

WEDNESDAY, JANUARY 6, 2021	
TIME	**EVENT DESCRIPTION**
1300 hours	USCP personnel advise Metro to have trains bypass Capitol South metro station due to explosive device.
1300 hours	CDU Hard Platoon forms line at Upper West Terrace and less lethal Grenadiers prepare to launch from inauguration stage area.
1301 hours	COP Sund asks for and receives assistance from Chief Thomas Sullivan USSS/UD.
1301 hours	USCP personnel evacuates Madison Building due to explosive device at RNC headquarters.
1303 hours	USCP personnel finds vehicle with explosive chemicals (eleven Molotov cocktails) and a firearm.
1304 hours	COP Sund asks SSAA for declaration of emergency for National Guard support.
1305 hours	Prisoner transport staged on House side plaza.
1306 hours	USCP Grenadiers directed to launch chemical munitions.
Approximately 1306 hours	USCP personnel go door to door to notify residents in the vicinity of the explosive device to evacuate.
1307 hours	USCP personnel investigate explosive device at DNC Headquarters.
1308 hours	USCP personnel deploy OC Spray on Upper West Terrace.
1309 hours	COP Sund asks HSAA for declaration of emergency for National Guard support.
1309 hours	USCP personnel closes the following roadways due to explosive devices at RNC headquarters and 300 block of first street: First Street between C and D Streets SE New Jersey Avenue between Ivy and D Streets SE

LAW ENFORCEMENT SENSITIVE

DEPARTMENT TIMELINE

WEDNESDAY, JANUARY 6, 2021	
TIME	**EVENT DESCRIPTION**
	D Street between New Jersey Avenue and Second Street SE
1309 hours	JEMNS alert set: The USCP is continuing to investigate a Suspicious Package in the 300 Block of First Street SE. Staff and other personnel are directed to AVOID THIS AREA until further notice.
1310 hours	POTUS Trump speech ends.
1310 hours	MPD units respond to South Side Upper West Terrace.[1]
1311 hours	USCP personnel evacuates Cannon Building directing staff to leave underground through the Longworth Building due to explosive devices at RNC and DNC headquarters.
Approximately 1314 hours	USCP personnel raise all south barricades.
Approximately 1314 hours	USCP personnel and USSS evacuate protectee at DNC headquarters.
1315 hours	The following PA/Annunciator message sent: "Evacuate, evacuate, evacuate the Cannon House Office Building immediately due to a suspicious package and internally relocate to the Longworth House Office Building. I repeat evacuate, evacuate, evacuate, the Cannon House Office Building immediately due to a suspicious package and internally relocate to the Longworth House Office Building."
1321 hours	Additional MPD units respond to U.S. Capitol Building.
1322 hours	JEMNS alert sent: The USCP is evacuating the following building due to police activity: Cannon.
1322 hours	COP Sund reiterates request to HSAA for emergency declaration for National Guard support.
1323 hours	USCP personnel arrest two insurrectionists for unlawful conduct at the Upper West Terrace south.

---

[1] Timeline is not a comprehensive account of all LE partners' arrivals or participation.

LAW ENFORCEMENT SENSITIVE

DEPARTMENT TIMELINE

WEDNESDAY, JANUARY 6, 2021	
TIME	**EVENT DESCRIPTION**
1325 hours	USCP personnel arrest an insurrectionist for unlawful conduct at the Upper West Terrace north.
1330 hours	USCP personnel advise DNC security and Fairchild Building security to have occupants shelter in place.
1334 hours	CDU units report to Lower West Terrace.
Approximately 1335 hours	USCP relocates DPD Leadership Limos from the Senate and House side of Capitol Plaza to the Loading Dock and Rayburn Garage respectively.
1339 hours	JEMNS alert sent: The Cannon Building is executing internal relocation due to police activity. All other staff should remain inside their building until further guidance is received from USCP. If you are outside a building on Capitol Hill follow the direction of law enforcement officers. If you are in the Cannon Building, take visitors, escape hoods, and go kits and report to the South Tunnel connecting to the Longworth, further information will be provided as it becomes available.
1340 hours	COP Sund requests and receives confirmation of support from Ashan Benedict, ATF.
1342 hours	Insurrectionists breach Lower West Terrace fence line and scaffolding.
1345 hours	Insurrectionists breach East Plaza fence by the skylights.
1348 hours	JEMNS alert sent: All CLEAR. The evacuation of the Cannon has been cleared, and any associated road closures will clear momentarily.
Approximately 1348 hours	Insurrectionists breach the Upper West Terrace.
1349 hours	COP Sund requests National Guard Support from General Walker. Advises General Walker that a CPB emergency declaration is forthcoming.
1351 hours	COP Sund calls Metropolitan Washington Consortium of Governments to activate LE mutual aid within the National Capitol Region.

LAW ENFORCEMENT SENSITIVE

DEPARTMENT TIMELINE

WEDNESDAY, JANUARY 6, 2021	
TIME	**EVENT DESCRIPTION**
1353 hours	USCP Library Division deploys 12 officers to respond to Upper West Terrace.
1354 hours	Insurrectionists breach the Inauguration Stage and begin tearing things down.
1357 hours	MPD Hard Platoons respond to Lower West Terrace door.
1359 hours	Insurrectionists breach a barrier at the north side of the plaza.
1359 hours	CDU lines form on Senate Steps and Center Steps of East Plaza. Less lethal munitions deployed to Center Steps.
1400 hours	Assistant COP Pittman orders lockdown of U.S. Capitol Building.
1402 hours	JEMNS alert sent: Due to Police Activity, all personnel are advised to relocate from the Cannon House Office Building to the Rayburn and Longworth House Office Buildings through the underground tunnels. Do not evacuate outside the buildings. All personnel should shelter in place in the Rayburn and Longworth House Office Buildings.
1403 hours	COP Sund reiterates to HSAA request for emergency declaration for National Guard support.
1405 hours	The following Annunciator message is sent: Due to an external security threat, no entry or exit is permitted at this time in the U.S. Capitol Building. You may move throughout the buildings but stay away from exterior windows and doors.
1406 hours	Insurrectionists breach Rotunda steps. USCP deploys 10 units with shields up to the Rotunda door to hold the line.
1406 hours	JEMNs alert sent: The USCP is preparing to disrupt a Suspicious package in the 400 Block of Canal Street SE. A loud bang may be heard in the area. There is no cause for alarm, and no action needs to be taken by Congressional Staff.
1408 hours	Insurrectionists breach House Plaza coming from the south side of the U.S. Capitol building.

LAW ENFORCEMENT SENSITIVE

KASH PRAMOD PATEL

DEPARTMENT TIMELINE

WEDNESDAY, JANUARY 6, 2021	
TIME	**EVENT DESCRIPTION**
1408 hours	Assistant Chief Pittman orders Capitol Complex wide lockdown.
1410 hours	CPB issues verbal emergency declaration and gives authority for National Guard deployment.
1410 hours	JEMNS alert sent: Due to an external security threat located on the West Front of the U.S. Capitol building. No entry or exist is permitted at this time. You may move throughout the building(s) but stay away from exterior windows and doors. If you are outside seek cover.
1410 hours	The following PA/Annunciator message is sent: "Due to an external security threat, no entry or exit is permitted at this time in any building of the Capitol Complex. You may move throughout the buildings but stay away from exterior windows and doors."
Approximately 1410 hours	USCP personnel arrest rioter for kicking in a window on the center steps of the east plaza.
1411 hours	USCP personnel and USSS escort VP Pence from Senate Chambers.
Approximately 1415 hours	USCP DPD units evacuate House and Senate Leadership.
1415 hours	Second floor of the Capitol breached. USCP units directed to respond to Senate chambers.
1415 hours	USCP units directed to respond to the Rotunda, Senate side, first level. USCP orders lockdown of House and Senate Chambers.
1417 hours	The following PA/Annunciator message is sent: Security threat, security threat, security threat. Due to a security threat inside the building, immediately seek shelter inside the nearest office. Take visitors and emergency equipment. Lock all doors if able. If shelter is unavailable, seek cover or concealment. Remain quiet and await further direction.
1418 hours	JEMNS alert sent: Capitol Staff. Due to a security threat inside the building, immediately: move inside your office or the nearest office. Take emergency equipment and visitors. Close, lock, and stay away from external doors and windows. If you are in a public space, find a place to hide or seek cover.

Review of the Events Surrounding the January 6, 2021, Takeover of the U.S. Capitol   *2021-I-0003-A, February 2021*

LAW ENFORCEMENT SENSITIVE

248

DEPARTMENT TIMELINE

WEDNESDAY, JANUARY 6, 2021	
TIME	**EVENT DESCRIPTION**
	Remain quiet and silence electronics. Once you are in a safe location, immediately check in with your OEC. No one will be permitted to enter or exit the building until directed by USCP. If you are in a building outside of the affected area, remain clear of the police activity, await further direction.
1418 hours	USCP personnel barricade Senate Chamber.
1419 hours	Approximately 200 insurrectionists breach Rotunda. USCP Hard Platoon deployed to Rotunda.
1420 hours	Insurrectionists breach Senate door and north side door of the Upper West Terrace.
1422 hours	CDU Platoons 1 through 3 deployed to House side of U.S. Capitol; CDU Platoons 4, 6, 7, and 8 deployed to Rotunda.
1424 hours	JEMNS alert sent: The USCP is preparing to disrupt a Suspicious Package in the 300 Block of First Street SE. A loud bank may be heard in the area. There is no cause for alarm, and no action needs to be taken by Congressional Staff.
Approximately 1426 hours	COP Sund urgently request National Guard support during teleconference with Christopher Rodriguez, DC Homeland Security; Chief Contee, MPD; General Walker, DC National Guard; Muriel Bowser, DC Mayor; Lieutenant General Walter E. Piatt, Army Staff Secretary. COP Sund is advised by the Army Staff Secretary that "we don't like the optics of the National Guard standing a line at the Capitol" and that his recommendation to the Secretary of the Army will be not to support the request.
1428 hours	Remaining Members evacuated from Senate floor.
1430 hours	Per DC National Guard's request USCP drafts a formal written request to Department of Defense for National Guard support.
1432 hours	USCP personnel deployed to extract Members in office.[2]
1434 hours	Upper West Terrace breached.

---

[2] Timeline is not a comprehensive account of all Member or staff extractions.

LAW ENFORCEMENT SENSITIVE

KASH PRAMOD PATEL

Page 18 of 24

DEPARTMENT TIMELINE

WEDNESDAY, JANUARY 6, 2021	
TIME	**EVENT DESCRIPTION**
1437 hours	Corridor to House Chamber breached.
1439 hours	USCP personnel begin evacuating Members inside the House Chamber.
1440 hours	FBI personnel investigate an explosive device in the 600 Block of Independence Avenue.
1443 hours	USCP personnel shoots insurrectionist attempting to breach area outside of House Floor.
1444 hours	Assistant COP Pittman orders USCP SWAT team to respond to House Floor.
1444 hours	Officers barricade in third floor gallery of House floor with 12 to 15 members and staff ordered to shelter in place.
Approximately 1445 Hours	USCP Inspector meets with evacuated Congressional Leadership at alternate site to brief them on the situation.
1450 hours	Senate Chamber breached.
1450 hours	USCP SWAT team deployed to extract Members in offices.
1451 hours	USCP SWAT team holds insurrectionists at gun point at the House Chamber door.
Approximately 1451 hours	USCP personnel and LE partners deployed to extract Members and staff from offices.
1457 hours	USCP personnel arrest a rioter in possession of two knives.
1457 hours	Evacuation of Members on House Floor completed.
1457 hours	USCP personnel extract Members in offices.
1504 hours	USCP deploys additional CDU Hard Platoon to Rotunda.
1507 hours	Approximately 20 ATF and FBI personnel arrive at speaker's lobby.
1509 hours	Montgomery County PD through checkpoint 7 heading to North Barricade.

Page 18 of 24

33

Review of the Events Surrounding the January 6, 2021, Takeover of the U.S. Capitol   *2021-I-0003-A, February 2021*

LAW ENFORCEMENT SENSITIVE

GOVERNMENT GANGSTERS

DEPARTMENT TIMELINE

WEDNESDAY, JANUARY 6, 2021	
TIME	**EVENT DESCRIPTION**
1518 hours	USCP personnel extract Member and staff from office.
1526 hours	USCP deploys K9 unit for sweep at New Jersey and Independence Avenue to assist DC Fire.
Approximately 1532 hours	USCP and LE partners clear Senate Floor, second floor, Rotunda, and South Wing of the first floor of unauthorized persons.
Approximately 1532 hours	A Hard Platoon of about 40 DHS officers deployed.
1533 hours	Explosive device at RNC headquarters is cleared.
1541 hours	JEMNS alert sent: Capitol Staff: Due to a security threat inside the building, immediately: move inside your office or the nearest office. Take emergency equipment and visitors. Close, lock and stay away from external doors and windows. If you are in a public space, find a place to hide or seek cover. Remain quiet and silence electronics. Once you are in a safe location, immediately check in with your OEC.
1543 hours	USCP personnel extract Members from office.
1547 hours	USCP personnel clear Rotunda and secure broken Rotunda door.
1551 hours	Armed squad of Arlington County Police arrive and deploy to Lower West Terrace.
1554 hours	USCP personnel extract staff who called for assistance.
1559 hours	USCP personnel arrest an insurrectionist near the Hart loading dock.
Approximately 1601 hours	USCP personnel extract staff from office.
1607 hours	USCP personnel extract staff from office.
Approximately 1608 hours	Fairfax Police Department and Virginia State Troopers arrive.

Review of the Events Surrounding the January 6, 2021, Takeover of the U.S. Capitol   *2021-I-0003-A, February 2021*

LAW ENFORCEMENT SENSITIVE

DEPARTMENT TIMELINE

WEDNESDAY, JANUARY 6, 2021	
TIME	**EVENT DESCRIPTION**
1609 hours	JEMNS alert sent: All buildings within the Capitol Complex Staff. Due to a security threat inside the building, immediately: move inside your office or the nearest office. Take emergency equipment and visitors. Close, lock and stay away from external doors and windows. If you are in a public space, find a place to hide or seek cover. Remain quiet and silence electronics. Once you are in a safe location, immediately check in with your OEC.
Approximately 1611 hours	SSAA requests USCP extraction team respond to Senate offices in the U.S. Capitol.
Approximately 1613 hours	USCP arrests insurrectionists who jumped through a window in the hallway.
1615 hours	COP Sund teleconference with VPOTUS Pence.
Approximately 1615 hours	USCP personnel extract Member from Lincoln room.
Approximately 1619 hours	Senate Chambers cleared.
1621 hours	JEMNS alert sent: The USCP has cleared the incident with the Suspicious Package in the 400 Block of Canal Street SE.
1628 hours	USCP confirms basement, subways, first floor, and crypt of both wings secure. Also officers reinforcing every access point to include the windows that were shattered. Further second floor, Rotunda, and wings are clear. House chamber is secure.
1628 hours	USCP personnel extract staff barricaded in Senate offices.
1636 hours	Suspicious package at DNC cleared.
1645 hours	USCP personnel deploy munitions at Rotunda door where insurrectionists pushing in doors and breaking windows.
Approximately 1648 hours	USCP personnel and LE partners move insurrectionists off the West Front Terrace.

DEPARTMENT TIMELINE

WEDNESDAY, JANUARY 6, 2021	
TIME	**EVENT DESCRIPTION**
1648 hours	USCP deploys chemical munitions on Lower West Terrace to disperse insurrectionists.
1652 hours	USCP arrests two insurrectionists in the Rotunda.
1709 hours	USCP personnel extract staff barricaded in Senate offices.
Approximately 1720 hours	USCP deploys K-9 teams to sweep House and Senate Chambers.
Approximately 1720 hours	USCP arrests one insurrectionist at the staff wing, north side, west front stairs and one insurrectionist north stairs.
1730 hours	USCP and LE partners clear media tower on the West Front.
1736 hours	USCP and LE partners clear West Front, Lower West Terrace and the House and Senate Steps of all unauthorized occupants.
1736 hours	COP Sund meets with VPOTUS Pence and teleconference with House Speaker Nancy Pelosi to brief them on the security posture. Advised that the building could be safely re-occupied by 1930 hours.
Approximately 1738 hours	USCP and LE partners push invaders away from the U.S. Capitol building on the West Front.
1745 hours	PA announcement internal and external: There is a curfew in effect at 1800 hours until 0600 hours tomorrow. All individuals are required to leave Capitol Hill or be subject to arrest.
1746 hours	USCP deploys HDS to sweep Senate floor.
1747 hours	Seven National Guard buses headed to north barricade.
1750 hours	USCP and LE partners push insurrectionists off West Front grassy areas to First Street.
1752 hours	USCP and LE partners push insurrectionists off of East Front Plaza.
1756 hours	Fifteen Airport Police Officers arrive and deployed to center deck.

LAW ENFORCEMENT SENSITIVE

DEPARTMENT TIMELINE

WEDNESDAY, JANUARY 6, 2021	
TIME	**EVENT DESCRIPTION**
1801 hours	USCP and LE Partners sweep East Plaza. Confirm clear.
1806 hours	USCP investigates suspicious package at First Street from Constitution Avenue to East Capitol.
Approximately 1807 hours	USCP personnel extract Member and staff.
1813 hours	USCP clears suspicious package at First Street and Constitution Avenue.
Approximately 1825 hours	USCP, National Guard, and LE partners move insurrectionists back to Third Street.
Approximately 1825 hours	COP Sund briefs Senators Schumer and McConnell, and Representative Clyburn over the telephone on the current security posture of the Capitol and the ability of the House and Senate to reconvene in their respective Chambers.
1826 hours	USCP personnel and LE partners confirm that area around the southeast drive has been swept with negative results.
1834 hours	USCP personnel and LE partners confirm that House Chamber is swept, cleared, and negative results in the gallery.
Approximately 1837 hours	USCP and LE partners sweep East Front completed at 1936 hours.
1838 hours	USCP confirms that Senate Floor and Galleries have been swept and are hazard free.
1844 hours	JEMNS alert sent: All buildings within the Capitol Complex staff: Due to a security threat inside the building, immediately: move inside your office or the nearest office. Take emergency equipment and visitors. Close, lock and stay away from external doors and windows. If you are in a public space, find a place to hide or seek cover. Remain quiet and silence electronics. Once you are in a safe location, immediately check in with your OEC.

DEPARTMENT TIMELINE

WEDNESDAY, JANUARY 6, 2021	
TIME	**EVENT DESCRIPTION**
1920 hours	USCP and LE partners sweep Third and Fourth Floor of Senate Chambers and confirm clear.
1924 hours	JEMNS alert sent: All buildings within the Capitol Complex staff: Update police activity related to the report of an internal security threat is ongoing. While we encourage Members and staff to remain in the buildings, if anyone must leave: House Personnel: The Longworth South Capitol Door is open for departure only. Senate Personnel: The Northwest Door of the Dirksen is open for departure only.
1925 hours	USCP personnel arrest insurrectionists.
1931 hours	USCP and LE partners sweep Speakers Office.
1936 hours	USCP and LE partners sweep West Front of the Capitol, including Upper West Terrace, West Terrace Areas, outward to First Street, Independence and Constitution.
1938 hours	USCP and LE partners complete sweep of House 2nd Floor and confirm all clear except for broken window.
1940 hours	USCP personnel arrest an insurrectionist at Inaugural Stage.
1945 hours	USCP personnel investigate suspicious package at Lower West Terrace doors.
1957 hours	USCP clear suspicious package.
2005 hours	USCP personnel investigate suspicious package at Peace Circle reflecting pool.
2012 hours	USCP clear suspicious package.
2031 hours	USCP and LE partners complete sweep of entire Capitol Square, including the Inaugural Stage, and the entire West Front and confirm it is clear.

LAW ENFORCEMENT SENSITIVE

DEPARTMENT TIMELINE

WEDNESDAY, JANUARY 6, 2021	
TIME	**EVENT DESCRIPTION**
2115 hours	JEMNS alert sent: Police activity related to the report of an internal security threat is ongoing. While we encourage Members and staff to remain in the buildings, if anyone must leave: Senate Personnel: The Northwest door of the Dirksen is open for departure only. Additionally, the Hart Senate Office Building is now open for egress only.

Source: USCP Office of General Counsel.

Review of the Events Surrounding the January 6, 2021, Takeover of the U.S. Capitol   *2021-I-0003-A, February 2021*

LAW ENFORCEMENT SENSITIVE

LETTER FROM DC MAYOR MURIEL BOWSER DECLINING NATIONAL GUARD ASSISTANCE

MURIEL BOWSER
MAYOR

January 5, 2021

The Honorable Jeffery Rosen
Acting United States Attorney General
950 Pennsylvania Ave, NW
Washington, DC 20530

The Honorable Ryan D. McCarthy
Secretary of the Army
101 Army Pentagon
Washington, DC 20310

The Honorable Chris Miller
Acting Secretary of Defense
1000 Defense Pentagon
Washington, DC 20301

Dear Acting Attorney General Rosen, Secretary McCarthy, and Acting Secretary Miller:

As the law enforcement agency charged with protecting residents and visitors throughout the District of Columbia, the Metropolitan Police Department (MPD) is prepared for this week's First Amendment activities. MPD has coordinated with its federal partners, namely the US Park Police, US Capitol Police and the US Secret Service   all of whom regularly have uniformed personnel protecting federal assets in the District of Columbia. This week, MPD has additional logistical support of unarmed members of the DC National Guard, who will work under the direction of, and in coordination with, MPD.

The District of Columbia Government has not requested personnel from any other federal law enforcement agencies. To avoid confusion, we ask that any request for additional assistance be coordinated using the same process and procedures.

We are mindful that in 2020, MPD was expected to perform the demanding tasks of policing large crowds while working around unidentifiable personnel deployed in the District of Columbia without proper coordination. Unidentifiable personnel   in many cases, armed   caused confusion among residents and visitors and could become a national security threat with no way for MPD and federal law enforcement to decipher armed groups.

To be clear, the District of Columbia is not requesting other federal law enforcement personnel and discourages any additional deployment without immediate notification to, and consultation with, MPD if such plans are underway. The protection of persons and property is our utmost concern and responsibility. MPD is well trained and prepared to lead the law enforcement, coordination and response to allow for the peaceful demonstration of First Amendment rights in the District of Columbia.

Sincerely,

Muriel Bowser
Mayor

Cc: Congresswoman Eleanor Holmes Norton

Document ID: 0.7.4100.19843 000001

20210609 0012754

HCOR-Jan6-07222021-000596

BIDEN ADMINISTRATION INSPECTOR GENERAL REPORT ON JANUARY 6TH

20210115-069052-CASE-01   CUI

REVIEW OF THE DEPARTMENT OF DEFENSE'S
ROLE, RESPONSIBILITIES, AND ACTIONS TO PREPARE FOR AND
RESPOND TO THE PROTEST AND ITS AFTERMATH AT THE
U.S. CAPITOL CAMPUS ON JANUARY 6, 2021

I. INTRODUCTION

This report presents the results of the DoD Office of Inspector General (OIG) review of the DoD's role, responsibilities, and actions to prepare for and respond to the protest and its aftermath at the U.S. Capitol Campus on January 6, 2021.[1]

The DoD Acting Inspector General initiated this review on January 15, 2021. Our review evaluated requests for DoD support before January 6, 2021, how the DoD responded to such requests, the requests for support the DoD received as the events unfolded on January 6, 2021, and how the DoD responded to the protests and rioting at the U.S. Capitol Campus. We evaluated whether the DoD's actions were appropriate and supported by requirements. We also examined whether the DoD complied with applicable laws, regulations, and other guidance in its response to requests for assistance.

To conduct the review, we assembled a multidisciplinary team of DoD OIG administrative and criminal investigators, evaluators, auditors, and attorneys. We examined approximately 24.6 gigabytes of e-mails and documents, including letters, memorandums, agreements, plans, orders, reports, briefings, calendars, statements witnesses made in congressional hearings, and comments witnesses made to journalists as reported in media articles and network news broadcasts. We examined records from the offices of the Secretary of Defense (SecDef); the DoD General Counsel; the Chairman of the Joint Chiefs of Staff (JCS); the Secretary of the Army (SecArmy); the Chief, National Guard Bureau (NGB); and the District of Columbia National Guard (DCNG). We also reviewed records provided to us by the Office of the Mayor, Washington, D.C.; the Office of the District of Columbia Homeland Security and Emergency Management Agency (DCHSEMA); the Department of the Interior (DoI); the U.S. Capitol Police (USCP) OIG; and the Federal Bureau of Investigation (FBI). Finally, we reviewed official e-mails, telephone records, call logs, and records from other means of communication, such as text messages, that DoD officials used before and on January 6, 2021.

We interviewed 44 witnesses, including:

- Mr. Christopher C. Miller, former Acting SecDef;

- Mr. Ryan C. McCarthy, former SecArmy;

- Mr. Kenneth Rapuano, former Assistant Secretary of Defense for Homeland Defense and Global Security (ASD[HD&GS]);

- Mr. Robert Salesses, former Deputy Assistant Secretary of Defense for Homeland Defense Integration and Defense Support of Civil Authorities (DASD[HD & DSCA])

---

[1] The U.S. Capitol Campus is a large area within Washington, D.C., that consists of the U.S. Capitol building and visitor center, principal congressional office buildings, Library of Congress buildings, Supreme Court buildings, U.S. Botanic Garden and over 270 acres of grounds.

CUI

- General (GEN) Mark Milley, Chairman, JCS;

- GEN James McConville, Chief of Staff, U.S. Army;

- GEN Daniel Hokanson, Chief, NGB;

- Lieutenant General (LTG) Walter Piatt, Director of the Army Staff;

- Then-LTG Charles Flynn, Deputy Chief of Staff for Operations, Plans, and Training/G-3/5/7, Headquarters, Department of the Army (HQDA);[2]

- Major General (MG) William Walker, Commanding General, DCNG;[3]

- Ms. Muriel Bowser, Mayor, Washington, D.C.;

- Dr. Christopher Rodriguez, Director, DCHSEMA;

- Acting Chief of Police Robert Contee, D.C. Metropolitan Police Department (MPD);[4]

- Mr. Steven Sund, former Chief of Police, USCP; and

- DoD personnel involved in planning and executing the DCNG's response to requests for assistance at the U.S. Capitol Building.[5]

We also reviewed classified material as part of our review; however, this report does not contain any classified information.

Although we conducted an independent review of the actions of the DoD's Components and personnel, we also held interagency meetings with the OIGs from the Department of Justice (DoJ), Department of Homeland Security (DHS), and DoI to identify and address potentially overlapping facts and timelines applicable to each OIG's independent reviews of the January 6, 2021 events.

We divided our report into six sections.

Section I is an introduction to this report.

Section II provides an overview of our findings, conclusions, and recommendations.

Section III, "Defense Support of Civil Authorities," provides an overview of the DoD's mission, the DCNG's mission, and the support that DCNG provides to civil authorities.

---

[2] LTG Flynn received a promotion to General and subsequently assumed command of U.S. Army Pacific on June 4, 2021. We address him as LTG Flynn throughout this report.
[3] MG Walker served as the Commanding General, District of Columbia Army and Air National Guard, from January 2017 through March 2021. On March 5, 2021, MG Walker was selected as the new Sergeant at Arms of the U.S. House of Representatives. He subsequently retired from military service and was sworn in as the 38th Sergeant at Arms of the U.S. House of Representatives on April 26, 2021. We address him as MG Walker throughout this report.
[4] Mr. Contee became the MPD Chief on May 4, 2021.
[5] Hereafter we refer to the U.S. Capitol Building in this report as the Capitol.

Section IV, "Significant Events Leading Up to January 6, 2021," provides an overview of the relevant events leading up to January 6, 2021, and includes information about protests, riots, and other events in D.C. from June through December 2020, and the DoD's review and approval of the D.C. Government's request for assistance (RFA) from the DCNG. We also provide our conclusions regarding DoD actions during this period.[6]

Section V, "DoD's Actions on and After January 6, 2021," provides details of the events on January 6, 2021. It includes information about the DCNG's mission and activities, DoD coordination with D.C. and Federal officials, receipt and approval of the USCP's RFA, DoD planning for the DCNG's new mission, the DoD's response to the events at the Capitol, and plans for the DCNG and National Guard (NG) forces from several states to help secure the Capitol in the immediate aftermath of January 6, 2021. We also provide our conclusions regarding DoD actions during this period.

Section VI, "DoD OIG Review Observations and Recommendations," details our observations regarding the DoD's response time to the Capitol on January 6, 2021. Additionally, we make recommendations that the SecDef and SecArmy should consider improving the DoD's Defense Support of Civil Authorities (DSCA) operations, policies, and procedures.

We provided a copy of our preliminary report to the Deputy SecDef, the DoD General Counsel, and The Inspector General of the Army for review on October 29, 2021. We asked them to review our preliminary report and identify any information they believed should be exempt from public release under the Freedom of Information Act, section 552, title 5, United States Code. We also asked them to identify any information they believed was factually incorrect and provide documentation to support their assessment for our review. We also provided excerpts from our preliminary report to the OIGs from the DOJ, DHS, and DOI, and asked each to review for exemptions from public release and to identify any potential factual errors. We received responses from all entities that reviewed our preliminary report and, where we deemed appropriate, modified our final report.

II. OVERVIEW OF THE DOD OIG REVIEW

A. EVENTS LEADING UP TO JANUARY 6, 2021

The United States held a presidential election on November 3, 2020. As individual states tallied and reported their election results to Congress, the President of the United States asserted that the election results were fraudulent.

The President announced via Twitter on December 19, 2020, that there would be a large protest on January 6, 2021, in Washington, D.C. He also alleged election fraud. He followed with a tweet on December 27, 2020, about the planned large gathering on January 6, 2021, to protest Congress certifying the Electoral College vote results at the Capitol.[7]

Twelve days later, on Thursday, December 31, 2020, Mayor Bowser sent a letter to MG Walker, requesting DCNG support in the District of Columbia for January 5 through 6, 2021. Mayor Bowser wrote in her letter that DCNG personnel would support both the MPD and the Fire and Emergency Medical Services (DCFEMS). In addition, she wrote, "[N]o DCNG personnel shall be

---

[6] We based our conclusions on a preponderance of the evidence, consistent with our normal process in administrative investigations.
[7] A description of the electoral process is at https://www.usa.gov/election. A description of the Electoral College is at https://www.archives.gov/electoral-college.

armed during this mission, and at no time, will DCNG personnel or assets be engaged in domestic surveillance, searches, or seizures of [U.S.] persons." She also stated that the Director, DCHSEMA, would send an RFA to MG Walker providing detailed requirements for the request.

The DCHSEMA Director sent an RFA to MG Walker on December 31, 2020, requesting DCNG personnel to support D.C. authorities from 7:30 a.m., Tuesday, January 5, 2021, through midnight, Wednesday, January 6, 2021.[8] The DCHSEMA Director wrote that the DCNG's primary mission would be "crowd management and assistance with blocking vehicles at traffic posts [traffic control points or TCPs]." The DCHSEMA Director specifically requested six DCNG crowd management teams at identified Metro transit stations to prevent overcrowded platforms and teams to help staff 30 designated TCPs.

MG Walker forwarded the D.C. RFA to Mr. McCarthy on Friday, January 1, 2021, and recommended that Mr. McCarthy approve supporting the request. Mr. Miller told us that he learned of the D.C. RFA on January 1, 2021. During the following weekend, Army Staff members coordinated the response to D.C. officials with staff members assigned to the Office of the Assistant Secretary of Defense for Homeland Defense and Global Security (OASD[HD&GS]) and the DoD Office of General Counsel (OGC). OASD(HD&GS) staff members also telephoned and texted their points of contact at the U.S. Secret Service (USSS), U.S. Marshals Service (USMS), U.S. Park Police (USPP), DHS, and USCP to determine if any of these Federal civilian law enforcement agencies intended to request DoD support for January 6, 2021. All of these agencies responded that they did not anticipate needing DoD assistance.

Mr. Miller and Mr. McCarthy attended a number of meetings from Saturday, January 2, 2021, through Monday, January 4, 2021, within the DoD and with the DoJ, the DHS, and the DoI. The DoD held these meetings to discuss approval of the D.C. RFA, the potential for civil disturbances on January 6, 2021, and conditions for deployment of DCNG personnel. During these interagency and interdepartmental meetings, Mr. Miller sought to ensure that civilian agencies had no additional support requirements for the DoD, and that the DoJ would be designated as the lead Federal agency if circumstances developed to necessitate a Federal response to potential civil disturbances. During a January 4, 2021 meeting, Acting Attorney General (AG) Jeffrey Rosen orally concurred with the DoD's plan for fulfilling the D.C. RFA. Mr. McCarthy wrote in a January 4, 2021 letter to Mr. Miller that he intended to approve the D.C. RFA if a lead Federal agency was designated and if the anticipated size of the demonstrations exceeded the capability of civilian law enforcement agencies.[9]

Following a January 4, 2021 meeting with Mr. McCarthy, Mr. Miller signed a memorandum that authorized Mr. McCarthy to approve the D.C. RFA, subject to consultation with Mr. Rosen and additional guidance. Mr. Miller specifically withheld the authority from Mr. McCarthy to approve riot control equipment or tactics; use military Intelligence, Surveillance, and Reconnaissance (ISR) assets; share equipment with law enforcement agencies; and seek support from non-DCNG units. Finally, Mr. Miller authorized Mr. McCarthy to employ a standby Quick Reaction Force (QRF) only as a last resort in response to a request from an appropriate civil authority.[10] He directed Mr. McCarthy to notify him immediately if Mr. McCarthy employed the QRF.[11]

---

[8] Copies of the DCHSEMA Director's RFA and Mayor Bowser's letters are in Appendix C. In this report, we refer to the DCHSEMA Director's RFA and the Mayor's letter as the "D.C. RFA."
[9] See Appendix C for a copy of Mr. McCarthy's letter.
[10] A Quick Reaction Force (QRF) is any force that is poised to respond on very short notice.
[11] See Appendix C for a copy of Mr. Miller's memorandum.

On the evening of January 4, 2021, Mr. McCarthy discussed the DoD's mission and Mr. Miller's employment guidance with MG Walker. Later that evening, an Army Staff member, on behalf of Mr. McCarthy, sent a letter to the DoJ to request Mr. Rosen's written concurrence with the DoD's plan to fulfill the D.C. RFA.

Mr. McCarthy sent a letter to MG Walker on January 5, 2021, that authorized MG Walker to support the D.C. RFA with 340 DCNG personnel for traffic and crowd control activities at 30 TCPs and 6 Metro stations; chemical, biological, radiological, and nuclear (CBRN) monitoring and hazardous material on-site support; and a 40-person QRF stationed at Joint Base Andrews (JBA), Maryland. The letter prohibited performing other tasks and duties or employing the QRF without Mr. McCarthy's approval.[12]

The DCNG executed its approved mission as directed on the morning of January 5, 2021. Additionally, on January 5, 2021, Mayor Bowser sent a letter to both the DoD and DoJ advising that no other Federal law enforcement support personnel were required and discouraged the deployment of any additional Federal law enforcement personnel without first consulting with MPD leadership.[13]

No major incidents of rioting or other violence occurred on January 5 or during the morning of January 6, 2021.

B. EVENTS ON JANUARY 6, 2021

At about 11:00 a.m. on Wednesday, January 6, the President and other speakers addressed a large group of protesters assembled on The Ellipse, near the White House. At this time, ▮▮ DCNG soldiers were on duty at TCPs and Metro stations in downtown Washington, D.C., with another ▮▮ off duty and expected to report to the DCNG Armory during the afternoon to relieve troops on duty and cover TCPs and Metro stations during the evening. The 40-person DCNG QRF was stationed at JBA. The QRF was outfitted with riot control equipment, and the soldiers at TCPs and Metro stations had riot control equipment stored in their vehicles. ▮▮ DCNG soldiers were carrying out CBRN monitoring and hazardous material on-site support, and ▮ DCNG personnel were at the Armory providing command and control and other support.

Shortly before 1:00 p.m. on January 6, 2021, as the President concluded his speech, a large crowd left The Ellipse and began marching towards the Capitol. As this group reached the area of the U.S. Capitol Campus, an undetermined number of individuals forced their way past barricades, some attacking law enforcement personnel, and into the Capitol as Members of Congress were meeting to certify the Electoral College vote count.[14] Beginning at 1:49 p.m. and throughout the afternoon of January 6, 2021, the DoD and the DCNG received numerous calls from various Federal and D.C. government officials requesting support and immediate assistance.

At 2:20 p.m., a conference call between Army Staff members, civilian officials from the D.C. government, and the USCP was initiated during which Mr. Sund requested NG support at the Capitol. Mr. McCarthy relayed the request to Mr. Miller, who approved mobilization of the DCNG at 3:04 p.m. The DCNG moved the QRF from JBA to the DCNG Armory, arriving at approximately 3:15 p.m. The ▮▮ DCNG soldiers on duty at TCPs and Metro stations remained at their posts

---

[12] See Appendix C for a copy of Mr. McCarthy's letter.
[13] See Appendix C for a copy of Mayor Bowser's letter.
[14] These actions are under criminal investigation by the DoJ-FBI and were not within the scope of our review.

without other direction. At 3:48 p.m., after contacting congressional leaders and media personnel to rebut false media reports that the DoD denied Mr. Sund's request for support, Mr. McCarthy left the Pentagon for MPD headquarters to coordinate the DCNG response to the Capitol events.

After Mr. McCarthy arrived at MPD headquarters, he worked with D.C. government officials to develop a plan to re-mission and deploy the DCNG to support the USCP at the Capitol. Mr. McCarthy then called Mr. Miller at about 4:32 p.m., and Mr. Miller immediately approved the re-mission plan and authorized Mr. McCarthy and MG Walker to deploy the DCNG to the Capitol.

The soldiers on duty at TCPs and Metro stations returned to the Armory at approximately 5:00 p.m. as directed by the DCNG Joint Task Force commander and did not participate in the response to the Capitol events. The QRF, now supplemented with Soldiers reporting to duty for the evening shift at TCPs and Metro stations and other personnel on duty at the Armory, left the Armory at 5:15 p.m. for USCP headquarters to be sworn in as "special policemen" by USCP personnel. The response force then moved to the Capitol, arriving at 5:55 p.m., and joined civilian law enforcement personnel in reinforcing the perimeter and clearing the Capitol grounds.

The events at the Capitol led to questions from Members of Congress about the adequacy and timeliness of the DoD's response to requests for assistance and DCNG's deployment to the Capitol.

C. FINDINGS AND CONCLUSIONS

Conclusions on DoD Actions Before January 6, 2021

We concluded that the actions the DoD took before January 6, 2021, to prepare for the planned protests in Washington, D.C., on January 5 and 6, 2021, were appropriate, supported by requirements, consistent with the DoD's roles and responsibilities for DSCA, and compliant with laws, regulations, and other applicable guidance.

We also examined the actions the DoD took before January 6, 2021, that were independent of the D.C. RFA. We looked for a role or responsibility for the DoD to act preemptively to prevent or deter what later happened at the Capitol. We found none. On the contrary, we found restrictions that limited the DoD's roles and responsibilities in planning and providing support for domestic civil disturbance operations (CDO). These restrictions, set forth in statutes and implementing DoD directives, do not limit what civil authorities can request, but rather mandate what support DoD can provide to civilian authorities by setting strict limits.

Conclusions on DoD Actions On January 6, 2021

We concluded that the DoD's actions to respond to the USCP's RFA on January 6, 2021, were appropriate, supported by requirements, consistent with the DoD's roles and responsibilities for DSCA, and compliant with laws, regulations, and other applicable guidance. In particular, we determined that the decisions made by Mr. Miller, Mr. McCarthy, and other senior DoD officials, and actions taken by the DoD in response to the civil disturbance at the U.S. Capitol Campus on January 6, 2021, were reasonable in light of the circumstances that existed on that day and requests from D.C. officials and the USCP.

We also determined that DoD officials did not delay or obstruct the DoD's response to the USCP RFA on January 6, 2021.

D. DOD OIG REVIEW OBSERVATIONS AND RECOMMENDATIONS

Although we reached the previous conclusions, we made several observations and recommendations about how the DoD could improve its command structure, command and control architecture, communications systems, planning, and training during future DSCA missions within D.C. We detail our observations and recommendations in Section VI of this report.

ENDNOTES

1. Dwight D. Eisenhower. 1961. "Military-Industrial Complex Speech." Transcript of speech delivered January 17, 1961. https://avalon.law.yale.edu/20th_century/eisenhower001.asp.

2. Pete Williams, "Former Trump adviser Steve Bannon indicted by federal grand jury for contempt of Congress," NBC News, November 12, 2021, https://www.nbcnews.com/politics/justice-department/former-trump-adviser-steve-bannon-indicted-federal-grand-jury-contempt-n1283834.

3. Sam Dorman, "Parents respond to DOJ, school boards' statements: 'I am what a domestic terrorist looks like?,'" Fox News, October 5, 2021, https://www.foxnews.com/politics/parents-respond-doj-nsba-domestic-terrorist.

4. Natasha Bertrand, "Hunter Biden story is Russian disinfo, dozens of former intel officials say," Politico, October 19, 2020, https://www.politico.com/news/2020/10/19/hunter-biden-story-russian-disinfo-430276.

5. Alec Schemmel, "Jury foreperson claims Sussmann case was waste of time following not guilty verdict," KATV, June 1, 2022, https://katv.com/news/nation-world/jury-foreperson-claims-sussmann-case-was-waste-of-time-following-not-guilty-verdict.

6. Ryan Sit, "Here's What The FBI Had On Martin Luther King Jr.," Newsweek, January 15, 2018, https://www.newsweek.com/fbi-martin-luther-king-jr-surveillence-wiretap-report-j-edgar-hoover-780630.

7. Ken Bensinger, Miriam Elder, and Mark Schoofs, "These Reports Allege Trump Has Deep Ties To Russia," BuzzFeed News, January 10, 2017, https://www.buzzfeednews.com/article/kenbensinger/these-reports-allege-trump-has-deep-ties-to-russia#.anbQXnwz8.

8. Erik Wemple, "David Corn and the Steele dossier: Just checking the facts!" *Washington Post*, January 10, 2020, https://www.washingtonpost.com/opinions/2020/01/10/david-corn-steele-dossier-just-checking-facts/.

9. HPSCI Staff to Devin Nunes, "Nunes Memo," January 2, 2018, 5.

10. James Clapper, "Clapper: Steele dossier not part of assessment." CNN, January 3, 2018, https://www.cnn.com/videos/politics/2018/01/03/steele-dossier-not-a-factor-russia-intel-assessment-clapper-ac.cnn.

11. Brooke Singman, "FBI's Strzok allegedly dismissed Mueller probe: 'no big there there'," Fox News, January 23, 2018, https://www.foxnews.com/politics/fbis-strzok-allegedly-dismissed-mueller-probe-no-big-there-there.

12. U.S. Department of Justice, report from David Hardy to William Marshall, March 17, 2020. https://www.judicialwatch.org/wp-content/uploads/2020/05/JW-v-DOJ-reply-02743.pdf.

13 52. *Voting and Elections, U.S. Code 52* (2002), § 30121. https://uscode.house.gov/view.xhtml?req=(title:52+section:30121+edition:prelim).

14 Chuck Ross, "FBI Informant Bragged About Links To Russian Spies In Secret Recording Of Trump Aide," Daily Caller, April 19, 2020, https://dailycaller.com/2020/04/19/stefan-halper-papadopoulos-fbi-russian-trubnikov-crossfire-hurricane/.

15 Rosalind Helderman and Carol Leonnig, "Former Trump adviser Papadopoulos pleads guilty to lying to the FBI about contacts with Russians," *Toronto Star*, October 30, 2017, https://www.thestar.com/news/world/2017/10/30/former-trump-adviser-papadopoulos-pleads-guilty-to-lying-to-the-fbi-about-contacts-with-russians.html.

16 Brooke Singman, Jake Gibson, and David Spunt, "Durham releases former Clinton lawyer Michael Sussmann's text message, says he put 'lie in writing,'" Fox News, April 5, 2022, https://www.foxnews.com/politics/durham-text-message-sussmann-lie-writing.

17 Adam Sabes and Jake Gibson, "Federal court rules DOJ must release internam memo to then-AG Barr stating Trump didn't obstruct justice," Fox News, August 19, 2022, https://www.foxnews.com/politics/federal-appeals-court-rules-doj-must-release-internal-memo-stating-trump-did-not-obstruct-justice.

18 Jerry Dunleavy, "New FBI whistleblower claims bureau leadership slow-walked Hunter Biden investigation," *Washington Examiner*, August 24, 2022, https://www.washingtonexaminer.com/news/justice/whistleblowers-fbi-slow-walked-hunter-biden-investigation-johnson.

19 Miranda Devine, "GOP senators demand Wray, AG Garland end FBI whistleblower's suspension," *New York Post*, September 26, 2022, https://nypost.com/2022/09/26/gop-senators-demand-wray-ag-garland-end-fbi-whistleblowers-suspension/.

20 Miranda Devine, "FBI put the Hunter Biden story right in Facebook's lap," *New York Post*, August 28, 2022, https://nypost.com/2022/08/28/fbi-put-the-hunter-biden-story-right-in-facebooks-lap/.

21 Ian Haworth, "How The Censorship Of Hunter Biden's Laptop Story Helped Joe Biden Win," Daily Wire, April 7, 2022, https://www.dailywire.com/news/how-the-censorship-of-hunter-bidens-laptop-story-helped-joe-biden-win.

22 Miranda Devine, "FBI put the Hunter Biden story."

23 Charles Grassley, email to Honorable Merrick Garland and Honorable Christopher Wray, July 25, 2022. https://drive.google.com/file/d/1EuxPN1hOA9pnSuCLazVexCKzAzY32Dqj/view.

24 Chuck Ross, "Meet the FBI Analyst Behind The Decade's Biggest Political Disinformation Campaigns," Washington Free Beacon, July 26, 2022, https://freebeacon.com/latest-news/meet-the-fbi-analyst-behind-the-decades-biggest-political-disinformation-campaigns/.

25 John Solomon, "Biden White House facilitated DOJ's criminal probe against Trump, scuttled privilege claims: memos," Just the News, August 23, 2022, https://justthenews.com/politics-policy/all-things-trump/biden-white-house-facilitated-dojs-criminal-probe-against-trump?utm_medium=social_media&utm_source=twitter_social_icon&utm_campaign=social_icons.

26 *Judicial Watch, INC. v. National Archives and Records Administration*, F. Supp., 10, 23 (2012). https://justthenews.com/sites/default/files/2022-08/memorandum%20opinion.pdf.

27 Joe Schoffstall, "Judge who green-lit raid at Trump's Mar-a-Lago home donated thousands to Obama," Fox News, August 9, 2022, https://www.foxnews.com/politics/judge-green-lit-raid-trumps-mar-a-lago-home-donated-thousands-obama; Jon Levine, "Trump lawyer calls out judge who approved Mar-a-Lago search warrant for Clinton case," *New York Post*, August 13, 2022, https://nypost.com/2022/08/13/trump-lawyer-calls-out-judge-who-approved-mar-a-lago-search-warrant-for-clinton-case/.

28 Miranda Devine, "FBI put the Hunter Biden story right in Facebook's lap," *New York Post*, August 28, 2022, https://nypost.com/2022/08/28/fbi-put-the-hunter-biden-story-right-in-facebooks-lap/.

29 John Solomon, "FBI raid on Trump compound stands in stark contrast to Clinton treatment years earlier," Just the News, August 8, 2022, https://justthenews.com/politics-policy/all-things-trump/fbi-raid-trump-compound-stands-stark-contrast-clinton-treatment.

30 Gage Cohen, "FISA Surveillance Requests Are Almost Never Rejected," Daily Caller, March 6, 2017, https://dailycaller.com/2017/03/06/fisa-surveillance-requests-are-almost-never-rejected/.

31 Lee Smith, *The Permanent Coup* (Center Street, 2020), Kindle edition, 145

32 Smith, *The Permanent Coup*, 94

33 Smith, *The Permanent Coup*, 148

34 Smith, *The Permanent Coup*, 149

35 Bonchie, "Durham Drops a Stunning Revelation Regarding Igor Danchenko and FBI Corruption," Red State, September 14, 2022, https://redstate.com/bonchie/2022/09/14/durham-drops-n627222.

36 Fiona Hill. "Fiona Hill Testimony." Deposition given October 14, 2019, 310-311. https://www.scribd.com/document/434065486/Fiona-Hill-testimony.

37 Alexander Vindman. "Vindman PDF." Deposition given October 29, 2019, 169-170. https://www.scribd.com/document/434064258/Vindman-pdf.

38 Brooke Singman, "Flynn bombshell stirs speculation over possible dismissal, pardon," Fox News, April 30, 2020, https://www.foxnews.com/politics/flynn-bombshell-stirs-speculation-over-possible-dismissal-pardon.

39 Brooke Singman and David Spunt, "List of officials who sought to 'unmask' Flynn released: Biden, Comey, Obama chief of staff among them," Fox News, May 13, 2020, https://www.foxnews.com/politics/grenell-releases-list-of-officials-who-sought-to-unmask-flynn-biden-comey-obama-intel-chiefs-among-them.

40 U.S. Government, *Book I: Foreign and Military Intelligence* (Washington: U.S. Government Printing Office, 1976), 393. http://www.aarclibrary.org/publib/church/reports/book1/html/ChurchB1_0201a.htm.

41 U.S. Government, *Book III: Supplementary Detailed Staff Reports on Intelligence Activities and the Rights of Americans* (Washington: U.S. Government Printing Office, 1976), 4-5. https://www.intelligence.senate.gov/sites/default/files/94755_III.pdf.

42 Ryan Bort, "Trump's Pick for Defense Secretary Is as Swampy as You'd Expect," *Rolling Stone*, July 17, 2019, https://www.rollingstone.com/politics/politics-news/trump-defense-secretary-mark-esper-859988/.

43 Dan Mangan, "Pelosi told top general Trump should have been 'arrested on the spot' for inciting Capitol insurrection, new book says," CNBC, September 15, 2021, https://www.cnbc.com/2021/09/14/trump-should-have-been-arrested-for-capitol-riot-pelosi-told-milley.html.

44 Chuck Grassley, "Grassley: A Case In Waste, Fraud And Abuse: The Office Of Net Assessment," Chuck Grassley: United States Senator for Iowa, July 2, 2020, https://www.grassley.senate.gov/news/news-releases/grassley-case-waste-fraud-and-abuse-office-net-assessment.

45 Pete Williams, "Capitol Police Officer Brian Sicknick died of natural causes after riot, medical examiner says," NBC News, April 19, 2021, https://www.nbcnews.com/politics/politics-news/capitol-police-officer-brian-sicknick-died-natural-causes-after-riot-n1264562.

46 Louis Casiano, "Illegal immigrant killed 3 after 'sanctuary' release from custody, ICE says," Fox News, November 11, 2018, https://www.foxnews.com/us/undocumented-immigrant-released-from-jail-charged-in-triple-murder.

47 Joe Marino, Kevin Sheehan, and Mark Lungariello, "Suspected thief arrested for attempted rape of girl, 15, months after Bragg reduced charges," *New York Post*, August 25, 2022, https://nypost.com/2022/08/25/accused-thief-out-with-no-bail-arrested-for-attempted-rape-of-15-year-old-nyc-girl/.

48 Post Editorial Board, "New York's no-bail laws claim another horrific victim," *New York Post*, May 27, 2020, https://nypost.com/2020/05/27/new-yorks-no-bail-laws-claim-another-horrific-victim/.

49 Julio Rosas, "FBI's Stunning Answers When Grilled By Ted Cruz Asking if Any Feds Were Part of Capitol Riot," *Townhall*, January 11, 2022, https://townhall.com/tipsheet/juliorosas/2022/01/11/ted-cruz-fbi-january-6-riot-n2601698.

50 Joe Biden. 2022. "Remarks by President Biden on the Continued Battle for the Soul of the Nation." Transcript of speech delivered at Independence National Historical Park in Philadelphia, Pennsylvania, September 1, 2022. https://www.whitehouse.gov/briefing-room/speeches-remarks/2022/09/01/remarks-by-president-bidenon-the-continued-battle-for-the-soul-of-the-nation/.

51 Debra Heine, "Whistleblowers: FBI Officials Are 'Pressuring' Agents to 'Artificially Pad' Domestic Violence Extremist Data," *Tennessee Star*, July 29, 2022, https://tennesseestar.com/2022/07/29/whistleblowers-fbi-officials-are-pressuring-agents-to-artificially-pad-domestic-violence-extremist-data/.

52 Tim Hains, "GOP Rep. Jim Jordan: FBI Whistleblower Says Agents Are Being Transferred From Child Trafficking Cases To Investigating MAGA," RealClearPolitics, September 20, 2022, https://www.realclearpolitics.com/video/2022/09/20/gop_rep_jim_jordan_fbi_whistleblower_says_agents_are_being_transferred_from_child_trafficking_cases_to_investigating_maga.html.

53 AG Schmitt, "Missouri and Louisiana Attorneys General Ask Court to Compel Department of Justice to Produce Communications Between Top Officials and Social Media Companies," Eric Schmitt: Missouri Attorney General, September 1, 2022, https://ago.mo.gov/home/news/2022/09/01/

missouri-and-louisiana-attorneys-general-ask-court-to-compel-department-of-justice-to-produce-communications-between-top-officials-and-social-media-companies.

54 Nicholas McElroy, "Social media platforms banning or restricting Donald Trump in wake of US Capitol violence," ABC, January 10, 2021, https://www.abc.net.au/news/2021-01-10/social-media-platforms-that-have-banned-donald-trump/13045730.

55 McElroy, "Social media platforms banning or restricting Donald Trump."

56 U.S. Department of Defense, "Review of the DoD's Role, Responsibilities, and Actions to Prepare for and Respond to the Protest and Its Aftermath at the U.S. Capitol Campus on January 6, 2021," *Inspector General Report*, November 16, 2021, 6-7, https://s3.documentcloud.org/documents/21113253/dod-ig-jan-6.pdf.

57 Michael Isikoff, "'The most significant terrorism-related threat': DHS secretary says domestic extremists now more a danger to U.S. than foreign terrorist groups," Yahoo News, June 15, 2021, https://news.yahoo.com/the-most-significant-terrorism-related-threat-dhs-secretary-says-domestic-extremists-now-more-a-danger-to-us-than-foreign-terrorist-groups-220014920.html.

58 Dan De Luce and Mosheh Gains, "Pentagon orders pause across military to address extremism in its ranks," NBC News, February 3, 2021, https://www.nbcnews.com/politics/national-security/pentagon-orders-pause-across-military-address-extremism-its-ranks-n1256678.

IN GRATITUDE

overnment Gangsters, like anything else in my life, is a team lift. I am humbled to have created friendships with such great warriors during our mission, and blessed to have a family to bring it all together. I am forever indebted to you, and unable to repay you in this life or the next. But if you'll allow me, a few words of appreciation for some that will fall far short of the mark.

The idea for this book came from some brave operators I served with in the Trump White House, who had the daring audacity to make it a reality. To Vince Haley, Ross Worthington, and Alec Torres—words cannot express the appreciation I have for the faith you had to build *Government Gangsters*. Your brilliance, knowledge, and sheer determination to make this a reality is the only reason I am able to put these words to paper. A special thanks to Alec for working tirelessly on the written work and helping me navigate the tides of time.

To so many of those in my life who shaped my career, and before that, taught me above all to help others along the entire ride of life—thank you. First and foremost, my family. We are a massive group, too many to name, but I recall so often all the times we shared across America and around the world. Every instance has made me a better person, which is only a result of your enormous patience and generosity with me. Thank you for the memories that built a man.

As for streamlining the content of this book, a special thank you to Jan Jekielek and *Epoch Times*. Jan for having the crazy idea to encapsulate all things in a show so I could speak my mind on national security, defense, intelligence, and law enforcement matters. *Kash's Corner* has truly been a blessing, and it helped me put all my thoughts in one place—thank you, Jan and the entire *Epoch* team, for taking a chance on me. Six seasons and counting…

As to my start, too many to thank from across my sixteen years in government service, but I'd like to name a few. Devin Nunes and the entire Objective Medusa Team (special thanks to the late Damon Nelson), for rolling the dice and entrusting me to lead what would turn out to be the most consequential congressional oversight investigation of our time, Russia Gate. Lee Smith, Jack Langer, and Scott: How you have captured the essence of this investigation and helped teach the world the only thing I ever cared about, the truth, is ever so impressive.

For those not mentioned, my apologies. I am blessed to have such amazing family and friends, and for those who know me best, know there is no distinction in my book of life. I am here to answer your call, whenever it need be made.

To our fearless servicemembers, it was the honor of a lifetime serving with you, leading you, and walking in the shadows of your greatness. It is because of you, we are free.

To Fredde and David, who shaped the inner core of my professional being, thank you. And of course, thanks to the team at Post Hill Press and Vigliano Associates.

To my entire Fight With Kash and K$H Foundation team, thank you for delivering every day for those less fortunate and putting the Mission First.

To Brian and Mr. and Mrs. Gray for being my family down the street.

Lastly, thank you to President Trump for helping put so many Government Gangsters in their place, and a word of caution for those that got away: we are not done yet.

Dons Hockey for Life